SEX, SCHOOLS AND THE LAW

SEX, SCHOOLS AND THE LAW

A Study of the Legal Implications of
Sexual Matters Relating to the Public School
Curriculum (With a Separate Chapter on
Sex Education), the Public School Library,
the Personal Lives of Teachers and Students,
and the Student Press

By

FERNAND N. DUTILE

Professor of Law
University of Notre Dame
Notre Dame, Indiana

CHARLES C THOMAS • PUBLISHER
Springfield • Illinois • U.S.A.

Published and Distributed Throughout the World by

CHARLES C THOMAS • PUBLISHER
2600 South First Street
Springfield, Illinois 62717

© *1986 by* CHARLES C THOMAS • PUBLISHER

ISBN 0-398-05180-1

Library of Congress Catalog Card Number: 85-17381

With THOMAS BOOKS *careful attention is given to all details of manufacturing and design. It is the Publisher's desire to present books that are satisfactory as to their physical qualities and artistic possibilities and appropriate for their particular use.* THOMAS BOOKS will be true to those laws of quality that assure a good name and good will.

Printed in the United States of America
SC-R-3

Library of Congress Cataloging-in-Publication Data

Dutile, Fernand N.
  Sex, schools, and the law.

  Includes index.
  1. Students—Legal status, laws, etc.—United States.
  2. Teachers—Legal status, laws, etc.—United States.
  3. Sex instruction for youth—Law and legislation—United States.
  4. Sex and law—United States.   I. Title.
  KF4124.5.D88   1986   344.73'079   85-17381
  ISBN 0-398-05180-1   347.30479

To my siblings
Lorraine, Richard, Wilfred, Jr., and David

INTRODUCTION

This volume explores the interaction of three important matters which generate intense public interest: sex, schools and law. Schools are a microcosm in which almost all the problems of society—problems of race and crime, to name but two—can be felt. It is not surprising, therefore, that the same wide variety of issues, feelings and conflicts which attend sexual concerns in society at large appears as well in the school context.

Chapter 1 ("Sex and the Curriculum") explores sexual issues arising in connection with the curriculum. Chapter 2 ("Sex Education: A Special Situation"), recognizing that sex education, although part of the curriculum issue, raises legal problems different in scope, intensity and resolution, focuses on these problems. Chapter 3 ("Sex and the School Library") delves into issues connected with the school library, many of these related to book removal, but some to book selection. Chapter 4 ("The Sexual Orientation or Activity of Teachers") considers the legitimacy of adverse official treatment of teachers for their sexual conduct or orientation, or for related matters. Chapter 5 ("The Student's Personal Life") does the same with regard to students. Finally, Chapter 6 ("The Student Press") assesses the attempts by school officials to control sexually-oriented articles or language in student publications. Since sex as activity rather than as gender constitutes the topic for this volume, I have not included a chapter on sex discrimination.

I bring to this study several firm beliefs of which the reader should be aware. First, exposing children, consistent with their maturity, to a diversity of ideas provides a more effective and exciting education and produces more creative graduates. Second, teachers are professionals who must be given the discretion necessary to provide such an education. Third, both teachers and students should be endowed with the same Constitutional rights as other citizens, unless the threat of harm is real, significant and direct.

The matters considered in the volume should be of interest to lawyers, school administrators, educators generally, and anyone else intrigued by the difficulty and sensitivity of apportioning rights and responsibilities among the many and varied constituencies of the public school community. I hope that this book will contribute to the ongoing debate.

Fernand N. Dutile

ACKNOWLEDGMENTS

I wish to thank, first and foremost, my secretary, Kathleen M. Bradley, for her tireless and ever-cheerful work on draft after draft of the manuscript. I am indebted also to the Dean of the Notre Dame Law School, David T. Link, whose encouragement and support, in so many ways, of research and writing contributed mightily to this volume. Thanks go as well to Julie Clements, my research assistant, and Patty Dutile for their extensive help. Finally, the cooperation, assistance and understanding of Mr. Payne Thomas and his staff were unfailing and indispensable to the publication of *Sex, Schools and the Law.*

CONTENTS

SEX, SCHOOLS AND THE LAW

Chapter 1

SEX AND THE CURRICULUM

INTRODUCTION

Ouida Dean, in March of 1976, was in her sixth year of teaching at the Timpson High School in Timpson, Texas. Her professional reputation and her teaching record were excellent. She strove to inculcate in her students the habit of critical inquiry, an effort which led to her involvement in a controversy which upset the community.[1]

In connection with the consideration of sex roles in her psychology class and of interviewing techniques in her speech class, Mrs. Dean allowed the use of a sex survey entitled, "Masculinity—What it Means to be a Man?,"[2] originally appearing in *Psychology Today.* Treating of sensitive aspects of sex in an explicit manner, the survey was administered to Mrs. Dean's classes by a student who, needing an opportunity to do make-up work, was charged to do so. Mrs. Dean instructed the student that the exercise was optional, that questions assuming that the respondent was married or sexually active should be omitted and that even students responding to the survey could refuse to answer specific questions felt to be too personal. Although it is not clear how many of the questions were read to either the speech class or the psychology class, two students in the psychology class were given the entire questionnaire, and at least two students saw certain sexually explicit questions. Both classes took the survey without disruption, and no students complained to the teacher.

The Timpson community, however, did discuss the survey, and when the school principal told Mrs. Dean that one student's grandmother had complained about the survey, Mrs. Dean called the complainant, discussed the situation and then felt the matter closed. After a further discussion of the survey with the principal some days later, Mrs. Dean was asked to resign, she refused and, shortly thereafter, she was told by Superintendent Higginbotham that she was "being relieved of duty, effective immediately." Allowed to return to her classroom only to get her purse, she left all other personal belongings behind.[3] Greatly upset by this abrupt removal, Mrs. Dean remained in bed for several days and did not appear at a special school board meeting called to discuss the situation. Rather, her husband presented to the meeting a letter she had prepared. The board ratified Mrs. Dean's discharge which, the board minutes noted, was due to "a survey that was presented to one of her high school classes."[4] Mrs. Dean sued for reinstatement.

This situation raises dramatically the issue of the use of sexual material in the curriculum,[5] and will be alluded to throughout this chapter to illustrate the many facets of the problem, which, although largely related to the First Amendment's free speech provisions,[6] has significant Fourteenth Amendment due process implications.[7]

THE PUBLIC SCHOOL'S ROLE

Crucial to any consideration of the issue is the role of the public school in American life. Is the school's mandate (and therefore the teacher's) to transmit the traditional morals and values of the public or is it to provide a so-called "marketplace of ideas"?[8]

Transmitting the Majoritarian View

There is, to be sure, much to commend the former model of the public school, according to which the majority will control what is taught in the schools and how, through a faculty operating as agents of the school board, which, in turn, is usually[9] made up of elected agents of the community.[10] School boards are therefore "legitimate political authority, as represented by the small groups of people to whom communities large and small delegate away the choice of what values and knowledge their children will experience."[11] As a result, a school board may be able to limit class booklists,[12] for example, even if the decision is a political one and even if influenced by the members' personal views, at least if the limitations do not rule out the study of "entire representative groups of writers."[13] Thus, the school district's curriculum will legitimately reflect the values and educational emphasis collectively willed by the parents who, after all, pay the costs.[14]

Official school authority exists, it is said, in order to remove issues of speech and values from the "central political maelstrom."[15] The "free speech" analysis of public schools, furthermore, fails for its assertion of the priority of that diversity of views which nurtures a democracy over the democratic process itself.[16]

In *Board of Education, Island Trees Union Free School District No. 26 v. Pico*, the U.S. Supreme Court indicated that the school board's control over classroom matters (as opposed to school library offerings)[17] may be near total.[18] Even Justice Brennan, in his plurality opinion, recognized that local school boards have broad discretion in the management of school business, that they may administer the curriculum so as to transmit community values, and that there is an appropriate and substantial community interest in the promotion of respect for authority and other traditional social, moral,[19] and political values.[20] Although conceding that school board discretion must be exercised in conformity with the "transcendent imperatives" of the first amendment, Brennan, in a surprisingly sweeping dictum, stated that the school board "might well defend their claim of absolute discretion in matters of *curriculum* by reliance upon their duty to inculcate community values."[21] Since Justice Marshall joined Brennan's opinion, it is likely that the entire court would support this particular assertion. Since, however, the case involved school library offerings and not an assigned part of the curriculum, the statement does not yet represent binding law.[22]

Board control even over curriculum content, however, should not be total. Perhaps Justice Brennan was referring only to the choice of courses to be taught, rather than to perspectives and ideas within those courses. Indeed, in the same opinion, Brennan, noting that the Court's precedents have for many years acknowledged constitutional limits on the state's power over the curriculum and the classroom,[23] stated that the Constitution does not permit the official suppression of ideas.[24]

Why such suppression cannot occur through the assigned curriculum as well as through optional books in the school library is not vouchsafed us. In fact, textbooks and other required reading present a greater likelihood of a pall of orthodoxy than does optional reading.[25] In any event, Brennan suggested a greater discretion for compulsory courses than for elective ones.[26]

The "majority" model is not flawless. Absent the relatively rare controversial case, such as Mrs. Dean's, the community at large is not likely to be aware of the specifics of day-to-day curriculum content. Moreover, board meetings are often closed to the public and unrecorded; the ballot is thus not as effective as sometimes thought due both to citizen ignorance and the inevitable delay between the parent's objection and the opportunity to vote a board member out of office.[27] Furthermore, the board itself may not be as cognizant of the schoolday content as we often assume and may operate on hearsay, irrational complaint, incomplete information or personal prejudice.

The situation would be more defensible if the views of all segments of the population were represented proportionately in the curriculum of the schools—but that is not the case and may even be impossible; if a particular use of sexually-oriented material is allowed, *all* are usually exposed to it, absent some excusal system; if the material is not allowed, *none* gets to use it, even though 40 percent of the community might favor its use.

Moreover, exclusion of competing ideas may be unconstitutional to the extent it results in an indoctrinating curriculum or one which imposes "ideological homogeneity."[28] Even though the U.S. Supreme Court itself has deemed the inculcation of values fundamental to our democratic political system to be one of the essential functions of the public school,[29] those values include the integrity of the person and individual freedom of thought.[30] Fundamental to the American system is respect for a diversity of ideas.[31]

The "Marketplace of Ideas"

The "marketplace of ideas" approach assumes that the best learning occurs when teachers are free to expose students to a great variety of concepts, approaches and values.[32] Students grow, it is said, not by indoctrination or routine learning of a traditional body of doctrine, but by wrestling with diverse ideas, choosing some, rejecting others and, in the long pull, realizing that most important issues are complex, not given to reflex answers.

One commentator's observation in the context of discussing science books that might yield physical dangers to children in school is perhaps equally (and unfortunately) true with regard to intellectual school activity: "We trust that school, like home, is a safe environment for our children."[33] It is not clear, after all, that a safe education is the best education. We should in any event be careful before assuming that children are easily harmed by contact with untraditional or progressive ideas; exposure need not be indoctrination.[34] Also, although courts may have tended to stress the dangers, the teacher's power in the classroom carries benefits as well.[35] Indeed, there is the reciprocal danger that a policy perceived as allowing in school only approved ideas signals institutional approval of every idea and view alluded to by teachers, counselors and even guest speakers.

Under the marketplace of ideas model for the public school, a focused application of the same doctrine that is clearly applicable to society at large,[36] the classroom can be seen not as the mere purveyor of ideas of the past, but as the place "where the ideas of the future are spawned."[37] Indeed, the school may be the only institution in which "youth is exposed to exciting and competing ideas. . . . "[38]

The U.S. Supreme Court lent considerable weight to the marketplace of ideas concept when it said, in *Keyishian v. Board of Regents,* "The classroom is peculiarly the 'marketplace of ideas.' The Nation's future depends upon leaders trained through wide exposure to that robust exchange of ideas which discovers truth 'out of a multitude of tongues, [rather] than through any kind of authoritative selection.' "[39]

Keyishian, however, involved faculty at the university level, at which, it is clear, the marketplace model is more apt. After all, students of college age, more mature and sophisticated, are better able to sift through ideas in order to accept or reject them and are less impressionable.[40] It is unlikely that a college student will be "led astray" by inappropriate comments in the university classroom. On the other hand, even public high schools, while not rigidly disciplinarian, are not "open forums in which mature adults, already habituated to social restraints, exchange ideas on a level of parity."[41] This point may of course be a two-edged sword since any "indoctrination"—presumably more likely under a monolithic model—will have greater effect at the lower levels of education.

Too, the university faculty member generally has more independent traditions, broader discretion with regard to teaching methodology, greater experience and greater intellectual and emotional maturity than lower-level teachers.[42] Public schools are more expected to transmit information and even, to some extent, to indoctrinate. Relevant also is the fact that "colleges and universities are corporations with their own various charters, a species of civil body much further removed from direct public representative control than our public school districts."[43]

A further reason underlies some reluctance to see in the public schools the "marketplace" concept obtaining in higher education. Elementary and secondary school students constitute a captive audience[44] because they must attend school, either under state mandatory attendance laws or, in any event, because of the absolute necessity of basic schooling for effective functioning in modern-day society. Furthermore, although one could argue that the public school student unhappy with curriculum content may go elsewhere, many families, whether due to expense, distance or other concerns, do not have such an option.[45] Parents and their children, therefore, should not have to be exposed to ideas and approaches, outside the majoritarian perspective, which they find offensive. University students, on the other hand, more freely choose a particular college or even a particular course.

Again, however, the argument seems to cut both ways. Precisely because the school-age child is part of a captive audience, he should not be subject to but one, traditional, majoritarian approach, which carries with it serious concerns for the orthodoxy frowned upon by the first amendment. As the U.S. Supreme Court has reminded us, "If there is any fixed star in our constitutional constellation, it is that no official, high or petty, can prescribe what shall be orthodox in politics, nationalism, religion, or other matters of opinion . . . "[46]

Although these considerations argue against the wholesale applicability of the marketplace of ideas theory to the public schools, one might suggest an "age-activated sliding scale" approach, thus recognizing that as "the child grows older, his interest in having an unfettered opportunity for ideas and to gain knowledge broadens"[47] or, conversely, that "the state interest in limiting the discretion of teachers grows stronger . . . as the age of the students decreases . . . "[48] There is not yet substantial judicial support for this approach.[49]

The difficult task remains, then, to accommodate, within constitutional constraints:

> the inherent tension between . . . two essential functions, on the one hand exposing young minds to the clash of ideologies in the free marketplace of ideas, and on the other hand the need to provide our youth with a solid foundation of basic, moral values. . . . Striking a balance between them is difficult. . . . [50]

SCHOOL BOARDS AND THE COURTS

Since the U.S. Constitution gives to the states all powers not specifically delegated to the national government, states exercise plenary power over public education.[51] Accordingly, public education is generally provided for in state constitutions, and implemented through a comprehensive and intricate set of laws.[52] This arrangement usually entrusts the day-to-day operation to local schools districts and their administrators. As a result, one of the most fundamental educational principles in the United States is that, despite substantial regulation from state legislatures and agencies,[53] local communities control public education.[54]

Whenever a teacher's use of sexually-oriented language or other material is at issue, therefore, the "specter" of court control of the schools is raised. Why, after all, should a judge decide what goes on in schools supported by taxpayers, and under what criteria?[55] The judge—at least the federal judges typically called on in such situations—are not elected[56] and, since the federal judicial district is not coterminous with the school district, may not be a resident of that school district. If the trial judge's decision does not ultimately prevail, the federal judges deciding the appeal will be from distant communities. If, as is unlikely, the case reaches the U.S. Supreme Court, "Washington" will be telling the local school district what to do. On the other hand, a "responsive majoritarian public education helps to retain a region's local character, maintain national diversity, and pass along to the young the values and beliefs of their society."[57]

Local control, however, need not pit the courts against local officials, or the U.S. Constitution against local regulation. The issue in the courts is typically a *power* issue—may the state through its school district do what it did? Choosing among the many things the school district may do is a *wisdom* issue. Even an elected school board may decide in its wisdom to allow significant play for the marketplace of ideas philosophy. It need not use its power to enforce a monolithic vision of public education. The same governmental and political processes calculated to decide curricular matters provide the forum for challenging limitations on what teachers may teach.[58] Effort designed to make these processes more responsive to minority viewpoints and more given to conciliation is well spent, especially in light of the increasing tendency to challenge official decisions in the area.[59]

Moreover, even in speech cases, courts have often sustained the local board's power over the asserted rights of teachers or students,[60] and often reflect great concern and sensitivity for the role of the local school district, as the court in *Dean u Timpson Independent School District* did when it said: "Local school boards in this state are given wide discretion and authority to structure and control the course of public education within their districts. School administrators perform a task of great importance and immeasurable difficulty."[61]

An appellate court itself may check a lower court's inappropriate exercise of power over a school district. Reviewing a trial judge's grant of a writ compelling a school district to cease the use of a particular novel, the Court of Appeals of Michigan said, "This Court cannot, in good conscience, nor in adherence to our constitutional oath of office, allow a non-educational public official the right, in absence of gross constitutional transgressions, to regulate the reading material to which our students are exposed."[62]

Alas, just as constitutional rights in areas of suffrage or criminal procedure must occasionally supersede local majoritarian control, so too must first amendment rights prevail when in conflict with local majoritarian wishes.[63]

WHAT RIGHTS AND WHOSE?

When the internal processes of curriculum control fail to achieve some kind of conciliation with regard to a particular curricular choice, litigation concerning the question of rights may be considered. The issue of what rights becomes inseparable from that of whose rights.[64] Of course, some right under the state constitution or under state legislation may resolve the issue as long as that "right" in turn is not violative of the federal Constitution. On the assumption that the controversy survives resort to state law, what—and whose—federal rights may be implicated in a curricular dispute? The inquiry is made the more difficult since most of the pertinent U.S. Supreme Court cases arose at the university level and did not involve curricular matters or teaching-related classroom speech. Nonetheless, four parties are likely candidates for the attribution of discrete rights: the school board, the teacher, the student and the parent.

The School Board

As indicated earlier, the school board, as the legitimate state representative, has plenary and primary control of the schools. Its rights, however, arise not specifically under the U.S. Constitution but as a manifestation of the residual powers left to states by that Constitution. In a very real sense, then, its rights are best described as the power remaining in the board after any rights of contending parties are accounted for.

Perhaps the school board's rights are amply protected by its power to require the *inclusion* in the curriculum of almost any material (certain religious material being an exception[65]) it sees fit, whatever the right of the teacher to *add* to it. There is, after all, little authority for the proposition that teachers may exclude material prescribed by the school board[66] unless that material—for example, a political endorsement— violates the students' first amendment rights,[67] or unless, at least, the board's choices were made arbitrarily, capriciously or in violation of procedural due process.[68]

Clearly, teachers do not have a right to use whatever curricular devices they want over the objection of the board, even if the board's wishes are "more orthodox."[69] Clearly, too, "school boards do not have an absolute right to remove materials from the curriculum".[70] Recent cases suggest, nonetheless, that school boards are entitled to dramatic control over the curriculum,[71] even, perhaps, if that control results from the board members' personal social, political and moral views.[72]

The Teacher

Does the teacher have any right with regard to the school curriculum beyond that of any other citizen-taxpayer, that is, to vote for or against school board candidates or other relevant officials, to complain to the board or other school employees, or to make speeches and the like? While there is often the assumption that teachers are clothed with some special first amendment right with regard to in-class discussion, the extent of any such right bears analysis. Why should a public employee whose mission is to serve the public through classroom teaching have more of a right to say particular things (rather than others) than other public employees? Surely the local driver's license examiner cannot claim the right to tell those taking the driver's test anything he wants. Justice Black has eloquently set out the "employee" model:

> I am also not ready to hold that a person hired to teach school children takes with him into the classroom a constitutional right to teach sociological, economic, political, or religious subjects that the school's managers do not want discussed . . . I question whether . . . "academic freedom" permits a teacher to breach his contractual agreement to teach only the subjects designated by the school authorities who hired him.[73]

The U.S. Supreme Court itself has noted that the interest of the State as employer in regulating the speech of its employees is greater than that in regulating the speech of citizens in general.[74] Others have resisted the employee model, asserting that teachers "cannot be made to simply read from a script prepared or approved by the board."[75]

In fact, to assert that teachers have no more rights than other public employees may not do justice to the teacher's peculiarly significant interest in and dedication to the free exchange of ideas and the concept of personal achievement.[76] Perhaps ascribing additional rights is justified by the need to attract talented teachers. Since public school teachers should be interested in matters intellectual, good teachers are more likely to be attracted by the opportunity to discuss freely, to investigate and to experiment. Moreover, limitations placed on teachers will deter others from free inquiry.[77] Still, it would seem that the value of such freedom inures more directly to the student who, therefore, should hold the primary right. Since schooling exists for the student, any teacher's self-interest must be given only secondary consideration.[78]

Perhaps we might attribute first amendment classroom rights to teachers on the very pragmatic ground that they are in the best position to assert them,[79] and the most likely to. After all, neither the student nor his parent may even be aware of restrictions on assigning certain books or discussing certain topics; barring the teacher from asserting the right may deny it altogether.[80]

A similar device is at work in the criminal law. We exclude from the trial any evidence seized in violation of the defendant's fourth amendment rights in part because he is the most likely to assert fourth amendment rights. The victim of an illegal search against whom no evidence is found may choose not to sue the offending officer due to lack of time, money, sophistication or the like. The criminal defendant, on the other hand, has a compelling incentive to assert his right, thus protecting the rights of us all.

Whatever the validity of this device, it has been noted that most cases raising the first amendment in connection with the right to discuss controversial matters in class have been brought by teachers, with students, parents and administrators seldom raising such issues in court.[81]

The teacher's first amendment right in the classroom may be a necessary check on the orthodoxy that might otherwise prevail. "The teacher's autonomy is more often an insulator against ideological bombardment than it is a danger. As long as all teachers retain a right to express independent views in the classroom, the state is unable to speak with a single voice."[82] This argument, however, presumes to some extent a multitude of teachers touching upon the same areas. If sex education, for example, is taught in only one grade and by only one teacher, that teacher's approach and perspective are the "orthodox" ones, even if the school board would seriously disapprove of them. Since sexual matters are not, relatively speaking, much discussed in public schools, there is some question that balance is enough to support the teacher's right to deal with sexually-oriented material substantially as he sees fit.

In *Parducci v. Rutland*,[83] involving the dismissal of a teacher for the assignment of a controversial short story,[84] the United States District Court, noting that academic freedom is not among the enumerated rights of the first amendment, nonetheless recalled the U.S. Supreme Court's emphasis upon the right to teach, inquire, evaluate and study as fundamental to a democratic society,[85] and the same Court's observation that "[o]ur nation is deeply committed to safeguarding academic freedom, which is of transcendent value. . . . That freedom is therefore a special concern of the First Amendment. . . . "[86] The District Court ordered the teacher reinstated, commenting that the school officials' right to run the schools did not justify arbitrariness in the First Amendment area.[87]

In *Wieman v. Updegraff*,[88] the U.S. Supreme Court referred to loyalty oath requirements as an "unwarranted inhibition upon the free spirit of teachers," one which has an "unmistakable tendency to chill that free play of the spirit which all teachers ought especially to cultivate and practice. . . . "[89] Teachers, the court continued, must, as the "priests of democracy," be "examples of open-mindedness and free inquiry. . . . "[90] The U.S. Supreme Court's observations on this subject, however, tend to occur in cases related to higher education,[91] or decided on other grounds,[92] yielding no answer to whether academic freedom is guaranteed the public school teacher through the First Amendment.[93] Yet the suggestions from the nation's highest court and from other courts support such a right.[94]

In *Dean v. Timpson*, the "Masculinity Survey" case whose facts opened this chapter, the trial court found "that a teacher has a constitutional right protected by the First Amendment to engage in a teaching method of his or her own choosing, even though the subject matter may be controversial or sensitive",[95] an assertion which has been called the most "specific endorsement" yet of the teacher's academic freedom in the choice of teaching methods.[96] The Constitution recognizes that freedom, another court has said, "in order to foster open minds, creative imagination, and adventurous spirits. . . . Our faith is that [such] freedom will increase [the teacher's] intellectual vitality and . . . moral strength."[97]

The complexity of this issue is illustrated in *Cary v. Board of Education of Adams-Arapahoe School District 28-J, Aurora, Colorado*,[98] in which the District Court had found that the teacher's collective bargaining agreement had waived the teacher's First Amendment rights.[99] Such a waiver would raise serious concerns above and beyond the power of the collective bargaining representative to surrender constitutional rights of all teachers. It suggests that the rights involved are indeed those of the teachers and at least in large part not those of students, parents and others. It is not enough to say that the only matter given up was the teacher's right to assert the First Amendment right since, as a practical matter, the teacher's inability to exercise the right largely forecloses the student's enjoyment of his own free speech right or right to hear. As it turned out, the Court of Appeals overturned the trial court on this point, finding that there was no deliberate waiver of any First Amendment rights.[100] This spared the court from considering the power of the teacher's union to waive these rights.[101]

Perhaps, as we shall explore later, the real issue is not a substantive First Amendment speech right, but a procedural one focusing on whether the teacher has had a decent warning of what material should not be used.[102]

The Children or Their Parents

For the most part, children and their parents can be looked upon as the same party. Rarely will their interests in school litigation be adverse to one another and equally rarely will the child be in a position to pursue legal rights without the aid, direction and financial support of the parents.[103] Moreover, the courts have traditionally considered the parents the primary determinants of the child's educational needs[104] and, whether by right or not, parents in most public schools hold much sway in the conduct of those schools.[105] Perhaps the most precise approach is to view any classroom rights of children to be limited by parental prerogatives.[106]

On occasion, however, a court will insist that parents not have the last word. In *Keefe v. Geanakos*, which involved a teacher's discussion of a vulgar word, the Court of Appeals, noting that some parents had been offended, stated, "With the greatest of respect to such parents, their sensibilities are not the full measure of what is proper education."[107] In the "Masculinity Survey" case, the court found unpersuasive the fact that members of the community were upset by the presentation of controversial material in the schools: "To exclude a subject from the public school curriculum because it offends the community . . . runs counter to the spirit of the First Amendment, and poses a threat greater than the unsettling effect on the community. . . ."[108]

At least in theory, parents who object to classroom methods or material have the option of withdrawing their children from that particular course—at least if it is elective—or placing them in some alternative educational program.[109] Again, however, not all parents have the means to place their children in what may be the only alternative, a private school, and it is, in any event, not fully satisfying for a taxpaying parent to be told that the public school is available only on a take-it-or-leave-it basis.

Of course, we cannot substitute the parent for the child in the classroom itself and a child's First Amendment rights are not as extensive as those of an adult.[110] The U.S. Supreme Court has determined, for example, that the state can criminalize the sale to minors of sexually-oriented material not obscene under the law controlling sales to adults.[111]

What rights, then, do children (and, at least derivatively, their parents) have concerning curriculum matters dealing with sexually-oriented material? With regard to their own utterances, presumably, some First Amendment free speech protection must exist, although such cases tend to arise rarely. Suppose, however, a twelfth-grade student, assigned to make a presentation in class on some piece of literature, chose to discuss D. H. Lawrence's *Lady Chatterley's Lover*, used fairly explicit sexual language in discussing it and, indeed, quoted several salacious paragraphs from it. Could the student constitutionally be disciplined for the content of his speech?

In *Tinker v. Des Moines Independent School District*, the U.S. Supreme Court said, "It can hardly be argued that either students or teachers shed their constitutional rights to freedom of speech or expression at the schoolhouse gate."[112] Involved there was extracurricular speech (black armbands in protest of the Vietnam War), but the same principle would apply to the curriculum.[113] The ultimate test is the same for both: does the speech materially and substantially interfere with the operation of the school or collide with the rights of others?[114]

Presumably, then, any sanction on the student discussing *Lady Chatterley's Lover* could be challenged, requiring resort to criteria similar to those used to evaluate teacher speech in connection with the curriculum,[115] including whether a school regulation clearly proscribed the student speech or whether any student of the same age should have known that the content was clearly inappropriate in the context.

Perhaps the converse question is the tougher one. Suppose the teacher, with school board support, assigned the *Chatterley* novel to a twelfth grader as the topic for the student's in-class presentation. Could the student refuse to make the presentation with impunity? The case is quite different from one in which an entire class is required to read the same work and, perhaps, even to submit a written report. Here, not only is one student singled out, which might lead to ridicule or contempt, real or perceived, but that student is also being required to express himself on matters of considerable sensitivity. In such a case, the test of the school's power should not be whether a reasonable teacher could find the novel and a discussion of it appropriate, but rather whether *any* reasonable student could find the assignment objectionable. In such a case, a student, under the first amendment, possesses the right not to speak as well as to speak.

In *West Virginia State Board of Education v. Barnette*, the U.S. Supreme Court invalidated on First Amendment grounds the flag salute and pledge requirements in language quite relevant to our concerns: "Here . . . the State . . . requires the individual to communicate by word and sign his acceptance of the political ideas it thus bespeaks. Objection to this form of communication when coerced is an old one, well known to the framers of the Bill of Rights."[116] The Court noted that the State was requiring an "affirmation of a belief and an attitude of mind."[117] Of course, the student perhaps could fulfill the *Lady Chatterley* assignment without specifically affirming a belief. In fact, read narrowly, *Barnette* does not prohibit requiring a student to affirm a belief, but only bars requiring him to affirm a specific *state-selected* belief.[118] Nonetheless, his discussion of such a novel impliedly and inevitably conveys his acceptance of its importance and relevance. Moreover, any recital he might make with regard to the book would surely coerce him into revealing an "attitude of mind." This is not to suggest that *any* student could refuse such an assignment with regard to *any* particular book. The student could speak on most books without any such problem arising. It is the sensitivity of the material in the Lawrence novel that creates the problem. Nor is it enough to say that the student could in his presentation decry the book, its implications or its language. To do so would also require him to affirm a belief and, in any event, cause him to pay a price—again, ridicule or perhaps a lower grade—for his exercise of a right.[119]

Beyond any relating to his own speaking, what rights does a student have with regard to sexually-oriented material in the curriculum? There has been posited a right to receive information, and lower courts have consistently found such a right even in academic matters.[120] In doing so, they have relied on *Lamont v. Postmaster General,*[121] holding that a person receiving mail from communist countries could not be compelled by federal officials to complete certain identification forms.[122] The right to receive information, it is said, is nowhere more crucial than in schools and universities,[123] although it has had less impact in high schools than in colleges.[124] The U.S. Supreme Court itself has observed that "students may not be regarded as closed-circuit recipients of only that which the State chooses to communicate."[125]

In *Island Trees,* Justice Brennan emphasized the right to receive information and ideas, calling it an inherent corollary of the rights of free speech and press, and in two senses: first, the right to receive flows inevitably from the sender's right to send;[126] second, the right to receive is a crucial predicate to the receiver's meaningful exercise of free speech, free press and political freedom.[127]

Despite this important pronouncement, however, several limiting caveats are in order. First, Justice Brennan's *Island Trees* opinion is a plurality one, and therefore did not garner the agreement of a Court majority. Second, *Island Trees* involved the removal of library books, not curricular matter and, as indicated earlier, even Justice Brennan would give the school board more power vis-a-vis classroom and otherwise assigned material.[128]

Yet the right to receive information can be a restricted one if the teacher and other school employees agree on a limited offering of ideas and teaching methodologies. Only when someone wishes to present certain material to the students and meets obstruction is the right crystallized. Furthermore, although the right to receive information seems to imply that government must be the transmitter for anyone with something to say, such a position is difficult to justify on available precedent.[129]

Perhaps the student and the teacher can be said to enjoy a reciprocal right of academic freedom,[130] since "the teacher's right to speak in the classroom is the necessary complement of the public school student's right to receive educational information."[131]

BALANCING THE INTERESTS

Some would say that to ascribe free speech rights to any of the parties involved is a "circular quest," because teachers, students, parents, librarians, administrators and board members do not operate independently of each other and of the government but, rather, are "intimately entwined in a *forum* created, maintained, funded, staffed, and populated by public action and force, including the powers of taxation and (through truancy laws) criminal fines or imprisonment."[132] On this view, curricular or teaching methodology choices made by school boards should be justiciable only when allegedly violating a legal right other than free speech.[133]

Indeed, in view of public education's lofty goal of preserving our democracy, the right to academic freedom may belong, in varying degrees of intensity, to all of society. Academic freedom, the U.S. Supreme Court has reminded us, is of "transcendent value to all of us and not merely to the teachers concerned."[134]

It is clear that any first amendment rights within the school cannot be absolute.[135] Justice Holmes would surely preclude falsely shouting fire in a classroom as well as in a theater.[136] The freedom, then, is one of "responsible inquiry"[137] and must therefore be balanced against all competing interests.[138] Such a balancing, obviously, requires examination of the particular facts of the case.[139] Accordingly, the Court of Appeals for the First Circuit resisted one trial court's attempt to set general principles in the area: "With all respect to the District Court's sensitive effort to devise guidelines for weighing those circumstances . . . any such formulation would introduce more problems than it would resolve. At present, we see no substitute for a case-by-case inquiry. . . . "[140]

Indeed, when the teacher's right to select aspects of the curriculum is pitted against the power of the state, perhaps, one court has suggested, "state regulatory control of the classroom is entitled to prevail unless the teacher bears the heavy burden of proving that it has no rational justification . . . or is discriminatory on religious, racial, political, or like grounds."[141]

Other courts have been less restrictive, interpreting *Tinker* to justify restraints on first amendment freedom in the schools only when the disruption reaches a material or substantial degree.[142]

THE FACTORS

Good Faith

What factors will the courts consider in assessing a teacher's use of sexually-oriented material in class? First, the teacher using such material should be in good faith[143] and reasonably careful. In the "Masculinity Survey" case, it probably did not help the teacher's case, though she ultimately prevailed, that she failed to read the controversial article in its entirety, but rather merely skimmed it, prior to its use in class.[144] On the other hand, when a complaint about use of the survey was received, the teacher personally called the complainant to discuss the matter.[145] A court will inevitably see good faith reflected in this kind of conduct, as the court in that case did.[146] Conversely, courts will find it relevant to inquire whether the other parties in the controversy were in good faith. The trial court in the "Masculinity Survey" case found that the Superintendent had "failed to act in good faith in the discharge of Mrs. Dean."[147]

Relevance

Second, the use must be relevant. When a high school biology teacher brought suit challenging the denial of his continuing contract status, the U.S. District Court held that he had abused his authority by leaving legitimate areas of discussion to relate personal experiences with Japanese prostitutes.[148] In another case, on the other hand, the court found that an offending word was not artificially introduced in an assigned article but was important to the author's thesis and conclusion; furthermore, the teacher could not properly have avoided consideration of the word in a classroom discussion of the article.[149]

It is clear that the sexual nature of the recital plays a significant role in the extent to which irrelevance will be penalized. After all, some matters of irrelevance will always creep into a classroom, and we have perhaps all had teachers who spent considerable time off the assigned subject, sometimes to great profit, if not in the lessons of class, in those of life. As one court has recognized, "[F]rom time to time it may be necessary for a school teacher to delve into thought provoking discussions with students that may well concern areas of interest other than English, Biology, American History, or the like."[150] It is usually only when the topic is sensitive—like sex[151]—that school officials will take action, perhaps due to parental complaints, and, if the discussion was irrelevant, the courts will sustain the official action. One commentator perhaps put it best, warning that the teacher should not use "*controversial* matter which has no relation to his subject."[152]

Presumably, the amount of time devoted to irrelevancy will also be taken into account.[153] The longer the time devoted to irrelevancy, one surmises, the less sensitive need the content be to justify official action.

In passing on the issue of relevance, courts must also take into account whether the teacher should reasonably know the limits of the assigned subject matter. An expert is more likely to know (and defend the use of) the material and techniques appropriate to a course related to his expertise. In the "Masculinity Survey" case, the teacher was currently teaching five classes in five different subjects: Drama, Junior English, Senior English, Speech and Psychology. In addition, she was directing a Junior Class play and participating in the filming and editing of a student project for a state arts commission.[154] Teachers with such a load and variety of assignments must be given considerable leeway in deciding what is relevant to what course. After all, a teacher makes decisions day-by-day and minute-by-minute on what to assign, discuss or answer; however, when a controversy develops, parents and school officials can mull over for weeks the one item at issue.

When controversy does arise over materials or methods, the teacher should enjoy an initial presumption of validity due to his presumably greater qualifications to judge their educational value and effect.[155] Furthermore, the total context is crucial in evaluating the use of controversial material or techniques which, considered only in isolation, can appear much more outrageous than is in fact the case. As one court put it, the "offensiveness of language and the particular propriety or impropriety [are] dependent on the circumstances of the utterance."[156] The teacher has an obvious and large edge over parents and administrators in judging the total context. This said, courts will clearly emphasize "the closeness of the relation between the specific techniques used and some concededly valid educational objective. . . . [157]

Unlawfulness of the Material or of Potentially Induced Conduct

It is clear, in any event, that a teacher may not use obscene material.[158] After all, since obscenity falls outside the protection of the First Amendment even among the general public, surely it need not be allowed in the schools, however relevant it might arguably be. One Court of Appeals, assessing the assignment and discussion of a controversial article, noted that it was in no way pornographic, implying that if it was, its use might be prohibited.[159] This is not to say, however, that whatever is *not* obscene, even under the variable obscenity standard for children,[160] is permissible in the schools.[161] Material used in class must meet several criteria.

It has been said that the state could "obviously" forbid a teacher's use of profanity.[162] This seems not to be self-evident. If a teacher uses some common profanities to make himself more clearly understood by and more relevant to his twelfth graders, could he not assert that his method of expression was protected under the First Amendment, which presumably protects the right not only to say something, but to say it effectively?[163] Perhaps this example illustrates the difficulty of framing absolute principles in this area.

The *Island Trees* case, though no opinion garnered a majority vote and although only library books were involved, does signal some limits to a teacher's use of vulgarity or of materials containing vulgarity. There, Justice Brennan strongly suggested that the school board could keep out of the schools anything "pervasively vulgar" or, still more vaguely, anything educationally unsuitable.[164] When something becomes pervasively vulgar and, in any event, what criteria are appropriate in judging educational suitability, however, are not clear. Both of the inquiries would seem to require an assessment of the effectiveness and necessity of the use of the vulgarity in a particular context. Language in Justice Rehnquist's *Island Trees* dissent suggests the difficult lines to be drawn here: "[T]he petitioners may in one sense be said to have 'suppressed' the 'ideas' of vulgarity and profanity, but that is hardly an apt description of what was done. They ordered the removal of books containing vulgarity and profanity, but they did not attempt to preclude discussion about the themes of the books or the books themselves."[165] Moreover, why is not the school board the appropriate decisionmaker with regard to educational suitability?[166]

A related question is whether the material tends to induce to libidinous conduct or perhaps even thought.[167] With reference to a controversial assignment, one court observed that if the article raised the subject of incest, it was to condemn it, not to encourage it.[168] Material or techniques which are likely to spur students on to antisocial conduct, even if that conduct is not strictly illegal, may presumably be barred from the classroom.

Complaints

Perhaps as a partial index of how objectionable the material or techniques used in class are, courts have noticed whether and how many complaints were received from parents, students or others.[169] In *Moore v School Board of Gulf County, Florida,*[170] the trial court included in its findings of fact that "numerous complaints" had been made to school officials, most from parents but some from students and one from another teacher.[171] In *Parducci v Rutland,*[172] involving the assignment of a Vonnegut short story, three students had requested excusal from the assignment and several parents had called to complain; most students, the court found, had reacted with apathy.[173]

There are, of course, several problems in attributing significance to the number of complaints received. First, how many is many? Does not the *Parducci* court's statement that "only three" students out of ninety asked to be excused ignore the fact that most assignments get no such reaction and that, given the tendency to inertia, perhaps many more students found the assignment objectionable? Furthermore, perhaps many students discovered the alleged offensiveness too far into the assignment to feel that a complaint or demand for an optional assignment was in order. With regard to parental objections, perhaps many parents never found out the details of the assigned material and therefore never had to decide whether to complain.

Furthermore, if parental complaints are to be considered, might it not be helpful to know how many parents find the assignment appropriate, indeed even highly desirable? In the nature of things, however, people are more likely to register their complaint than their approval, and those complaints that do eventuate may be registered with the Superintendent's office, the principal or even the teacher, who is not likely to convey them to school officials. The true significance of the complaints, therefore, is not likely to be known.

Age Appropriateness of the Material

In *Keefe v Geanakos,*[174] the plaintiff, the tenured head of the English Department, coordinator of grades seven through twelve of the Ipswich, Massachusetts, Public School System, and a part-time teacher of English, brought suit to enjoin school officials from pursuing dismissal proceedings against him. The basis of the official unhappiness with him concerned his assigning to a senior English class an article entitled, "The Young and the Old," appearing in the September, 1969, *Atlantic Monthly,* "a publication of high reputation."[175] Written by Robert J. Lifton, a psychiatrist and professor at a noted medical school, the article used the word "motherfucker" or, as the court gently put it, a "word, admittedly highly offensive, [which] is a vulgar term for an incestuous son."[176] Called before the school committee, the teacher asserted as a matter of conscience that he could not promise never again to use the word in class.

The court obviously felt that the age of the students exposed to controversial material or techniques is crucial, as reflected in Chief Judge Aldrich's statement of the issue: "Hence the question in this case is whether a teacher may, for demonstrated educational purposes, quote a 'dirty' word currently used in order to give special offense, or whether the shock is too great for high school seniors to stand."[177] Labelling the article scholarly, thoughtful and thought-provoking, the court emphasized that the word was not unknown to many high school seniors.[178] The court took judicial notice that young radicals and protestors all over the country used the term. "If the answer were that the students must be protected from such exposure," said the court, "we would fear for their future."[179]

Moreover, the age level need not be one at which there is no reaction whatever to the material or the technique. Some unease may be acceptable, indeed inevitable. In another "dirty word" case, a federal district court observed that "[b]oys and girls in an eleventh grade have a sophistication sufficient to treat the word from a serious educational viewpoint. While at first they may be surprised and self-conscious to have the word discussed, they are not likely to be embarrassed or offended."[180] This approach, reminiscent of the sliding-scale approach to the "marketplace of ideas,"[181] would clearly disapprove of the same material used in an elementary level grade.

Observations that appropriateness depends on the "age and sophistication"[182] of the students, however, fail to give full attention to the fact that grade levels are overwhelmingly age-dependent, not sophistication-dependent. In a typical high school class, there may be a tremendous range between the least mature and the most mature students. The eleventh grade, for example, is not usually further broken down into more or less sophisticated groups. Even where some form of tracking, advanced placement, or honors courses are used, the separation is based on intellectual rather than emotional criteria. Nonetheless, the grade level tells us enough, at least in broad strokes, to warrant its careful use in evaluating the propriety of teaching material or techniques.

Comparison With Other Material

Courts are understandably interested in how the allegedly offensive curriculum material or technique compares with material or techniques that are otherwise easily available to students or are, in any event, of recognized appropriateness.

In *Parducci v. Rutland*,[183] the plaintiff-teacher assigned to her eleventh grade English class a short story, "Welcome to the Monkey House," a comic satire by Kurt Vonnegut, Jr. On the day following the assignment, the Associate Superintendent and the Principal expressed to her their unhappiness with the assignment. They called the story "literary garbage," and felt it condoned if not encouraged the killing of the elderly and free sex. The plaintiff, despite their admonishment, felt a professional obligation to teach the story. She was ultimately dismissed for giving an assignment with an allegedly disruptive effect.

Evaluating the content of the short story, the court noted that the slang words occurred in two short rhymes less ribald than some Shakespearean lines; the act of sexual intercourse is described, continued the court, in language no more descriptive than the rape account in Alexander Pope's "Rape of the Lock."[184] Moreover, the school's Junior English Reading List included J. D. Salinger's *Catcher in the Rye*, which "contains far more offensive and descriptive language. . . . "[185] Finally, the court noted that the school library itself contained books with controversial words and philosophies.[186]

In making these observations, the court was clearly pursuing two points. First, if similar material can be found in what is concededly classic literature, then the material itself is not sufficient cause for banning. Second, if similar material is made available to the students through the book list or through the school library, then the school officials are acting arbitrarily, enigmatically and perhaps grossly unfairly.[187] As one court commented, in noting that the school library contained at least five books using the allegedly offensive word whose discussion in class occasioned disciplinary action against the teacher,[188] "It is hard to think that any student could walk into the library and receive a book, but that his teacher could not subject the content to serious discussion in class."[189]

Although helpful, this comparison approach must be carefully employed. First, the true classic has by definition withstood the test of time, perhaps indicating that the context, tone and purpose of the language in controversy justify its use. Its nature as a classic might further indicate that, in any event, the literary worth of the piece clearly outweighs that particular language. Neither of these claims is inevitably true of the material whose use in class is contested.

Second, when complaints do surface concerning material used in connection with the curriculum, it is obviously because the complaining party or school official has somehow learned of the offending material. No inconsistency can be alleged if indeed neither of these parties was aware, at the time of their action, of other accessible material with similar content. Often, the detailed search of the library will occur only after the onset of disciplinary proceedings or even litigation. Perhaps the same action would have been taken in connection with those other works had they been brought to the complainant's attention. Moreover, neither a parent nor a school official need necessarily move against *all* "evils" at once in order appropriately to move against one.

Third, books in the school library will not necessarily be read by every student. Libraries often exercise discretion as to who may borrow a book, and books with controversial themes or language can be kept in a separate collection to ensure further the use of discretion. Teachers assigning book reports are in a position to require their approval of any student's selection of a book from the library or from a book list.

Although comparisons are usually with works of accepted merit, at least one court has seen fit to compare the challenged work with others of clearly less literary worth. In *Todd v. Rochester Community Schools,*[190] a parent challenged on religious grounds the use of Kurt Vonnegut's *Slaughterhouse-Five* in the community's public schools. Feeling constrained, due to the lower court's treatment of the case, to discuss whether the novel was obscene, and alluding to the U.S. Supreme Court's opinion in *Redrup v. New York,*[191] which held paperback books entitled *Lust Pool* and *Shame Agent* not to be obscene, the Court of Appeals of Michigan stated:

> [I]t is ludicrous to consider *Slaughterhouse-Five* in the same literary niche as *Lust Pool* and *Shame Agent.* If the latter are not convicted because of their profanity, the former should not even stand trial. *Slaughterhouse-Five* is Sunday school reading compared to these paperbacks. We do not wish to demean Mr. Vonnegut by making such ridiculous comparisons.[192]

As a tactical matter, finally, courts or others may be unwilling, in curriculum cases, to rely heavily on a comparison with school library books available, lest such an approach lead not to an expansion of the curriculum but to a "bowdlerization" of the school library.[193]

Teacher Methodology

Relevant too is the manner in which the teacher presents the material to the students. In *Mailloux v. Kiley*,[194] the plaintiff-teacher assigned to his eleventh grade basic English class, about twenty-five boys and girls sixteen and seventeen years of age, outside reading consisting of chapters from Jesse Stuart's novel, *The Thread That Runs So True*. Based on the author's experiences as a young schoolteacher in a rural area, the novel describes how he had taken over a classroom in which all boys sat on one side and all girls on the other. The young schoolteacher intermingled the sexes in seating, prompting complaints from parents that he was conducting a "courting school."

During a subsequent discussion of the book in class, and after some students had called the parents' protest ridiculous, the plaintiff stated that some current societal views were equally ridiculous. Using taboo words as an illustration, he wrote the word "goo" on the board and asked its definition, which no one could provide. Plaintiff explained to the students that the word did not exist in English but might be a taboo word in some other culture. He then wrote the word "fuck" (which did not appear in the novel) on the blackboard and, in accordance with his usual teaching method, called on volunteers for a definition. Ultimately, one boy volunteered the definition of "sexual intercourse." Plaintiff then said, " 'We have two words, sexual intercourse and this one on the board. . . . [O]ne . . . is acceptable by society [and] the other is not accepted. It is a taboo word.' "[195] Plaintiff discussed other aspects of taboos for a short time and then moved on to other subjects. Discharged, he sued for reinstatement.

The U.S. District Court recognized that teachers dealing in sensitive material must themselves be sensitive. "[A] teacher who uses a taboo sexual word must take care not to transcend his legitimate professional purpose . . . He must not sacrifice his dignity to join his pupils as 'frere et cochon.' "[196]

The Court found, however, that the plaintiff had not transcended legitimate professional purposes, and was clearly impressed by the plaintiff's mode of presentation. It noted specifically that the teacher had written the word on the board, but had not spoken it himself. "A class might be less disturbed by having the word written than if it had been spoken."[197] The court, stating that discussion of a taboo sexual word in a class of adolescent boys and girls "must not go beyond asking for verbal knowledge and become a titillating probe of privacy,"[198] found that the teacher had not attempted to explore the private feelings, attitudes or experiences of the students or to embarrass them.[199]

This point seems crucial in such cases. The court in the "Masculinity Survey" case specifically noted that the teacher had instructed the student administering the instrument to omit any questions that assumed the students were married or sexually active.[200]

Whether the class is a mixed one sexually may also be relevant.[201] There is some suggestion, indeed, that a male teacher may appropriately put to a male student a question involving sexually sensitive material which would be inappropriate put to a female.[202] If this suggestion is based on the idea that girls are less able to deal with such material, it is open to a charge of sexism. It is perhaps more justifiable if based on the different sex of the teacher,[203] since such a situation is more prone to titillation, real or apparent. Furthermore, that principle could be equally applied to a female teacher quizzing a male.

In any event, it should be added that current attitudes may put to a dilemma the male teacher who calls on students with regard to sexually sensitive material: if he calls on female students, he may be seen to be indulging in titillation and, if he does not, in sexism.

Another important factor in cases involving sensitive material concerns the freedom given students to decide the extent of their involvement. In *Mailloux v. Kiley*, for example, the court approved of the device of calling on volunteers since it avoided implicating anyone who might not want to participate.[204] In the "Masculinity Survey" case, the exercise was optional and those who chose to participate could skip any questions for any reason whatever.[205] In *Keefe v. Geanakos*, any student finding the *Atlantic Monthly* assignment distasteful could have received an alternative one.[206] In *Cary v. Board of Education of Adams-Arapahoe School District 28-J, Aurora, Colorado*, the school board ultimately adopted a written policy allowing substitution for assignment material offensive to a student or a parent.[207]

The opting out policy, however, creates problems. With regard to a reading assignment, neither the student nor the parent may be aware of the nature of the material until the student has been exposed to it. It is difficult for a teacher to test fairly on material for which all students cannot be held accountable. In any subsequent classroom discussion, the teacher must be careful not to allude to the material students have been excused from without providing a new option. Furthermore, any student excused from some curricular matter at his or a parent's request is possibly subject to ridicule or other special notice. This threat is especially strong when the students are adolescents and the material is sexually-oriented. One commentator has objected that representative government cannot long condone a process permitting personal retraction of power delegated to school officials.[208]

Professional Judgment

Central to any assessment of a teacher's use of sexually-oriented material in the curriculum is the issue of professional judgment, that is, whether a significant body of competent opinion in the field—not "all reasonable men"[209]—would find the use appropriate. The competent opinion might come from one or more of at least three different groups: (1) education specialists, for example from schools of education;[210] (2) teachers generally; and (3) teachers in the particular discipline involved.[211] School administrators too might testify to what is generally done, although such testimony would seem less pertinent.

In *Mailloux v. Kiley*, the court resorted to this device in observing, despite conflict among the experts,[212] that "the weight of the testimony offered leads this court to make an ultimate finding that [the teacher's] methods served an educational purpose, in the sense that they were relevant and had professional endorsement from experts of significant standing."[213]

Why is professional judgment relevant? Since the teacher's claim will be that the first amendment, perhaps among other legal rights, protects what he sought or seeks to do, the validity of the claim must stand or fall with its appropriate relationship to his valid objectives in the school system. Surely those most knowledgeable in the field have much to tell us concerning the appropriateness of certain material or devices to the teacher's particular mission.

Nonetheless, expert opinion is not *per se* controlling. If a majority of the English teachers in the country suddenly decided, for whatever reason, that all sixth graders should read *Lady Chatterley's Lover*, courts would not be bound to incorporate that judgment into constitutional law. After all, expert opinion is just that—opinion. Moreover, the decision as to whether particular materials or techniques are appropriate often goes beyond the narrow expertise of the particular expert. Although our hypothetical English teachers might want *Lady Chatterley's Lover* read by all sixth graders, other experts (for example, psychologists)—or the court's own judgment—might counsel against.

Expert opinion would surely be crucial in assessing whether action by administrators themselves was based on reasonable educational judgment, a standard which, it has been suggested, accommodates the tension between freedom of expression and the school board's desire to protect the interests of the community.[214] In *Parducci v. Rutland*,[215] for example, the U.S. District Court felt constrained to point out that neither the Principal or the Associate Superintendent, both of whom had expressed their displeasure to a teacher for assigning a particular short story, had ever taught English, was much of a reader or had literary expertise.[216]

The expert, in judging whether a certain course of conduct was appropriate, will of necessity inquire into, and rely upon, the relevance, age appropriateness, and other factors already discussed so that, in a sense, expert judgment becomes not a wholly separate criterion but a different method of weighing those other factors.

The "Tinker" Test

If the professional judgment test tends to be a composite one by incorporating the others[217] by reference, the *Tinker* test constitutes the "bottom line" standard. Even though that case involved a student's right to wear a black armband and not, therefore, curricular speech, the U.S. Supreme Court opinion in that case signalled that no one—administrator, teacher or student—has a right to expression which materially and substantially disrupts school operations.[218] This test, however, grants considerable leeway and it is perhaps in reliance on it that "teachers and students have pressed their first amendment rights of free speech to both assign and read materials and to discuss topics of their choice, contrary to the expressed wishes or regulations of school authorities."[219]

The *Tinker* test may be a bottom line, however, only in specifying what may clearly be proscribed—speech that materially or substantially disrupts. It may not—and probably does not—state the converse, namely, that whatever speech is not materially or substantially disruptive is permissible.

"The Court's decision in *Tinker* has given lower courts difficulty in applying the test, and has caused some commentators to suggest that either the Court did not mean to delineate all the circumstances in which school authorities could regulate teacher conduct, or the Court simply did not mean what it said."[220] Nonetheless, the *Tinker* test has played a key role in cases dealing with the curricular use of sexually-oriented materials or techniques.

In *Parducci v. Rutland*, the Court alluded to the *Tinker* doctrine in holding that the dismissal of the teacher who used the Vonnegut short story violated First Amendment rights because the assignment did not involve inappropriate material and was not significantly disruptive.[221] The clear implication, however, is that nondisruptive but otherwise inappropriate material, as determined by criteria discussed earlier, may be outlawed. Potential for disruption, therefore, constitutes but one factor, although an important one.

Moreover, the relevant potential for disruption may be that in the school itself, not in the community at large: the "Masculinity Survey" case held in favor of the teacher, in large part because the exercise occasioned no "outburst, disruption, or similar conduct" in the classroom, even though "the reported use of the survey caused no small amount of disruption in the community."[222] What is not clear is why community disruption is not a significant *Tinker* factor.

Indeed, one can hypothesize situations in which outrageous materials are used in a second grade class, creating no disruption there—perhaps because the students are not mature or sophisticated enough to know the full implication of their exposure to the materials. Would not a pervasive community revolt in such a case trigger the *Tinker* test? Perhaps the court in the survey case felt that the community reaction was unreasonable in light of the smooth in-class administration of the survey and should for that reason be discounted. The court might even have thought that to credit community reaction would allocate too much control to the most vocal of parents. Finally, it is possible that the court's reference to "disruption" in the community was a misuse of the term. After all, the school system and, as far as we know, all other governmental processes continued to operate well. Disruption that is material and substantial signifies more than the vociferous complaints of many irate citizens; it signifies some significant dysfunction in the community, as the court ultimately seems to accept,[223] pointing out that if community disruption were the test, evolution would never have been taught in Arkansas[224] and, indeed, nothing straying from the majoritarian perspective would be taught in public schools.[225]

As the Court in *Tinker* made clear, the disruption criterion is not activated merely by some generalized or undifferentiated apprehension of disturbance:

> Any departure from absolute regimentation may cause trouble. Any variation from the majority's opinion may inspire fear. Any word spoken, in class, in the lunchroom, or on the campus, that deviates from the views of another person, may start an argument or cause a disturbance. But our Constitution says we must take this risk . . . and our history says that it is this sort of hazardous freedom—this kind of openness—that is the basis of our national strength and of the independence and vigor of Americans who grow up and live in this . . . often disputatious society.[226]

THE QUESTION OF NOTICE

Relevant to any discussion of the curricular use of sexually-oriented materials or techniques are the extent of any advance notice[227] to the teacher concerning their use and the effect of any notice. The cases suggest three categories of material or techniques.

The first includes that which is generally understood to be so necessary or at least appropriate to a particular course that the teacher is entitled to use it, perhaps even if specifically warned not to.[228] The second includes material or techniques that are so outrageous that any reasonable teacher would know them to be impermissible, even without notice[229], or that a school board might not anticipate in drawing up regulations.[230] An English teacher who, discussing a play with sexual content, actually demonstrates sexual activity in the classroom or asks students to do so, would fall within this category. For disciplinary action to result in such a case, no specific regulation need be called upon; the teacher should have known. A third category presents the real difficulty, since it involves material or techniques not essential to teaching the course, nor so outrageous that any reasonable teacher would have known them to be inappropriate.

Judge Wyzanski's opinion in *Mailloux v. Kiley*[231] well illustrates the situation. The judge found that experts of significant stature supported the teacher's use of the word "fuck" to illustrate the concept of taboo. Nonetheless, other experts deemed use of the word in those circumstances unreasonable. The trial record did not allow the court to determine the preponderant view of the teaching profession, or of that part of it teaching English.[232] The court concluded that a teacher who uses a method which divides expert opinion, and which the court in its own assessment cannot find plainly permissible, may be suspended or discharged for using such a method. Such drastic penalties, however, may not be visited upon him unless he was somehow put on notice that that method was not to be used.[233]

Judge Wyzanski stated that this "exclusively procedural" protection is granted the teacher not because he is a citizen or a public employee, but because as a teacher he is exercising "what may plausibly be considered 'vital first amendment rights.' "[234] The difficulty with this position is its failure directly to delimit any substantive first amendment right to use material or methods in this third category. What results is merely a right to be warned about what will not be tolerated, a purely Fourteenth Amendment due process concept of notice.[235]

This right to be warned, however, may be nothing more than what the teacher would be entitled to in nonspeech areas, for example if school officials sought to fire a male teacher for not wearing a coat and tie in class. It is true that a clear warning of what to avoid allows greater freedom to the extent that vagueness, since it requires the actor to guess at the line between approved and disapproved behavior, may cause him to stay far from wherever the line *might* be.[236] The rule that no one should be punished except for conduct clearly proscribed, therefore, is especially important in First Amendment cases,[237] a tie-in between the First and Fourteenth Amendments which the U.S. Supreme Court has recognized.[238] In any event, it seems clear that academic freedom should afford a teacher more latitude in judging the appropriateness of material where standards have not been provided by school officials.[239]

Where notice is required, what will be sufficient? Surely a statute, a regulation,[240] or a letter sent to beginning teachers can provide suitable notice. Judge Wyzanski alluded to still other methods in stating he could find no substantial evidence that the teacher's discussion of the taboo word was "contrary to an informal rule, to an understanding among school teachers of his school or teachers generally, to a body of disciplinary precedents, to precise canons of ethics, or to specific opinions expressed in professional journals or other publications."[241] The terms or limits of any notice might come from a school official's prior dealings with others, if known to the teacher.[242] As indicated earlier, conduct so outrageous that any teacher should have known it to be inappropriate might itself provide the notice.[243] If a statute or school board regulation prescribes a method for giving such notice, adherence to that method may be required.[244]

Some will settle for quite imprecise language, as did one court, reviewing a teacher demotion for reading to her classes at least part of a note she found circulating among her students, a note which contained three vulgar colloquialisms. State statutes penalized neglect of duty and required teachers to maintain discipline and to encourage morality. The U.S. Court of Appeals for the Fourth Circuit agreed with the trial court that the statutory language gave the teacher sufficient notice of the unacceptability of her conduct: "The regulations prescribing a teacher's speech and conduct are necessarily broad; they cannot possibly mention every specific kind of misconduct."[245]

Two points are in order. First, precisely because speech is involved, greater clarity in any such regulation is needed. Second, the state was not helpless to improve the situation. It might have specified that "no vulgarity or obscenity is to be used in class." This language would seem to meet any notice requirements imposed by the Fourteenth Amendment, whatever one might say of it under the First.[246] In any event, the teacher could have been merely reprimanded, and a written explanation of her transgression given her so that she might avoid future violations.

The U.S. Court of Appeals for the First Circuit, considering *Mailloux v. Kiley* on appeal, did agree that the teacher had received insufficient notice, despite the provision in a Code of Ethics that the teacher "recognizes the supreme importance of the pursuit of the truth, devotion to excellence and the nurture of democratic citizenship." This laudable standard, said the court, is "impermissibly vague." The court declined, however, to approve Judge Wyzanski's "sensitive effort to devise guidelines for weighing [the relevant circumstances]" in such cases.[247]

In the "Masculinity Survey" case, Mrs. Dean had on a previous occasion administered an "Ethics Survey" dealing with a number of social issues, such as drug use, euthanasia, artificial reproduction methods and organ transplanting. The Superintendent and the Principal stated that Mrs. Dean had been told following that incident "not to bring materials of a similar nature into the classroom without prior clearance by the school administration."[248] Mrs. Dean denied receiving such a warning. The court was able to deal with this evidentiary conflict in two ways. First, implicitly putting upon school officials the duty to establish a permanent record of such notice, the court observed that there was no notation in the teacher's file of any such warning and that the school board never issued a written policy on the use of such materials. Second, if there ever was any warning, it "was of an ambiguous or vague nature, such that a reasonably prudent person could not discern what conduct the warning sought to prevent."[249]

If indeed she was told not to use "materials of a similar nature" without prior approval, was the court correct in finding the warning too vague? If from this language she had to determine at her peril whether the Masculinity Survey was prohibited, the court is surely correct, since whether that survey was "similar in nature" to the Ethics Survey is a difficult question to resolve. But the warning she received did not purport to provide the final word on what was ultimately prohibited but rather gave her notice that before she used materials that might raise similar concerns she should seek the advice of school officials. Perhaps the real issue is not whether the alleged warning effectively conveyed with reasonable specificity what material was proscribed, but rather whether the warning would put the teacher on notice that the Masculinity Survey was a device which school officials would want to see before she exposed the students to it. Although still not a model of clarity, the warning came much closer to carrying the latter message.

Finally, in any assessment of the notice provided by a contract, or any language which it incorporates by reference, three rules of construction should be remembered. First, courts will take into account any surrounding circumstances;[250] second, the contract will be construed against the party whose terms are ambiguous;[251] third, courts will usually adopt the practical construction which the parties' subsequent conduct lends to the agreement.[252]

CONCLUSION

The rights of several different constituencies are implicated in curriculum decisions. To be sure, the public school must play a basic, inculcative role and some courts seem ready to grant school officials almost total discretion over curriculum content. We must remember, however, the dangers of orthodoxy and the fact that such officials need not, and should not, exercise their constitutional power to the limit; constitutionality and wisdom are not interchangeable terms. Our children, entitled of course to a solid grounding in basic values, learn better, learn more deeply and learn more willingly when exposed to a variety of ideas. We do them an injustice, on the other hand, when we presume that they are only fit to receive a homogenized education, every facet of which is digestible to the great majority of the population.

Accordingly, teachers should be allowed great leeway in their classroom discussions, especially when these are clearly undertaken in good faith. Teachers must be allowed to be innovative, indeed provocative. When restraints are deemed necessary, notice as specific as the subject matter permits should be provided.

NOTES

1. These facts are drawn from Dean v. Timpson Independent School District, 486 F.Supp. 302, 304–307 (E.D. Texas 1979).
2. *Psychology Today* (March, 1976).
3. Dean v. Timpson Independent School District, 486 F.Supp. at 306.
4. *Id.* at 307.
5. "Curriculum," as used in this volume, refers to classroom discussion, assignments, examinations and textbooks. It does not directly refer to library books (considered in Chapter 3, *infra*), or to extracurriculars such as student newspapers (considered in Chapter 6, *infra*), unless, like in some schools, production of the student paper is itself a regular course. At least one court has considered a school play to be part of the curriculum. See Seyfried v. Walton, 668 F.2d 214, 216 (3d Cir. 1981).
6. U.S. CONST. amend. V: "Congress shall make no law . . . abridging the freedom of speech, or of the press. . . . "
7. U.S. CONST. amend XIV: "[N]or shall any state deprive any person of life, liberty, or property, without due process of law. . . . "
8. See Goldstein, *The Asserted Constitutional Right of Public School Teachers to Determine What They Teach*, 124 U.PA.L. REV. 1239, 1355–1357 (1976).
9. Of the fifteen thousand school boards in this country, over seventy-five percent are elected. Diamond, *The First Amendment and Public Schools: the Case Against Judicial Intervention*, 59 TEXAS L.REV. 477, 509 (1981).
10. See Orleans, *What Johnny Can't Read: "First Amendment Rights" in the Classroom*, 10 J. LAW & EDUCATION 1, 7 (1981). Indeed, perhaps no government agency is closer to the people it serves. See Board of Education, Island Trees Union Free School District No. 26 v. Pico, 457 U.S. 853, 894 (1982) (Powell, J., dissenting) (hereafter *Island Trees*).
11. Orleans, *supra* note 10, at 2.
12. It should be noted that barring a book, film or the like from the classroom does more than deny access to that item. "The symbolic effect . . . is more significant than the resulting limitation of access. . . . ", and the "message [that certain ideas are unacceptable for discussion] is not lost on students and teachers, and its chilling effect is obvious." Pratt v. Independent School District No. 831, Forest Lake, Minnesota, 670 F.2d 771, 779 (8th Cir 1982). See text in Chapter 3, *infra*, at note 46.
13. Zykan v. Warsaw Community School Corp., 631 F.2d 1300, 1305 (7th Cir. 1980);

Cary v. Board of Education of the Adams-Arapahoe School District 28-J, Aurora, Colorado, 598 F.2d 535, 544 (10th Cir. 1979).

14. Cary v. Board of Education of Adams-Arapahoe School District 28-J, Aurora, Colorado, 598 F.2d at 543.

15. Orleans, *supra* note 10, at 2.

16. *Id.* at 12.

17. See Chapter 3, *infra.*

18. *Island Trees,* 457 U.S. 853 (1982).

19. See KY. REV. STAT. ANN. § 158.200 (Baldwin 1981), authorizing local school boards to provide for the "moral instruction" of pupils subject to their jurisdiction. See also *id.* § 158.210 *et seq. Cf. id.* § 158.190, prohibiting the use of "immoral" publications and the teaching of "immoral" doctrine in any common school. For a discussion of the vagueness of the term "immoral" in another context, see text *infra,* Chapter 4, at notes 81–153.

20. *Island Trees,* 457 U.S. at 864. See also Zykan v. Warsaw Community School Corp., 631 F.2d at 1305, holding that school boards may even act on their members' personal moral, social or political views; and Cary v. Board of Education of Adams-Arapahoe School District 28-J, Aurora, Colorado, 598 F.2d at 544.

21. *Island Trees,* 457 U.S. at 869 (emphasis in original). See also *id.* at 862: "Respondents do not seek to impose limitations upon their school board's discretion to prescribe the curricula of the Island Trees schools."

22. Indeed, no majority could be mustered on the central issue in the case. See *id.* at 886, n.2 (dissenting opinion) ("Fortunately, there is no binding holding on the critical constitutional issue presented").

23. *Id.* at 861. Justice Blackmun would qualify this: "[T]he state may not suppress exposure to ideas—for the sole *purpose* of suppressing exposure to those ideas—absent sufficiently compelling reasons." *Id.* at 877 (concurring in part).

24. *Id.* at 871.

25. *Id.* at 892 (dissenting opinion).

25. *Id.* at 862: "Our adjudication of the present case . . . does not intrude into the classroom, or into the *compulsory* courses taught there." (Emphasis added).

27. See Comment, *What Johnny Can't Read: School Boards and the First Amendment,* 42 U.PITT.L. REV. 653, 664–665 (1981). Some states have open meeting requirements. *Id.*

28. Stern, *Challenging Ideological Exclusion of Curriculum Material: Rights of Students and Parents,* 14 HARVARD CIVIL RIGHTS–CIVIL LIBERTIES L.REV. 485, 491 (1979).

29. *Id.* at 493, n.47 (citing Ambach v. Norwick, 441 U.S. 68, 77 (1979)).

30. *Id.* at 493.

31. See *Island Trees,* 457 U.S. at 880 (Blackmun, J., concurring).

32. *Id.* at 868 (plurality opinion).

33. Swartz, *You Can't Judge a Book by its Cover,* 17 TRIAL, no. 11, 89–91 (1981).

34. Stern, *supra* note 28, at 502.

35. See Note, *Schoolbooks, School Boards, and the Constitution,* 80 COLUMBIA L.REV. 1093, 1112 (1980).

36. See *Island Trees,* 457 U.S. at 868.

37. Comment, *supra* note 27, at 657. See also Dean v. Timpson Independent School

District, 486 F.Supp. at 308, suggesting that the educational process can be called the "shedding of dogmas."

38. Todd v. Rochester Community Schools, 41 Mich.App. 320, 340, 200 N.W.2d 90, 99 (1972).
39. Keyishian v. Board of Regents, 385 U.S. 589, 603 (1967) (quoting United States v. Associated Press, 52 F.Supp. 362, 372 (S.D.N.Y. 1943)). In the words of Justice Brennan, the "access to ideas . . . prepares students for active and effective participation in the pluralistic, often contentious society in which they will soon be adult members." *Island Trees*, 457 U.S. at 868 (plurality opinion). See also Stern, *supra* note 28, at 487: "Fostering a free marketplace of ideas is an essential principle of the First Amendment. Nowhere is this tenet more important than in our nation's classrooms."
40. See Note, *supra* note 35, at 1105. See also *Island Trees*, 457 U.S. at 909, 914, 915, and 920 (Rehnquist, J., dissenting).
41. Mailloux v. Kiley, 323 F.Supp. 1387, 1392 (D. Mass. 1971), *aff'd*, 448 F.2d 1242 (1st Cir. 1971).
42. *Id.*
43. Orleans, *supra* note 10, at 3, n.6.
44. Stern, *supra* note 28, at 497.
45. *Id.*
46. West Virginia State Board of Education v. Barnette, 319 U.S. 624, 642 (1943).
47. Kemerer and Hirsch, *The Developing Law Involving the Teacher's Right to Teach*, 84 W.VA. L.REV. 31, 39, 41 (1981–82).
48. Webb v. Lake Mills Community School District, 344 F.Supp. 791, 799 (N.D. Iowa 1972). See also Seyfried v. Walton, 668 F.2d at 219–20 (concurring opinion).
49. Kemerer & Hirsch, *supra* note 47, at 41.
50. Seyfried v. Walton, 668 F.2d at 219 (concurring opinion). See *Island Trees*, 457 U.S. at 881–82 (Blackmun, J., concurring in part).
51. Kemerer and Hirsch, *supra* note 47, at 35.
52. Note, *supra* note 35, at 1095.
53. For a dramatic example, see Justice Marshall's description of the control exercised by the State of Michigan over its public schools. *Milliken v. Bradley*, 418 U.S. 717, 794–797 (1974) (dissenting opinion).

    Textbooks, which comprise an important part of the curriculum, are often selected through state-ordained procedures and often require state-level approval. See, *e.g.*, LA. REV. STAT. ANN. §§ 17:352, 17:415.1; OKLA. STAT. ANN. tit. 70, § 16-102 *et seq.* (West Supp. 1984); S.C. CODE § 59-31-50 (1977); TEX. EDUC. CODE ANN. § 12.24(a)(Vernon Supp. 1985); W.VA. REV. STAT. ANN. §§ 17:352, 17:415.1 (West 1982).
54. Stern, *supra* note 28, at 487. "Local control of a school system's curriculum by school boards organized at a community level characterizes the traditional allocation of responsibility for the education of our youth in the United States." Seyfried v. Walton, 668 F.2d at 218 (concurring opinion). See also Pratt v. Independent School District No. 831, Forest Lake, Minnesota, 670 F.2d at 775.
55. See Orleans, *supra* note 10, at 9. See also *Island Trees*, 457 U.S. at 885 (Burger, C. J., dissenting).
56. See *Island Trees*, 457 U.S. at 893–94 (Powell, J., dissenting).
57. Note, *supra* note 35, at 1097.

58. Orleans, *supra* note 10, at 3–4.
59. For a good discussion of the reasons for the increase in the 1960s and 1970s of controversy regarding schoolbooks and curriculum, see Orleans, *id.* at 6.
60. See, *e.g.*, Parker v. Board of Education of Prince George's County, Maryland, 348 F.2d 464 (4th Cir. 1965); and Moore v. School Board of Gulf County, Florida, 364 F.Supp. 355 (N.D. Fla. 1973).
61. 486 F.Supp. at 304.
62. Todd v. Rochester Community Schools, 41 Mich.App. at 337–38, 200 N.W.2d at 98.
63. See Note, *supra* note 35, at 1097.
64. See Orleans, *supra* note 10, at 9–10, bemoaning the alleged failure of the Department of Health, Education and Welfare, in the debate concerning whether Title IX of the Education Amendments of 1972, 20 U.S.C. § 1681, could be used by the Department to ban sexist books, to identify what or whose free speech right was in danger.
65. See Stone v. Graham, 449 U.S. 39 (1980); Abington School District v. Schempp, 374 U.S. 203 (1963); Engel v. Vitale, 370 U.S. 421 (1962); Cary v. Adams-Arapahoe School District 28-J, Aurora, Colorado, 598 F.2d at 544.
66. See Note, *supra* note 35, at 1111 (citing Palmer v. Board of Education, 603 F.2d 1271 (7th Cir. 1979), *cert. denied*, 444 U.S. 1026 (1980)). See also Minarcini v. Strongsville City School District, 541 F.2d 577, 579–580 (6th Cir. 1976).
67. Note, *supra* note 35, at 1110.
68. See Minarcini v. Strongsville City School District, 541 F.2d at 580.
69. Adams v. Campbell County School District, Campbell County, Wyoming, 511 F.2d 1242, 1247 (10th Cir. 1975).
70. Pratt v. Independent School District, 670 F.2d at 776.
71. See text at note 18 *et seq.*, *supra.*
72. See Zykan v. Warsaw Community School Corp., 631 F.2d at 1305, discussed *infra* at Chapter 3, note 84 *et seq.* See Seyfried v. Walton, 668 F.2d at 218; and Cary v. Board of Education of Adams-Arapahoe School District 28-J, Aurora, Colorado, 598 F.2d at 544.
73. Epperson v. Arkansas, 393 U.S. 97, 113–14 (1968).
74. Pickering v. Board of Education, 391 U.S. 563, 568 (1968). At issue there, however, was not curricular speech, but teacher speech outside the classroom. Justice Rehnquist, dissenting in *Island Trees*, alluded to this language in connection with a recent school library book case. *Island Trees*, 457 U.S. at 908 (dissenting opinion).
75. Cary v. Board of Education of Adams-Arapahoe School District 28-J, Aurora, Colorado, 598 F.2d at 543.
76. Osterhage, *Academic Freedom in the Classroom*, 1976–77 J.FAMILY LAW 706, 723.
77. See Parducci v. Rutland, 316 F.Supp. 352, 355 (M.D. Ala. 1970).
78. Osterhage, *supra* note 76, at 724.
79. *Id.* at 725.
80. *Id.*
81. *Id.* at 712.
82. Note, *supra* note 35, at 1112.
83. 316 F.Supp. 352 (M.D. Ala. 1970).
84. For further facts, see text accompanying note 183 *et seq.*, *infra.*

85. 316 F.Supp. at 355 (citing Sweezy v. New Hampshire, 354 U.S. 234 (1957) and Wieman v. Updegraff, 344 U.S. 183 (1952)).
86. 316 F.Supp. at 355 (Quoting Keyishian v. Board of Regents, 385 U.S. 589, 603 (1967)).
87. 316 F.Supp. at 357.
88. 344 U.S. 183 (1952).
89. *Id.* at 195.
90. *Id.* at 196.
91. See, *e.g., id.* at 183.
92. See Epperson v. Arkansas, 393 U.S. at 104 (The courts "have not failed to apply the First Amendment's mandate in our educational system where essential to safeguard the fundamental values of freedom of speech and inquiry and of belief.") (Decided on establishment clause grounds).
93. See Dean v. Timpson Independent School District, 486 F.Supp. at 307.
94. *Id.* (Citing Keyishian v. Board of Regents, 385 U.S. at 603; Mailloux v. Kiley, 448 F.2d 1242 (1st Cir. 1971), *aff'g* 323 F.Supp. 1387 (D. Mass. 1971); Keefe v. Geanakos, 418 F.2d 359 (1st Cir. 1969); Sterzing v. Fort Bend Independent School District, 376 F.Supp. 657 (S.D. Tex. 1972), *judgment vacated on other grounds,* 496 F.2d 92 (5th Cir. 1972); and Parducci v. Rutland, 316 F.Supp. 352 (M.D. Ala. 1970)). See also Tinker v. Des Moines Independent School District, 393 U.S. 503, 506, 512 (1969); and Kingsville Independent School District v. Cooper, 611 F.2d 1109, 1113, n.4 (5th Cir. 1980): "[C]lassroom discussion is protected activity."

    For an excellent discussion of whether academic freedom for teachers exists, see Osterhage, *supra* note 76, at 712 *et seq.* See also Epperson v. Arkansas, 393 U.S. 97 (1968).
95. 486 F.Supp. at 307.
96. Kemerer and Hirsh, *supra* note 47, at 68–69.
97. Mailloux v. Kiley, 323 F.Supp. at 1391.
98. 598 F.2d 535 (10th Cir. 1979).
99. See 427 F.Supp. 945 (D. Colo. 1977).
100. 598 F.2d at 539. At the end of the contract section entitled "academic freedom" was a sentence specifying that the "final responsibility in the determination of the above rests with the Board." The Court of Appeals saw this clause not as a deliberate waiver but rather as a "cautionary clause, a reminder that the board retains control over the techniques, method and means of teaching the courses. . . . " *Id.*
101. *Id.*
102. See, *e.g.,* Mailloux v. Kiley, 323 F.Supp. at 1390.
103. Osterhage, *supra* note 76, at 710. For an interesting discussion of the rights of the child versus those of the parents in a school case, see the partial dissent of Justice Douglas in Wisconsin v. Yoder, 406 U.S. 205, 241 (1972).
    See also Parham v. J.R., 442 U.S. 584, 602 (1978):
    Our jurisprudence historically has reflected Western civilization concepts of the family as a unit with broad parental authority over minor children. . . . The law's concept of the family rests on a presumption that parents possess what a child lacks in maturity, experience, and capacity for judgment required for making life's difficult decisions. More important, historically it has recognized that natural bonds of affection lead parents to act in the best interests of their children.

104. Osterhage, *supra* note 76, at 707.
105. *Island Trees,* 457 U.S. at 891 (Burger, C. J., dissenting). State law often provides for public inspection of or comment upon books being considered for use, or being used, in public schools of that state. See, *e.g.,* LA. REV. STAT. ANN. §§ 17:352B, 17:451.1 (West 1982); TEX. EDUC. CODE ANN. § 12.24(a) (Vernon Supp. 1985). See also LA. REV. STAT. ANN. § 17:415.1 (West 1982) (providing for a textbook adoption committee, at least one-third of whose members are parents); and OKLA. STAT ANN. tit. 70, § 16-102.1 (West)(Supp.1984) (requiring that meetings of the State Textbook Committee be open to the public).
106. See Note, *supra* note 35, at 1104.
107. Keefe v. Geanakos, 418 F.2d at 361–362.
108. Dean v. Timpson, 486 F.Supp. at 308.
109. *Id.* at 707–708.
110. Osterhage, *supra* note 76, at 710.
111. See Ginsberg v. New York, 390 U.S. 629 (1968). See also New York v. Ferber, 102 S.Ct. 3348 (1982); and FCC v. Pacifica Foundation, 438 U.S. 726 (1978).
112. Tinker v. Des Moines Independent School District, 393 U.S. at 506.
113. *Cf. id.* at 512: "A student's rights . . . do not embrace merely the classroom hours."
114. *Id.* at 509.
115. See text accompanying notes 143–227, *infra.*
116. West Virginia State Board of Education v. Barnette, 319 U.S. at 633. See Minarcini v. Strongsville City School District, 541 F.2d at 583.
117. 319 U.S. at 633.
118. *But see* Nistad v. Board of Education, 61 Misc.2d 60 (S.Ct. N.Y., N.Y. County, 1960).
119. Perhaps a right to privacy argument is also tenable here. See generally Chapter 2, *infra.*
120. Comment, *supra* note 27, at 655.
121. 381 U.S. 301 (1965).
122. Comment, *supra* note 27, at 655 (citing Brooks v. Auburn University, 412 F.2d 1171 (5th Cir. 1969); Smith v. University of Tennessee, 300 F.Supp. 777 (E.D.Tenn. 1969)).
123. Kleindienst v. Mandel, 408 U.S. 753, 763 (1972).
124. Kemerer and Hirsh, *supra* note 47, at 44.
125. Tinker v. Des Moines Independent School District, 393 U.S. at 511.
126. The right to receive information has been called the reciprocal of free speech. See Comment, *supra* note 27, at 655 (citing Virginia State Board of Pharmacy v. Virginia Citizens Consumers Council, Inc., 425 U.S. 748 (1976)).
127. 457 U.S. at 867.
128. See *id.* at 869.
129. *Id.* at 887 (Burger, C. J., dissenting).
130. Osterhage, *supra* note 76, at 730.
131. Note, *supra* note 35, at 1102.
132. Orleans, *supra* note 10, at 2 (emphasis added).
133. *Id.*
134. Keyishian v. Board of Regents, 385 U.S. at 603.
135. Dean v. Timpson Independent School District, 486 F.Supp. at 307 (citing Parducci v. Rutland, 316 F.Supp. at 355). See Mailloux v. Kiley, 448 F.2d at

1243: "[F]ree speech does not grant teachers a license to say or write in class whatever they may feel like...."

136. See Schenck v. United States, 249 U.S. 47, 52 (1919).

137. Wieman v. Updegraff, 344 U.S. at 196.

138. See Tinker v. Des Moines Independent School District, 393 U.S. at 506.

139. Parducci v. Rutland, 316 F.Supp. at 355. See also Mailloux v. Kiley, 448 F.2d at 1243; and *id.*, 323 F.Supp. at 1391, n.4.

140. Mailloux v. Kiley, 448 F.2d at 1243.

141. Mailloux v. Kiley, 323 F.Supp. at 1391, n.4 (citing Justice Black's dissent in Tinker v. Des Moines Independent School District, 393 U.S. at 519–521; and Epperson v. Arkansas, 393 U.S. 97 (1969)).

See also *Island Trees*, discussed *supra* at text accompanying notes 17–22; and Zykan v. Warsaw Community School Corp., discussed *supra* at note 20.

142. Dean v. Timpson Independent School District, 486 F.Supp. at 307.

143. See Mailloux v. Kiley, 323 F.Supp. at 1388: "At all times in the discussion plaintiff was in good faith...."

144. 486 F.Supp. at 306. *Compare* Brubaker v. Board of Education, School District 149, Cook County, Illinois, 502 F.2d 973, 982 (7th Cir. 1974), where the court refers to a failure to read distributed materials beforehand as an "excuse."

145. 486 F.Supp. at 306.

146. *Id.* at 310.

147. *Id.*

148. Moore v. School Board of Gulf County, Florida, 364 F.Supp. at 361. The plaintiff's amended complaint alleged that a fourth year annual contract had been offered him on condition that he pledge not to discuss anything but biology on school premises.

149. Keefe v. Geanakos, 418 F.2d at 361. See also Brubaker v. Board of Education, School District 149, Cook County, Ill., 502 F.2d at 977–982. Courts may on occasion be skeptical—see *id.* at 978: "We are not advised what rock music has to do with Language Arts."

150. Moore v. School Board of Gulf County, Florida, 364 F.Supp. at 360–361. See also Brubaker v. Board of Education, School District 149, Cook County, Illinois, 502 F.2d at 991–992 (dissenting opinion). In doing so, however, the teacher must be cognizant of his serious responsibility in guiding the student in his intellectual development. Moore v. School Board of Gulf County, Florida, 364 F.Supp. at 361.

151. Or perhaps criticism of school officials. See Moore v. School Board of Gulf County, Florida, 364 F.Supp. at 361.

152. Kemerer and Hirsh, *supra* note 44, at 50 (emphasis added).

153. See Moore v. School Board of Gulf County, Florida, 364 F.Supp. at 361, indicating the teacher had spent "as much as a full class period" criticizing the Superintendent, the school board and the school system. See also Brubaker v. Board of Education, School District 149, Cook County, Illinois, 502 F.2d at 991 (dissenting opinion).

154. Dean v. Timpson, 486 F.Supp. at 304.

155. Osterhage, *supra* note 76, at 727.

156. Keefe v. Geanakos, 418 F.2d at 362.

157. Mailloux v. Kiley, 448 F.2d at 1243.

158. Osterhage, *supra* note 76, at 717. See FLA. STAT. ANN. § 233.165(2) (West 1977),

prohibiting the use of "hardcore pornography" and related materials in public schools in the state.

Many states provide, for persons involved in educational programs, exemptions, of varying breadth, from certain laws prohibiting the use or distribution of obscenity or the like. See, *e.g.,* CAL. PENAL CODE § 311.8 (West 1970) (limited to "legitimate scientific or educational purposes"); IOWA CODE ANN. § 728.7 (1979) (limited to "the use of appropriate material"); KY. REV. STAT. ANN. § 531.070 (Baldwin 1984); MD. ANN. CODE art. 27, § 423 (1982); MICH. COMP. LAWS § 722.676 (West Supp. 1983) (applicable to teacher, administrator or librarian in connection with school employment); NEB. REV. STAT. § 28-815(1) (1979); OR. REV. STAT. § 167.089 (1981); S.D. CODIFIED LAWS ANN. § 22-24-31 (1979); UTAH CODE ANN. § 76-10-1226(1)(1953) (requiring "educational justification"); VT. STAT. ANN. tit. 13, § 2805(b)(3) (Supp. 1984). Presumably, such legislation was primarily intended for educational or scientific programs in higher education (for example, a study of the effects of pornography), not those in primary or secondary schools.

159. Keefe v. Geanakos, 418 F.2d at 361. See also Parducci v. Rutland, 316 F.Supp. at 352.
160. See text accompanying note 111, *supra.* See Osterhage, *supra* note 76, at 710.
161. See Keefe v. Geanakos, 316 F.Supp. at 361, stating the standard to be not what is obscene for adult consumption but rather one of degree, depending on the circumstances of the case. See also Todd v. Rochester Community Schools, 41 Mich. App. at 322–323, 200 N.W.2d at 100 (concurring opinion).
162. Osterhage, *supra* note 76, at 717. See CAL. EDUC. CODE § 44434 (West 1978), setting out the use of profanity as grounds for revocation of certificates issued by local boards of education.
163. For a discussion of the relationship between style and content, see Cohen v. California, 403 U.S. 15, 26 (1971); *Island Trees,* 638 F.2d at 429 (dissenting opinion); and Chapter 3, *infra,* at note 154 *et seq.*
164. 457 U.S. at 871. See also *id.* at 880 (Blackmun, J., concurring in part). One court, hazarding a meaningful distinction between vulgarity and profanity, has suggested that the school board's power to exclude vulgarity may not extend to profanity, which "is legally very closely related to 'blasphemy'." State regulation of profanity "may well be in collision with establishment of and free exercise of religion clauses of the Constitution." Webb v. Lake Mills Community School District, 344 F.Supp. at 802.

School boards may have the power to remove depictions of violence from the curriculum. See Pratt v. Independent School District No. 831, Forest Lake, Minnesota, 670 F.2d at 776, n.6, 778.
165. *Island Trees,* 457 U.S. at 919 (dissenting opinion).
166. *Id.* at 890–891 (dissenting opinion).
167. See Keefe v. Geanakos, 418 F.2d at 361.
168. *Id.*
169. One court has observed that it was "right for school authorities to take cognizance of . . . parental concern." Brubaker v. Board of Education, School District 149, Cook County, Illinois, 502 F.2d at 989.
170. 364 F.Supp. 355 (N.D.Fla. 1973).
171. *Id.* at 358. Their complaints cited the teacher's use of class time to discuss his personal financial status and criticism of school officials. *Id.* See also Frison v.

Franklin City Board of Education, 596 F.2d 1192, 1193 (1979). In Webb v. Lake Mills Community School District, 344 F.Supp. at 797, the complaint was from a teaching colleague. The court pointed out that no student or parent had complained. *Id.* at 797, 798, 803.

172. 316 F.Supp. 352 (M.D.Ala. 1970).
173. *Id.* at 354, 356.
174. 418 F.2d 359 (1st Cir. 1969).
175. *Id.* at 361.
176. *Id.*
177. *Id.*
178. *Id.* See also Webb v. Lake Mills Community School District, 344 F.Supp. at 803 ("Defendants agree that Miss Webb's students have heard the terms ['son of a bitch' and 'damn'] often during their lives and that the terms are used commonly in Lake Mills."
179. Keefe v. Geanakos, 418 F.2d at 361. Compare Brubaker v. Board of Education, School District 149, Cook County, Illinois, 502 F.2d at 976: "It is probably a fair inference that by second or third year high school most American males have become familiar with, and at times employ, these and like [vulgarities]. Is it only a forlorn hope, however, that most of our young ladies will never employ that kind of speech?"
180. Mailloux v. Kiley, 323 F.Supp. at 1389. The court added that most students "had seen the word even if they had not used it." *Id.* See also *Island Trees,* 457 U.S. at 880 (Blackmun, J., concurring).
181. See text accompanying note 47 *et seq., supra.*
182. Mailloux v. Kiley, 448 F.2d at 1243.
183. 316 F.Supp. 352 (M.D. Ala.).
184. *Id.* at 356.
185. *Id.* at 357.
186. *Id.* at 358. See also Webb v. Lake Mills Community School District, 344 F.Supp. at 795–796: "The school library is replete with books containing vulgarity far more extreme than any vulgarity uttered or performed [in the school play] under Miss Webb's supervision; these books can be freely assigned to and read by high school students." *Id.* at 804.

    Cf. Pratt v. Independent School District No. 831, Forest Lake, Minnesota, 670 F.2d at 77: "[T]here is no evidence that the board has ever removed from the high school curriculum any material other than the films in dispute here because of their violent content."
187. See Parducci v. Rutland, 316 F.Supp. at 358.
188. See also Mailloux v. Kiley, 323 F.Supp. at 1389.
189. Keefe v. Geanakos, 418 F.2d at 362.
190. 41 Mich. App. 320, 200 N.W.2d 90 (1972).
191. 386 U.S. 767 (1967).
192. 41 Mich. App. at 335, 200 N.W.2d at 96–97.
193. See Keefe v. Geanakos, 418 F.2d at 362.
194. 323 F.Supp. 1387 (D. Mass. 1971), *aff'd,* 448 F.2d 1242 (1st Cir. 1971).
195. *Id.* at 1388.
196. *Id.* at 1391.
197. *Id.* at 1389.
198. *Id.* at 1391.

199. *Id.* at 1388.
200. 486 F.Supp. at 305. *Compare* Moore v. School Board of Gulf County, Florida, 364 F.Supp. at 359, where there was testimony to the effect that individual students were asked if they had ever masturbated and, if they said they had not, were told they were lying.
201. See Moore v. School Board of Gulf County, Florida, 364 F.Supp. at 359; Mailloux v. Kiley, 323 F.Supp. at 1391.
202. See Mailloux v. Kiley, 323 F.Supp. at 1388, where the court ultimately found that the teacher had not called on "any girl individually."
203. See *id.* at 1391: "When a *male* teacher asks a class of adolescent boys and *girls...*" (Emphasis added).
204. *Id.* at 1389.
205. Dean v. Timpson Independent School District, 486 F.Supp. at 305–306.
206. 418 F.2d at 361.
207. 598 F.2d at 538.
     For a limited option plan, see Davis v. Page, 385 F.Supp. 395 (D.N.H. 1974), where school board policy required students to remain in the room during the use of audiovisual devices, but specifically allowed them to turn their heads. The court allowed the children to leave the room when the devices were used for entertainment rather than for educational purposes. *Id.* at 401. See Osterhage, *supra* note 76, at 709.
208. Orleans, *supra* note 10, at 8.
209. Brubaker v. Board of Education, School District 149, Cook County Ill., 502 F.2d at 983.
210. See, *e.g., id.* at 980.
211. See Mailloux v. Kiley, 323 F.Supp. at 1390.
212.   In the opinion of experts of significant standing, such as members of the faculties of the Harvard University School of Education and of Massachusetts Institute of Technology, the discussion of taboo words in the eleventh grade, the way the plaintiff used the word "fuck," his writing of it on the blackboard, and the inquiry he addressed to the class, were appropriate and reasonable under the circumstances and served a serious educational purpose. In the opinion of other qualified persons plaintiff's use of the word was not under the circumstances reasonable, or appropriate, or conducive to a serious educational purpose. It has not been shown what is the preponderant opinion in the teaching profession, or in that part of the profession which teaches English.
     323 F.Supp. at 1389.
213. *Id.* at 1390.
214. Note, *supra* note 35, at 1115.
215. 316 F.Supp. 352 (M.D. Ala. 1970).
216. *Id.* at 354.
217. Indeed, the professional judgment standard would to some extent incorporate by reference the *Tinker* test since, presumably, experts would factor into their judgment the extent to which particular material or teaching methods would disrupt the school community.
218. Tinker v. Des Moines Independent Community School District, 393 U.S. at 509, 513.
219. Osterhage, *supra* note 76, at 706.
220. *Id.* at 729 (citations omitted).
221. 316 F.Supp. at 356. See also *id.* at 355.
222. Dean v. Timpson Independent School District, 486 F.Supp. at 306.

223. See *id.* at 308.
224. See Epperson v. Arkansas, 393 U.S. 97 (1968).
225. 486 F.Supp. at 308.
226. Tinker v. Des Moines Independent School District, 393 U.S. at 508–509.
227. See Pratt v. Independent School District No. 831, Forest Lake, Minnesota, 670 F.2d at 778–779.
228. See Webb v. Lake Mills Community School District, 344 F.Supp. at 791. Even if told not to, presumably a biology teacher would be entitled to refer to evolution in discussing the origin of the species. See Epperson v. Arkansas, 393 U.S. 97 (1969). See Mailloux v. Kiley, 323 F.Supp. at 1390.
229. See Webb v. Lake Mills Community School District, 344 F.Supp. at 804:

> Miss Webb allowed nothing in her plays or rehearsals that is so inherently repugnant to good teaching practices or to community standards of decency that she should have known that such activity was unquestionably not in the best interests of Lake Mills schools; that is, so much so that she would automatically lose her job.

See also Brubaker v. Board of Education, District 149, Cook County, Ill., 502 F.2d at 984; Keefe v. Geanakos, 418 F.2d at 362; Mailloux v. Kiley, 323 F.Supp at 1393.
230. In Brubaker v. Board of Education, District 149, Cook County, Illinois, the court remarked: "We will not fault a school board for not anticipating that eighth grade teachers might distribute to their students, without explanation or assigned reason therefore, poetry of [this] caliber." 502 F.2d at 984.
231. Mailloux v. Kiley, 323 F.Supp. 1387 (D. Mass. 1971), *aff'd,* 448 F.2d 1242 (1st Cir. 1971).
232. *Id.* at 1389.
233. *Id.* at 1392. See also Brubaker v. Board of Education, District 149, Cook County, Illinois, 502 F.2d at 992 (dissenting opinion).
234. *Id.*
235. The court in one curriculum case seemed to see this problem: "The cases which held for the teachers and placed emphasis upon teachers' rights to exercise discretion in the classroom, seemed to be situations where school authorities acted in the absence of a general policy, after the fact...." Cary v. Board of Education of Adams-Arapahoe School District 28-J, Aurora, Colorado, 598 F.2d at 541.
236. See Webb v. Lake Mills Community School District, 344 F.Supp. at 804, 805; Parducci v. Rutland, 316 F.Supp. at 357.
237. Webb v. Lake Mills Community School District, 344 F.Supp. at 801.
238. See Winters v. New York, 333 U.S. 407 (1948). See also Parducci v. Rutland, 316 F.Supp. at 357.
239. See Brubaker v. Board of Education, School District 149, Cook County, Illinois, 502 F.2d at 991 (dissenting opinion).
240. See Mailloux v. Kiley, 323 F.Supp. at 1389, 1392.
241. *Id.* at 1392.
242. See Webb v. Lake Mills Community School District, 344 F.Supp. at 801.
243. *Id.* at 1392–1393.
244. See Dean v. Timpson Independent School District, 486 F.Supp. at 305.
245. Frison v. Franklin County Board of Education, 596 F.2d at 1194. *Cf.* text accompanying note 45 *et seq.,* Chapter 4, *infra.*
246. To be sure, if there are substantive First Amendment problems in proscribing

all vulgarity or sexually explicit terms from the classroom, see text at note 162 *et seq., supra,* the drafting of a suitable regulation will be more difficult.

Moreover, the drafter must, in attempting to be precise and comprehensive, avoid unconstitutional overbreadth. See Brubaker v. Board of Education, School District 149, Cook County, Illinois, 502 F.2d at 992 (dissenting opinion).
247. 448 F.2d at 1243.
248. Dean v. Timpson Independent School District, 486 F.Supp. at 305.
249. *Id.* See also *id.* at 309. The fact that any warning came "in the course of a conversation" or as an "offhand comment" did not help. See *id.* With regard to the distribution of materials, compare the notice in Brubaker v. Board of Education, School District 149, Cook County, Illinois, 502 F.2d at 976, and at 976, n.2.
250. Webb. v. Lake Mills Community School District, 344 F.Supp. at 800.
251. *Id.*
252. *Id.*

Chapter 2

SEX EDUCATION: A SPECIAL SITUATION

INTRODUCTION

Five school districts in San Mateo County, California, implemented comprehensive family life and sex education programs. In each of these districts, specially selected teachers with particularized training conducted the program. The teacher Program Guides used in these districts were substantially alike, and the detail and complexity of materials used in each program increased with grade level. Although a large part of it did not deal directly with sex, the program did provide for discussion of subjects such as sexual intercourse, masturbation, contraception, abortion, child molestation, exhibitionism, homosexuality and prostitution. Citizens for Parental Rights and others ultimately brought suit in federal court seeking to enjoin the teaching of the family life and sex education courses in the five San Mateo County School districts[1] as violative of the establishment, free exercise, due process and equal protection clauses of the United States Constitution and of the rights of privacy and of parental control of education in matters of family, marriage and sex.

Among school matters dealing with sex,[2] which tend to involve a small number of class comments, assignments or library books, sex education courses present a unique controversy. They are comprehensive programs, are usually very visible and directly involve the students in discussion of *their* sexuality, rather than that of, say, a book character. With attitudes and conduct of students thus implicated, religious and moral aspects of sex are immediately involved.

Some have seen the attempt to prevent sex education courses as merely one instance in a series of academic suppressions.[3] Yet, surprisingly, much sex education has antedated recent controversies. It is said, for example, that in the early 1920s more than 40 percent of high schools provided some kind of sex education, apparently initiated, for the most part, by the local district.[4] In 1970, it could be written that more than fifty percent of both public and private schools made available some sex education.[5]

One tends to think of sex education as a discrete course, covering a myriad of topics more or less connected with sex, and most recent attacks have been on that form. In the *San Mateo* situation, for example, the guide in one district called for discussion of problem-solving techniques "learned in the family that become part of one's personality;" citizenship; financial responsibility; the roles of children in the family; family and home; human reproduction; and emotional maturity.[6] In *Medeiros v. Kiyosaki*,[7] the recently-adopted curriculum for family life and sex education for fifth- and sixth-graders, characterized as a "socio-psychological" program, was made up of fifteen lessons concerning inter-personal relationships, self-understanding, family structures and sex education. Each lesson used a twenty-minute film prepared for educational telecasting, supplemented by preparatory and follow-up activities organized by the particular teacher and geared to the particular class.[8] In *Hopkins v. Hamden Board of Education*,[9] the program, covering all grades from kindergarten through 12, dealt sequentially with (1) Growth and Development, (2) Public Health, (3) Family Living and Sex Education, (4) Safety and First Aid, (5) Health Maintenance, (6) Consumer Education, (7) Alcohol, Narcotics and Tobacco, (8) Nutrition, and (9) Disease.[10] Importantly, however, sex education can constitute a significant part of such traditional courses as anatomy, physiology, biology, psychology, history, sociology and even English Literature, among others,[11] although sexual components are often omitted from these courses.[12]

THE CASE FOR SEX EDUCATION IN THE SCHOOLS

Sex education in the schools is necessary, we are told, to vanquish the pervasive ignorance concerning the subject, ignorance which does not yield to other potential sources of information, due to their unwillingness, their inaccuracy, their incompleteness, or their unavailability.[13] Effective sex education, possible only through the schools, may produce more successful marriages, fewer extramarital pregnancies, fewer unwanted pregnancies[14] (and fewer consequent abortions), less sexual promiscuity, a reduction in venereal disease and a decrease in sex crimes, over and above the knowledge *per se* thus imparted.[15] Sex education in school, endorsed by many widely-respected organizations,[16] as well as by the general public,[17] allows the child to acquire accurate information about sex in a wholesome, as opposed to a prurient or sterile, context,[18] may "counteract the potentially traumatic impact of pornography",[19] and may increase parent-child communication.[20] Interestingly, however, although these attributes of sex education seem at least relevant to, if not dispositive of, the balancing of the state's interests against the asserted constitutional right of parents and children attacking sex education courses, the cases are relatively silent about them.

THE CASE AGAINST SEX EDUCATION IN THE SCHOOLS— THE ESTABLISHMENT CLAUSE QUESTION

Legal challenges to sex education programs have alleged that such programs constitute an establishment of religion[21] in violation of the First Amendment to the U.S. Constitution.[22] A governmental policy will not offend the establishment clause if (1) it has a secular legislative purpose; (2) its primary effect neither advances nor inhibits religion and (3) it does not promote an excessive entanglement with religion.[23] It is clear that sex education courses have a secular legislative purpose.[24] The second test presents more difficulty. Since sex has been connected with religion and morality since the earliest Judeo-Christian times, sex education in the public schools arguably establishes a state code of morality.[25] The assertion is that "nonjudgmental, secular courses in sex education and similar matters are themselves religious . . . ,"[26] and that sex education outside a religious context establishes a "religion" of secularism.[27]

The line between the sectarian and the secular is evasive.[28] With regard to this point, indeed, the state is put to a dilemma: the avoidance of any moral or religious considerations in sex education results in an immoral dehumanization of sex;[29] the use of moral considerations in sex education establishes a state morality.[30] Either approach, one might argue, violates the establishment clause.[31]

Nonetheless, establishment clause attacks on sex education have not persuaded the courts, which have rejected the claim "that sex education establishes a religion of secularism."[32] The courts have found, to the contrary, that sex education is not a religious exercise,[33] but "a public health measure,"[34] "secular in nature and purpose."[35]

Indeed, many other matters related to morality and religion (*e.g.,* honesty, patriotism) are appropriately dealt with in public education. It would be intolerable if public schools were preempted from dealing with any subject touched upon by organized religion.

The *San Mateo* case focused on this second test, that is, whether the program's primary effect advanced or inhibited religion. The parents argued that the program dealt with morality, family life and reproduction in a manner inimical to theistic religion, thus establishing " 'new or different religious and spiritual practices and beliefs.' "[36] The court noted, however, that the program provided for a studied recognition of the diversity of religions,[37] and that teachers were cautioned to indicate, in discussing the sensitive issues of concern to the parents, the existence of a variety of beliefs and practices, and to advise students to consult their parents and religious advisors for more specific guidance or information.[38]

The court's answer is not wholly persuasive. Elaborating on the sensitivity towards all allegedly shown by the program, the court observed that "under the subject of birth control, all present day methods are listed. Thus, there is evidence of neutrality. . . . "[39] Roman Catholics, among others, might well argue that to mention all forms of birth control, natural and artificial, without allusion to moral permissibility, suggests that all forms are at least to be considered or that reasonable persons may differ as to their permissibility, thus conveying an impression that the moral concern is a matter of taste. Perhaps the ultimate question raised is whether the morally neutral treatment of behavior is even possible.

The court found that the program did not establish any "religious concept, dogma, idea and precept," or favor any religion.[40] The parents' views on sex and family life, based on the moral standards of their religion, did not make sex education a religion.[41] Since the program's primary effect neither advanced nor inhibited religion, it did not violate the establishment clause of the First Amendment.[42] Indeed, said the court, any other result would yield chaos, since any parent could object to any portion of the curriculum allegedly contravening his religious belief. The court offered the example of a person whose religious beliefs prohibited meat consumption objecting to a nutrition course which suggests meat as a good protein source.[43]

In *Epperson v. Arkansas*,[44] the U.S. Supreme Court held the prohibition of the teaching of evolution in the public schools to be a violation of the establishment clause. Under *Epperson*, therefore, the barring of sex education from the curriculum because of a conflict with the religious views of parents could itself, ironically, violate the establishment clause.[45]

It seems clear that the typical sex education program, even if an excusal system is included,[46] does not transgress the third test, that is, it does not promote an excessive entanglement with religion.[47]

THE FREE EXERCISE QUESTION

Challenges to sex education programs under the free exercise clause, although faring little better than those under the establishment clause, have given the courts greater trouble. Unlike under the establishment clause, a violation under the free exercise clause requires official coercion in the exercise of one's religion.[48]

Greater coercion occurs, obviously, when a public school sex education program is compulsory.[49] Although compulsory attendance may well impinge upon sincere religious beliefs, however, not all such impacts are constitutionally invalid[50] and, even in compulsory attendance cases, the courts have refused to find a violation of the free exercise clause.[51] In *Hopkins v. Hamden*, for example, the court refused to issue a temporary injunction to school children seeking to stop a compulsory "Health Education" course which included a comprehensive study of reproduction, hygiene, sex education, family life and growth.[52] Noting that the freedom to believe is absolute but that the freedom to act is not,[53] the court stated that the "stigma of coercion or compulsion" was suitably dispelled by Connecticut law allowing private schools or equivalent instruction in the home.[54] (For some families, of course, these alternatives are wholly unrealistic.) In the court's view, the plaintiffs were unable to specify coercion sufficient to trigger the protection of the free exercise clause, and the mere fact that secular teaching might conflict with personal religious beliefs was equally unavailing, especially in light of the government's and the public's weighty interests in the educational system.[55] To allow such claims to prevail would, the court predicted, make the school system "vulnerable to fragmentation."[56]

So too in *Cornwell v. State Board of Education*, the federal district court, finding no substantial constitutional question, granted a motion to dismiss a complaint seeking to prevent implementation of a sex education program for all students.[57]

In making the balancing analysis required in such cases, a court cannot, of course, weigh the merits of the particular religious belief.[58] Nonetheless, the court may and must ascertain that the asserted belief is sincerely held[59] and that it is in fact religious, as opposed to merely philosophical or personal.[60] In *Davis v. Page*, for example, where plaintiffs,

members of the Apostolic Lutheran faith, sought excusal from, among
other things, a compulsory "Health and Education" course, the court
found no violation of free exercise rights since the parents failed to show
what tenets of their faith were violated and, indeed, anything more than
that the course was distasteful to them.[61]

JUDICIAL EXEMPTION

Although recourse to the courts for exemption from a compulsory sex
education course may be futile,[62] some support for such exemption can
be found in the cases. In *Valent u N.J. State Board of Education*,[63] the New
Jersey Superior Court, Chancery Division, denied summary judgment
to the defendant, thus signalling its belief that the plaintiffs, challenging
a mandatory sex education course, might well prevail in their quest for
relief. The court questioned whether the state could presume that all
parents will fail to teach satisfactorily to their children the subjects of sex
and morality and whether the state is permitted to "encroach" upon the
"molding" of the child's conduct in personal family or religious matters.[64]
The crucial questions, the court asserted, were the extent of the governmental interest[65] and whether permitting student excusal would undermine the success of the program.[66]

The court emphasized the U.S. Supreme Court's decision in *Sherbert u
Verner*,[67] which found unconstitutional the denial of unemployment com-
pensation to a Seventh Day Adventist because she refused employment
requiring her to work on Saturday, for her a religious day. In *Sherbert*,
Justice Brennan noted that no mere rational relationship to a state
interest would justify denying a claimed exemption in such a sensitive
area; an essential state interest must be jeopardized.[68] *Sherbert*, the *Valent*
court concluded, requires that judges, in cases involving a free exercise
claim to exemption from state policies, "balance harm, if any, to an
individual's freedom of conscience, on the one hand, against damage, if
any, to the essential governmental regulatory or legislative purpose."[69]
In some cases, exemption may have no significant impact on the program or on the general public, while in others, for example a smallpox
or measles inoculation program, individual exemption may jeopardize
many others in the community.[70] Although, for all these reasons, the
Valent court denied defendants a summary judgment, no final judicial
decision on the merits resulted; the matter was ultimately dismissed for
failure to exhaust administrative remedies.[71]

Hopkins v. Hamden Board of Education[72] also gives some support to the notion of judicial excusal from compulsory sex education courses. Although the court denied a temporary injunction sought against the entire program, it noted that none of the plaintiffs had seriously pursued requests for excusal from the program and that their individual interests would warrant greater consideration by the courts had individual exemptions or other specific forms of relief been sought.[73]

In *Hobolth v. Greenway,* the court stated that if the challenged sex education program compelled *all* students to take instruction, the plaintiff's legal, philosophical and sociological arguments would warrant consideration.[74]

When a challenged program includes excusal, the free exercise claim is obviously much less urgent,[75] and plaintiffs have been wholly unsuccessful in such challenges. In *Medeiros v. Kiyosaki,*[76] the state, apparently anticipating objections to a program including sex education, instituted an "excusal system," under which parents and guardians could view each of the fifteen films involved prior to its being shown to the children and could, upon submitting a written excuse, have their children exempted from the program. Since the program was not compulsory, the court found no "direct or substantial" burden on free exercise.[77] Relying heavily on the *Medeiros* reasoning and on *Sherbert v. Verner,* the *San Mateo* court reached the same result with regard to the sex education courses at issue there, which also allowed excusal: "The direct answer to the parents' contentions concerning free exercise is that the program against which the parents seek a permanent injunction is not compulsory."[78] Finally, in *Smith v. Ricci,*[79] the Supreme Court of New Jersey noted that "[t]he simple fact that parents can remove their children from any objectionable part of the program is dispositive [of the free exercise claim]. . . . When there is no compulsion . . . there can be no infringement. . . . "

PARENTAL RIGHT TO EDUCATE

Some have argued that sex education courses in the schools unduly intrude upon the parents' right to control the teaching of their children in the areas of sex and family life.[80] One variation of the argument asserts that as the state "forces its way into the home as a foster parent," discipline, authority and parental respect decrease, with the young perhaps seeking guidance from the state rather than from the parent.[81] Another variation bases the asserted legal right on the parental obligation to educate, especially in the sexual area, an obligation emanating from religious beliefs.[82]

Courts have been skeptical about the support for or limits of such claims.[83] To be sure, the U.S. Supreme Court has recognized a parental right to educate. In *Pierce u Society of Sisters,*[84] the most expansive Supreme Court recognition of parental educational prerogative,[85] the Court held unconstitutional the state requirement that all children attend public schools. Although *Pierce* denies the state a monopoly over education, however, it does not grant one to the parents; such a monopoly would do violence to the first amendment implication that informed citizenship requires the free exchange of views.[86]

In the courts' assessments of parental claims to educational control in connection with sex education, the U.S. Supreme Court pronouncement in *Prince u Massachusetts*[87] has been more dispositive.[88] *Prince* involved the constitutionality of the application of a child labor law to a Jehovah's Witness, the aunt and guardian of a nine-year-old, who allowed the child to attempt to sell religious magazines in the streets. The aunt buttressed her free exercise claims with a parental right, due process assertion.[89] Although recognizing the sensitivity of balancing the parent's right against that of the state, especially in religion cases, the Court upheld the conviction, observing that the state as *parens patriae* can, when a sufficient state interest—here, guarding the child against the dangers of the streets—is at stake, protect the child's well-being even against a parent's assertion of religious freedom.[90]

THE PRIVACY QUESTION

The parental right concept is closely allied with and in large part a component of the right to privacy,[91] which has also been urged upon the courts in family life and sex education cases.[92] It is not the more explicitly sexual part of such programs that are most likely to offend, however, but rather that aspect which probes into the child's private life.[93]

The *San Mateo* case provides the best example. The Teacher's Program Guide for one of the districts there involved suggested that students write a story entitled "My parents expect too much of me" or "My parents don't expect enough of me," and another describing the student's family and all significant changes occurring in it since the student's birth. The program also urged that the student compile a family scrapbook. Another part of the Program suggested that students write a story telling how the parents' work affects the family's life and how the family allocates its financial resources.[94] Presumably, at least the teacher would read these pieces and perhaps other students would learn of the content through class discussion or otherwise.

This official prying into the private lives of students (and, indeed, of family members not even in school!) may create embarrassment, feelings of inferiority and the like. To be sure, any class assignment or discussion may prompt a student to volunteer otherwise private information. The clear difference in the *San Mateo* system is the formality, pervasiveness and compulsoriness of the probing. Matters like fiscal responsibility are best studied in the abstract or in detailed reference to a hypothetical family, not through inquisition. Indeed, the privacy issue, and this aspect of it, presents the most solid case for unconstitutionality of such programs or at least for excusal therefrom for those objecting.

The *San Mateo* appellate court, however, gave little weight to the parents' claim that the program "deprived the students of privacy of mind as they were forced to reveal their innermost personal and private feelings and the intimate details of family life to teachers and fellow students. . . . "[95] The court did not specifically address the most intrusive components of the program,[96] but rather asked abstractly whether the county could "adopt and initiate a curriculum of family life and sex education,"[97] and stated, without giving reasons, that the program did not compel "the disclosures mentioned by the parents."[98] The court, relying on *Medeiros,* recognized privacy from official intrusion as a constitutionally protected value,[99] but held nonetheless that California's "elaborate and detailed" excusal system[100] precluded any finding of unconstitutionality on privacy grounds.[101]

This emphasis on excusal strongly suggests that the court would have declared unconstitutional a mandatory program with the same components.[102] Moreover, although the excusal resolution may be satisfactory for parents who object to the whole program, what of parents who want their children to participate in a comprehensive sex education-family life program but object to intrusive components like those present in the *San Mateo* case? Must they, in order to enforce their privacy rights, give up the instruction they otherwise want for their children? Even if an excusal law permits it,[103] withholding their children from selected parts of the course may be difficult when the intrusive components are not in a discrete unit or class session. Moreover, if excusals are limited to those with religious objections, they may not be available to a family whose only objection relates to privacy.[104]

OTHER ARGUMENTS

The *San Mateo* plaintiffs alleged,[105] among their arguments, violations of equal protection and due process under the fourteenth amendment.[106] The court rejected the equal protection claim, noting that the program applied to all students equally, and that the excusal system did not result in a " 'separation' " constituting an unreasonable and discriminating classification.[107] It rejected the due process argument, asserting that the program did not reflect an arbitrary or unreasonable exercise of authority.[108] Other courts as well have rejected equal protection and due process challenges to sex education programs.[109]

Although state constitutions and statutes also provide bases for legal challenges, claims that sex education programs represent an invalid delegation of authority,[110] an abuse of discretion,[111] or a failure to comply with statutory requirements,[112] or that irreparable harm to the children's mental or physical health has resulted or will result from the program[113] have been equally unsuccessful.

Courts are reluctant to intervene in school controversies, absent conflicts that "directly and sharply implicate basic constitutional values."[114] Moreover, courts have been hostile to the idea of restricting the exposure of our youth to a "broad educational spectrum."[115] True to these principles, the cases taken together demonstrate that courts will not enjoin the implementation of sex education courses nor even fashion an excusal where state or local authorities have failed to do so.

Finally, many fear that sex education leads to increased sexual activity[116] or to the use of contraception, or excites or otherwise disturbs the children.[117] For the most part, however, such concerns relate to the wisdom, not the legality, of sex education and are therefore best addressed not to courts, but to legislatures or school boards.[118]

THE EXCUSAL ACCOMMODATION

Since courts are unlikely to find excusal either mandated or proscribed[119] by the U.S. Constitution, state legislative[120] or administrative officials will decide whether to grant excusal to objecting parents or students,[121] and wisdom may so dictate.[122] Sex education is so personal, so fraught with moral concerns and so given to emotion that the benefits of excusal in accommodating legitimate parental concerns and in diffusing parental hostility to sex education programs far outweigh the costs.[123] Many jurisdictions grant some form of excusal[124] and, although most state statutes do not provide for exemptions from prescribed courses, local authorities are generally free to make sex education elective.[125]

Some considerable objections can be raised against the "easy way out" of excusal, however.[126] First, the parent's interest in excusal may not coincide with the child's best interest.[127] For example, a parent may use the excusal only to avoid dealing with the sexual questions he anticipates the course will generate in the child.[128] Yet it is perhaps that parent's child who most needs sex education in school. Second, an excusal system for sex education could serve as precedent for exclusion, on grounds of conscience, from other courses with sensitive or controversial content.[129] Third, excusal engenders tension between those who participate and those who do not and, especially in an area like sex education, nonparticipants may be perceived as different.[130]

The state has a legitimate interest in preventing a "stratified school structure, where division and derision . . . flourish."[131] Nonetheless, school officials may lessen this tension by setting the time and place for sex education in such a way that nonparticipants need not go to or leave a room in which participants remain, but rather merely do not appear in the room immediately before, during or immediately after the sex education class.[132]

Fourth, the number of excusals anticipated need not be negligible. In *San Mateo*, the evidence indicated that of the 19,852 students slated for sex education in the five districts involved, 425 sought excusal.[133] In *Davis v. Page*, the school board changed its policy, which had allowed students asserting religious objection to classroom activities to be excused, when the number of objections became "sizeable" and accompanying disciplinary problems arose.[134] Apparently, however, students, not parents, triggered the excusals, and excusal was not limited to sex education courses, two facts perhaps inflating the number of excusals sought. Too, specific alternative assignments for excused students will presumably keep objections honest and disciplinary problems under control. In any event, courts should not let a speculative fear of a flood of fraudulent religious claims carry the day.[135]

There is no wholly satisfactory resolution to this difficult problem. Nonetheless, on balance, sex education programs in public schools should provide exemptions to children of objecting parents or guardians. Moreover, to make excusal a meaningful option, parents or guardians should have an opportunity to view the instructional materials in advance of their use in sex education courses.[136]

Finally, excusal should be allowed to all, whether or not the objection is prompted by a religious or moral concern. School authorities should avoid, if possible, the awful administrative task of weighing the sincerity of a belief and whether that belief is religious, moral, or something else.

PROHIBITING DISCUSSION OF SPECIFIC SEXUAL TOPICS

Whether or not a state or district provides for formal sex education in the public schools, some attempt may be made to bar the classroom discussion of specific topics related to sex. Two topics which have met this fate are birth control and abortion.

In *Mercer v. Michigan State Board of Education*,[137] plaintiffs, including a Detroit public school teacher, challenged a Michigan statute barring any discussion of birth control in the schools.[138] Seeing the case as one involving the power to control the curriculum, the court found that the First Amendment did not grant the teacher any right to teach matters outside the established curriculum.[139] Although its power over the curriculum is not absolute,[140] the state has the authority to establish the curriculum or to delegate that authority to local officials.[141] The court relied heavily on *Goldwasser v. Brown*,[142] which sustained the firing of a teacher for expressing in class his views on the country's Viet Nam policies and on Anti-Semitism.

Goldwasser differs from *Mercer*, however, in four important respects. First, the plaintiff in *Mercer* was not necessarily urging that he be allowed to express his own views on birth control, while the teacher in *Goldwasser* was asserting his personal beliefs.[143] Second, the topics involved in *Goldwasser* were arguably irrelevant to the teaching of English,[144] whereas the ban on birth control discussion applied even to sex education courses, to which such discussion is presumably relevant, however desirable. Third, no religious considerations lay behind the *Goldwasser* situation, while religious concerns about birth control and premarital sex presumably were prominent in the background of the Michigan statute. Finally, Goldwasser was not a typical public school teacher, but an Air Force civilian language teacher of foreign military officers. The *Goldwasser* court, stressing the "uniqueness of appellant's teaching function," took cognizance of the special national interest considerations present.[145]

The most telling case for the *Mercer* situation is *Epperson v. Arkansas*,[146] in which the U.S. Supreme Court held that the banning from the classroom of any discussion of evolution violated the First Amendment. Applying *Epperson* is difficult, however. The Supreme Court seemed to emphasize that what violates the Constitution is barring a theory or perspective because it offends a particular religious viewpoint.[147] Thus, a school may not both teach about the origin of the species and also suppress the instructor's discussion of evolution. On the other hand, the state presumably remains free not to teach biology,[148] or perhaps even the origin of the human species,[149] at all and, moreover, to ban the discussion of evolution in, say, Calculus II, along with all other matters irrelevant to Calculus II. If birth control constitutes one perspective or aspect of sex education or other subject matter being taught,[150] then *Epperson* may prohibit a state from preventing, on the grounds of offensiveness to a particular religious view, its discussion. If birth control is itself a discrete area of study, then presumably the state remains free to ban the entire subject; not everything can be taught in the time available for public education.[151]

Other *Epperson* concerns relate to whether the offensiveness in *Mercer* is religious, as opposed to social or moral; whether the group offended is "a particular religious group;"[152] and whether the state interest in *Mercer* is more substantial than in *Epperson*[153] because potential conduct of the students is involved or because the particular subject matter threatened to carry controversy and emotion into the schools.[154]

Regrettably, the *Mercer* court, extensively relying on *Goldwasser,* a quite different situation, described *Epperson* only briefly and made no effort to compare it with the case at bar.[155]

A similar issue arose when a seventh-grade humanities teacher scheduled a classroom debate on the subject of abortion.[156] The school superintendent directed the teacher to cancel the debate, even though the teachers' collective bargaining agreement guaranteed academic freedom and allowed the discussion of controversial issues to the extent "appropriate for the maturation level of the group."[157] The teacher and the teachers association, alleging a violation of academic freedom, attempted, pursuant to the terms of the collective bargaining agreement, to submit the controversy to arbitration. The Board of Education sought an injunction against the teacher and the association and prevailed, the court holding that any contractual delegation to a teacher, a teachers union or an arbitration association of such control over the subject matter taught was *ultra vires* and unenforceable. Accordingly, the dispute could not be processed as a grievance.[158]

The court did not, however, have to deal with the constitutional questions presented by the superintendent's order since only the appropriate forum for the dispute was then at issue. Perhaps the subject of abortion, in relation to a humanities course, is only marginally relevant, or is more a discrete area of study than a perspective or theory and therefore may, under *Epperson,* be barred from the classroom.[159] *Mercer* remains a more difficult situation.

CONCLUSION

San Mateo and other sex education cases clearly indicate that courts will generally leave sex education courses where they find them: they will approve courses with or without excusal provisions. Nonetheless, the better part of wisdom and, one could argue, the spirit of free exercise dictate that excusal be made available. The importance of and general desire[160] for sex education in the schools, and the difficult accommodation which our pluralistic society and the First Amendment require, perhaps allow little beyond excusal for parents objecting to sex education in the schools. Even so, parents remain free, where feasible, to send their children to private schools and, in any event, to supplement or supplant the school's teaching with their own or that of their church.[161]

NOTES

1. These facts are taken from Citizens For Parental Rights v. San Mateo County Board of Education [hereinafter *San Mateo*], 51 Cal.App.3d 1, 4–11, 124 Cal.Rptr. 68, 72–77 (1975). Litigation involving sex education can be complex and lengthy. In Hopkins v. Hamden Board of Education, 29 Conn.Sup. 397, 289 A.2d 914 (1971), *appeal dismissed,* 305 A.2d 536 (1973), for example, trial and argument consumed eight weeks and over 3,300 transcript pages. *Id.* at 400, 289 A.2d at 916.
2. See generally Chapter 1, *supra.*
3. Note, *Sex Education: The Constitutional Limits of State Compulsion,* 43 SO.CAL.L. REV.548 (1970). The series includes, according to the author, discussions of slavery, communism, and Darwinian evolution. *Id.* (citing Beale, "A History of Freedom of Teaching," in *American Schools* 107–08, 144–45 153–55, 202–07, 227–28, 237–38 (1941).

4. Note, *supra* note 3, at 554, n.28 (citing Dept. of the Interior, BULL. NO. 14, STATUS OF SEX EDUCATION IN HIGH SCHOOLS (1922).

5. Recent Development, *The Constitutionality Under the Religion Clauses of the First Amendment of Compulsory Sex Education in Public Schools,* 68 MICH.L.REV. 1050, n.1 (1970) (citing Yuncker, *Sex Education: Should It Be Taught in School?,* FAMILY CIRCLE, Jan. 1970, at 46).

6. *San Mateo,* 51 Cal.App. 3d at 8–10, 124 Cal.Rptr. at 75–76.

7. 52 Hawaii 436, 478 P.2d 314, (1970).

8. *Id.* at 437–438, 478 P.2d at 315.

9. 29 Conn.Sup. 397, 289 A.2d 914 (1971).

10. *Id.* at 399, 289 A.2d at 916.

11. Note, *supra* note 3, at 558.

12. See Note, *supra* note 3, at 558 (citing Reiss, *Sex Education in the Public Schools: Problem or Solution?,* 50 PHI DELTA KAPPAN, Sept. 1968, at 53). There are advantages, of course, to having all sex education taught in a discrete (and discreet) course: easier notice of sexual content to parents; easier objection by parents to sexual content; more efficient excusal system for objecting parties; and better opportunity for selection of specially-skilled and sensitive teachers. On the other hand, incorporation of sex education into several traditional courses yields a better understanding of those courses and perhaps also of sex itself. See Note, *supra* note 3, at 558, n.43.

13. See generally Note, *supra* note 3, at 548–554.

14. A study by Johns Hopkins University professors indicates that sexually active women who took sex education courses providing birth control information are more likely to use contraceptives and less likely to get pregnant. "Assessing sex education," Chicago Tribune, July 4, 1982, sec. 12, p. 2, col. 4, quoting *Sexuality Today.* But see Smith v. Ricci, 446 A.2d 501, 503 (N.J. S. Ct.), *appeal dismissed* for want of a substantial federal question, *sub. nom.* Smith v. Brandt, 459 U.S. 962 (1982): "[T]he [Family Life] Committee pointed out that no research studies had been found that showed a correlation between teaching about human sexuality and a reduction in teenage pregnancy...." (*Smith v. Ricci* was decided just weeks prior to the cited *Chicago Tribune* article).

   Unwanted pregnancies drain the state's welfare budget; unwanted children disrupt the lives of their parents and, "ignored and unloved ... may take their frustrations out on society." Wanted children are less likely to engage in antisocial behavior. Note, *supra* note 3, at 559 (citing Glueck, *Spotting Potential Delinquents,* in THE SOCIOLOGY OF PUNISHMENT AND CORRECTION 207 (N. Johnston, L. Savitz & M. Wolfgard, eds., 1962)).

15. See Recent Development, *supra* note 5, at 1055–1056; Note, *supra* note 3, at 548.

16. These include the American College of Obstetricians and Gynecologists (Committee on Maternal Health), the American Medical Association, the National Congress of Parents and Teachers (PTA), the National Educational Association, the YMCA, the YWCA, the United Nations Educational, Scientific, and Cultural Organizations (UNESCO), the Synagogue Council of America, the United States Catholic Conference, and the United States Department of Health, Education and Welfare (U.S. Commission of Education). Note, *supra* note 3, at 548, n.3 (citing B. GRUENBERG & J. KAUKONEN, HIGH SCHOOLS AND SEX EDUCATION (1940); E. McHOSE, FAMILY LIFE

EDUCATION IN SCHOOL AND COMMUNITY (1952); and J. BAKER, SEX EDUCATION IN HIGH SCHOOLS 17–32 (1942)).

17. See Smith v. Ricci, 446 A.2d at 503, referring to a 1978 Gallup poll "indicating that 77 per cent of the public and 95 per cent of the students favored sex education in the schools." See note 65, *infra.*

18. Recent Development, *supra* note 5, at 1056; Note, *supra* note 3, at 550.

19. Note, *supra* note 3, at 554.

20. *Id.* at 564 (citing Lester Smith, Director of the Social Health Association of Greater St. Louis, quoted in Robbins, *The Growing Need for Sex Education in our Schools,* 16 GOOD HOUSEKEEPING, Nov. 1965, at 94–95).

21. See Cornwell v. State Board of Education, 314 F.Supp. 340, 342 (D.Md. 1969), *aff'd per curiam,* 428 F.2d 471 (4th Cir.), *cert. denied,* 400 U.S. 942 (1970); San Mateo, 51 Cal. App.3d at 11, 124 Cal.Rptr. at 77; Hopkins v. Hamden Board of Education, 29 Conn. Sup. at 400, 289 A.2d at 920; Smith v. Ricci, 446 A.2d at 503; Valent v. N.J. State Board of Education, 114 N.J. Super. 63, 66, 274 A.2d 832, 834 (1971), complaint ultimately dismissed for failure to exhaust administrative remedies, 118 N.J. Super. 416, 288 A.2d 52 (1972).

22. U.S. Const. amend. I: "Congress shall make no law respecting an establishment of religion, or prohibiting the free exercise thereof. . . . " The first amendment is enforceable against the states through the operation of the fourteenth amendment's due process clause. P. KAUPER & F. BEYTAGH, CONSTITUTIONAL LAW: CASES AND MATERIALS 1152 (5th ed. 1980).

23. Lemon v. Kurtzman, 403 U.S. 602, 612–613 (1971); See Widmar v. Vincent, 454 U.S. 263, 271 (1981); Committee for Public Education v. Regan, 444 U.S. 646, 653 (1980); Roemer v. Maryland Public Works Board, 426 U.S. 736, 748 (1976). The establishment clause seeks to guard against three principal evils: state sponsorship of, financial support of, and active state involvement in religion. *San Mateo,* 51 Cal. App.3d at 20, 124 Cal.Rptr. at 83 (citing Walz v. Tax Commission of City of New York, 397 U.S. 664 (1970)).

24. See *e.g.,* Davis v. Page, 385 F.Supp. 395, 404 (D.N.H. 1974). A sex education program will not be struck down on the speculative possibility that the valid secular purpose will be consciously violated by a teacher or administrator. Hopkins v. Hamden Board of Education, 29 Conn. Sup. at 414, 289 A.2d at 923.

25. See Note, *supra* note 3, at 560–561.

26. See Rice, *Conscientious Objection to Public Education: the Grievance and the Remedies,* 1978 BRIGHAM YOUNG UNIV.L.REV. 847–870.

27. See Recent Development, *supra* note 5, at 1059. Interestingly, the U.S. Supreme Court, in Torcaso v. Watkins, 367 U.S. 488, 495, n.11, alluded to Secular Humanism as a religion. See Rice, *supra* note 26, at 856.

28. Abington School District v. Schempp, 374 U.S. 203, 231 (1963) (Brennan, J., concurring). See Note, *supra* note 3, at 562.

29. Note, *supra* note 3, at 561.

30. Of course, the course might discuss "competing moral interpretations of sex." See Note, *supra* note 3, at 563 (footnotes omitted), quoted in Smith v. Ricci, 446 A.2d at 507.

31. Another dilemma under the First Amendment is reflected in Hopkins v. Hamden Board of Education, 29 Conn.Sup. at 412, 289 A.2d at 922, where the plaintiffs on religious freedom grounds complained of the curriculum assertion that "Life comes from life and is nature's greatest miracle." The court

noted that complying with the parents' feeling that the children should be taught that life comes from God would violate the establishment clause. Perhaps the court should have urged that schools avoid opining on the ultimate source of life.

32. M. YUDOF, D. KIRP, T. VAN GEEL & B. LEVIN, EDUCATIONAL POLICY AND THE LAW: CASES AND MATERIALS 134 (2d ed. 1982). For an extensive discussion of "secular religion and the public schools," see Rice, *supra* note 26, at 858 *et seq.* See also Chapter 7, "Secular Humanism," in E. B. JENKINSON, CENSORS IN THE CLASSROOM: THE MIND BENDERS (1979).

33. Rice, *supra* note 26, at 865.

34. Cornwell v. State Board of Education, 314 F.Supp. at 344. *See also San Mateo,* 51 Cal. App.3d at 21, 124 Cal.Rptr. at 84; Hopkins v. Hamden Board of Education, 29 Conn. Sup. at 415–416, 289 A.2d at 924.

35. Davis v. Page, 385 F.Supp. at 404.

36. 51 Cal. App.3d at 21, 124 Cal.Rptr. at 84.

37. *Id.* at 24, 124 Cal.Rptr. at 86.

38. *Id.* at 21, 124 Cal.Rptr. at 84.

39. *Id.*

40. *Id.* at 24, 124 Cal.Rptr. at 86. See also Hopkins v. Hamden Board of Education, 29 Conn. Sup. at 411, 289 A.2d at 922.

41. 51 Cal. App.3d at 24, 124 Cal.Rptr. at 86.

42. See *id.* See also Cornwell v. State Board of Education, 314 F.Supp. at 344.

43. 51 Cal. App.3d at 25, 124 Cal.Rptr. at 87–88.

44. 393 U.S. 97 (1968).

45. *See San Mateo,* 51 Cal. App.3d at 18, 124 Cal.Rptr. at 82; Smith v. Ricci, 446 A.2d at 506, citing Medeiros v. Kiyosaki, 52 Hawaii at 442–443, 478 P.2d at 318–319; Rice, *supra* note 26, at 869; and text accompanying notes 146–159, *infra.*

46. On the constitutionality of an excusal system under the establishment clause, see Davis v. Page, 385 F.Supp. at 401, 402.

47. Consultations with members of the clergy in the development of a sex education program does not foster excessive entanglement. Smith v. Ricci, 446 A.2d at 506, n.2.

48. Rice, *supra* note 26, at 862 (citing Abington School District v. Schempp, 374 U.S. at 222–23).

49. See, however, Vaughn v. Reed, 313 F.Supp. 431, 434 (D.Va. 1970), observing that an excusal system might itself suggest that a constitutionally suspect course is being offered.

50. Recent Development, *supra* note 5, at 1052.

51. Davis v. Page, 385 F.Supp. 395 (D. N.H.1974); Cornwell v. State Board of Education, 314 F.Supp. 340 (D. Md. 1969); Hopkins v. Hamden Board of Education, 29 Conn. Sup.397, 289 A.2d 914 (1971).See Note, *supra* note 3, at 565. *See generally,* Hirschoff, *Parents and the Public School Curriculum: Is There a Right to Have One's Child Excused from Objectionable Instruction?,* 50 SO.CAL.L.REV. 871 (1977). *Cf.* Aubrey v. School District of Philadelphia, 437 A.2d 1306 (Comm. Ct. Pa. 1981).

Even if the compulsion of mere attendance at sex education courses is constitutional, however, a question remains concerning the extent to which actual participation in the discussion of personal or otherwise sensitive matters can be compelled. *Cf.* West Virginia State Board of Education v. Barnette, 319 U.S. 624 (1943), holding compelled participation in a flag salute ceremony unconstitutional. The Court did not require, however, that objecting students be excused from the classroom. See Rice, *supra* note 26, at 865 and text accompanying notes 91–104, *infra.*

52. 29 Conn. Sup. at 399, 289 A.2d at 916.

53. *Id.* at 408, 289 A.2d at 920 (quoting Cantwell v. Connecticut, 310 U.S. 296, 303 (1940)).

54. 29 Conn. Sup. at 412, 289 A.2d at 922.

55. *Id.* at 414, 289 A.2d at 923. See Prince v. Massachusetts, 321 U.S. 158 (1944); *San Mateo,* 51 Cal. App.3d at 27, 124 Cal.Rptr. at 88.

State action impinging upon one's free exercise rights may still be constitutional if justified by a compelling state interest. See Sherbert v. Verner, 374 U.S. 398, 406 (1963), and text accompanying note 67 *et seq., infra.* See also Davis v. Page, 385 F.Supp. at 399, suggesting that the U.S. Supreme Court, in Wisconsin v. Yoder, 406 U.S. 205, 214 (1972), "signaled a departure" from this standard.

Given the preferred status of religious freedom, the burden of justifying an infringement may rest upon the state. Recent Development, *supra* note 5, at 1055.

56. 29 Conn. Sup. at 415, 289 A.2d at 923.

57. 314 F.Supp. at 340.

58. Hopkins v. Hamden, 29 Conn. Sup. at 415, 289 A.2d at 924.

59. Valent v. New Jersey State Board of Education, 114 N.J. Super. at 77, 274 A.2d at 840.

60. Recent Development, *supra* note 5, at 1052, n.11 (citing United States v. Ballard, 322 U.S. 78 (1974)); Davis v. Page, 385 F.Supp. at 402. Personal convenience, of course, is not sufficient. Valent v. New Jersey State Board of Education, 114 N.J. Super. at 77, 274 A.2d at 840.

61. 385 F.Supp. at 404. The court cited Justice Clark's observation in Joseph Burstyn, Inc. v. Wilson, 343 U.S. 495, 505 (1952), that "the state has no legitimate interest in protecting any or all religions from views distasteful to them." 385 F.Supp. at 404.

62. See Rice, *supra* note 26, at 864, 866. It has been suggested, in fact, that the grant of such an exemption might itself violate the establishment clause. See Recent Development, *supra* note 5, at 1060.

63. 114 N.J. Super. 63, 274 A.2d 832 (1972).

64. *Id.* at 76, 274 A.2d at 839.

65. The court emphasized that public opinion alone may not establish a sufficient governmental interest. 114 N.J. Super. at 77, 274 A.2d at 840. The court was clearly unimpressed by the defendant's assertion that 70% of a Junior Chamber of Commerce poll favored sex education and that "pro-sex-education" candidates had defeated "anti-sex-education" candidates in the most recent school board election. "If majority rule were to govern in matters of religion and conscience, there would be no need for the first amendment". *Id. Cf.* note 17, *supra.*

66. 114 N.J. Super. at 76–77, 274 A.2d at 839–840.

67. 374 U.S. 398 (1963).

68. *Id.* at 406.

69. Valent v. New Jersey State Board of Education, 114 N.J. Super. at 73, 274 A.2d at 838.
    The balance is a "most precarious one". Davis v. Page, 385 F.Supp. at 399. The *Davis* court would balance the parent's rights not only against the state's interest, but also against the children's right to receive a proper education. *Id.*
70. 114 N.J. Super. at 78–79, 274 A.2d at 841.
71. Valent v. New Jersey State Board of Education, 118 N.J. Super. 416, 288 A.2d 52 (1972).
72. 29 Conn. Sup.397, 289 A.2d 914 (1971).
73. *Id.* at 409, 289 A.2d at 921. *Cf.* Medeiros v. Kiyosaki, 52 Hawaii 436, 478 P.2d 314 (1970).
74. 52 Mich. App.682, 684, 218 N.W. 2d 98, 99 (1974).
75. In Smith v. Ricci, 446 A.2d at 505, the Supreme Court of New Jersey rejected the argument that exercise of the excusal option exerted "intolerable pressure" on the pupils "to abandon their beliefs. . . . " Said the court: "The constitution does not guarantee . . . that the exercise of religion will be without difficulty." *Id.*
76. 52 Hawaii 436, 478 P.2d 314 (1970).
77. *Id.* at 438–444, 218 N.W.2d at 316–318.
78. 51 Cal. App.3d at 19, 124 Cal.Rptr. at 83.
79. 446 A.2d at 505.
80. See Cornwell v. State Board of Education, 314 F. Supp. at 342; *San Mateo,* 51 Cal. App.3d at 32, 121 Cal.Rptr. at 68; Hopkins v. Hamden, 29 Conn. Sup. at 408, 289 A.2d at 920–921; Medeiros v. Kiyosaki, 52 Hawaii at 438, 478 P.2d at 315; Aubrey v. School District of Philadelphia, 437 A.2d at 1306–1307. *See generally,* Note, *supra* note 3, at 566–567. The author suggests that granting a parental monopoly over sex education may be unconstitutional under Meyer v. Nebraska, 262 U.S. 390 (1923), which held unconstitutional a state statute prohibiting the teaching of any foreign language to students below the ninth grade level. *Id.* at 566. See generally Hirschoff, *supra* note 51, at 885–904.
81. See Valent v. New Jersey State Board of Education, 114 N.J. Super. at 76, 274 A.2d at 839.
82. See Hopkins v. Hamden Board of Education, 29 Conn. Sup. at 408–409, 289 A.2d at 920. The court replied: "Minimal evidence appears that the plaintiff parents had been complying with claimed religious pronouncements relating to sex education in the home." *Id.* at 409, 289 A.2d at 921. The court, however, may merely have been referring to parental failure to provide all the child's education at home or to send the children to private schools, both of which state law allowed, or to seek excusal. See *id.*
83. See Cornwell v. State Board of Education, 314 F.Supp. at 342 ("No authority is cited in support of this novel proposition. . . . "); *San Mateo,* 51 Cal. App.3d at 31–32, 124 Cal.Rptr. at 91; and Hopkins v. Hamden Board of Education, 29 Conn. Sup. at 409, 411, 289 A.2d at 920, 922.
84. 268 U.S. 510 (1925).
85. Note, *supra* note 3, at 566.
86. *San Mateo,* 51 Cal. App.3d at 18, 124 Cal.Rptr. at 82, n. 18, citing Note, *supra* note 3, at 566–567.
87. 321 U.S. 158 (1944).
88. See Cornwell v. State Board of Education, 314 F.Supp. at 344; *San Mateo,* 51 Cal.

App.3d at 14, 27, 124 Cal.Rptr. at 79, 88. But see Valent v. New Jersey State Board of Education, 114 N.J. Super. at 76–77, 274 A.2d at 839–840.

89. 321 U.S. at 164.

90. *Id.* at 165–166, 169. In a statement apposite to the sex education area, the Court said, "Parents may be free to become martyrs themselves. But it does not follow they are free, in identical circumstances, to make martyrs of their children before they have reached the age of full and legal discretion when they can make that choice for themselves." *Id.* at 170.

It has been suggested that school officials could avoid both establishment clause and free exercise clause problems by making sex education an extracurricular activity. See Recent Development, *supra* note 5, at 1058, n.47. However, courts can be expected to look at the substance of the program, not its label. Presumably, for example, a public school is not free to sponsor a Mass, even as an extracurricular activity.

91. See, *e.g.*, Medeiros v. Kiyosaki, 52 Hawaii at 438–440, 478 P.2d at 315–316.

92. See *San Mateo*, 51 Cal. App.3d at 11, 124 Cal.Rptr. at 77; Hopkins v. Hamden Board of Education, 29 Conn. Sup. at 416, 289 A.2d at 924; Medeiros v. Kiyosaki, 52 Hawaii at 438–440, 478 P.2d at 315–316; and Aubrey v. School District of Philadelphia, 437 A.2d at 1307.

93. Some state statutes limit such probing. See, *e.g.*, CALIF. EDUC. CODE § 60650 (West 1978) (Prohibiting tests, questionnaires, surveys or examinations "containing any questions about the pupil's personal beliefs or practices in sex, family life, morality and religion," or those of his parents or guardian, without the permission of the parents or guardian. Curiously, the statute does not explicitly cover ordinary, in-class questioning on such topics, although that context may be the most embarrassing to the pupil); LA. REV. STAT. ANN. § 17:281 (West 1982 & Supp. 1985) (Providing not only that "students shall not be tested, quizzed, or surveyed about their personal or family beliefs or practices in sex, morality, or religion," but also that sex education "shall not include religious beliefs, values, customs, practices in human sexuality, nor the subjective moral and ethical judgment of the instructor or other persons").

94. 51 Cal. App.3d at 8–9, 124 Cal.Rptr. at 75.

95. *Id.* at 11, 124 Cal.Rptr. at 77.

96. It did address the family finances component in a footnote, stating that the study of family resources is a recognized part of school curricula in California and elsewhere. *Id.* at 31, 124 Cal.Rptr. at 90–91, n.29. This too misses the point; the concern is not the discussion of family economics, but the official and organized prying into the economics and other aspects of the student's family.

97. *Id.* at 30, 124 Cal.Rptr. at 90.

98. *Id.* at 31, 124 Cal.Rptr. at 91.

99. *Id.* at 29, 124 Cal.Rptr. at 89, citing Griswold v. Connecticut, 381 U.S. 479, 483, 485–86 (1965).

100. See CAL. EDUC. CODE §§51240 and 51550 (West 1978), the current excusal provisions.

101. 51 Cal. App.3d at 30–31, 124 Cal.Rptr. at 90–91. Enjoining the program, the court added, would " 'contract the spectrum of available knowledge' " in violation of the teaching of Griswold v. Connecticut, 381 U.S. 479, 482 (1965). *San Mateo*, 51 Cal.App. 3d at 31, 124 Cal.Rptr. at 90.

102. But see Hopkins v. Hamden Board of Education, in which a compulsory

program survived a privacy challenge: "The only evidence offered by the plaintiffs reflected their fear of disclosures by a child in the curriculum classroom discussions of private family activities or conversations which have taken place in the home. Disclosures of this nature are not constitutionally protected. . . . " 29 Conn. Sup. at 416, 289 A.2d at 924. There is no indication, however, that the challenged program called for the official and organized probing indicated in the *San Mateo* case.

103. California law allows a parent or guardian objecting on religious grounds to have the child excused from "the *part* of the training which conflicts" with the religious training or belief of the parent or guardian. CAL. EDUC. CODE §51240 (West 1978) (emphasis added). See also *id.* §51550, allowing requests that the child not attend "the class." The statutes do not deal with the problem presented when the child wants to attend over the wishes of his parent or guardian: is the excusal system in such a case unconstitutional? See R. MNOOKIN, CHILD, FAMILY AND STATE: PROBLEMS AND MATERIALS ON CHILDREN AND THE LAW 155 (1978). *Cf.* Wisconsin v. Yoder, 406 U.S. 205, 241–246 (1972) (dissenting opinion).

104. *Compare* CAL. EDUC. CODE §51240 (West 1978) with *id.* §51550.

105. 51 Cal. App.3d at 27, 124 Cal.Rptr. at 88.

106. U.S. Const. amend. XIV: No state shall "deprive any person of life, liberty, or property, without due process of law; nor deny to any person . . . the equal protection of the laws."

107. 51 Cal. App.3d at 28, 124 Cal.Rptr. at 88. Nor did the burdens incidental to excusal deny equal protection. *Id.* at 28, 124 Cal.Rptr. at 89.

108. *Id.* at 28–29, 124 Cal. at 89.

109. See Cornwell v. State Board of Education, 314 F. Supp. at 342; Hopkins v. Hamden, 29 Conn. Sup. at 411, 405, 289 A.2d at 919, 921–22.

110. See Medeiros v. Kiyosaki, 52 Hawaii at 444–446, 478 P.2d at 319–320; Hobolth v. Greenway, 52 Mich.App. at 684–685, 218 N.W.2d at 100.

111. See Medeiros v. Kiyosaki, 52 Hawaii at 446–447, 478 P.2d at 320.

112. See Hopkins v. Hamden Board of Education, 29 Conn. Sup. at 401–405, 289 A.2d at 917–919; Smith v. Ricci, 446 A.2d at 507–08; and Aubrey v. School District of Philadelphia, 437 A.2d at 1306–1308.

113. See Hopkins v. Hamden Board of Education, 29 Conn. Sup. at 406, 289 A.2d at 919.

114. Epperson v. Arkansas, 393 U.S. 97, 104 (1969), quoted in *San Mateo*, 51 Cal. App.3d at 20, 124 Cal.Rptr. at 83. See also Davis v. Page, 385 F. Supp. at 400; and Aubrey v. School District of Philadelphia, 437 A.2d at 1307–1308.

115. Davis v. Page, 385 F.Supp. at 400.

116. But see the Johns Hopkins University study referred to in note 14, *supra*, indicating that sex education does not increase teenagers' sexual activity.

117. See Note, *supra* note 3, at 567–568. But see note 14, *supra*.

118. For still other concerns, see Recent Development, *supra* note 5, at 1051, n.8.

119. See Mercer v. Michigan State Board of Education, 397 F.Supp. at 580.

120. Analogously, state legislatures may give local districts an "excusal" of sorts, that is, allow the districts to decide whether to have courses in sex education. See, *e.g.,* LA. REV. STAT. ANN. § 17:281A (West Supp. 1985). Sex education is proscribed, however, in kindergarten through sixth grade. *Id.* An Alabama provision is still more guarded: "Nothing in this chapter ['Drug Abuse

Education'] shall be construed to authorize or require the teaching of sex education in any form." ALA. CODE § 16-41-8 (1977). *Cf.* CAL. EDUC. CODE § 51550 (West 1978).

121. Rice, *supra* note 26, at 862.

122. See Davis v. Page, 385 F.Supp. at 405, holding an excusal system not constitutionally compelled, although "it might be more judicious for the School Board to make attendance voluntary."

123. See Recent Development, *supra* note 5, at 1051, n.5. For the state interests potentially involved, *see generally,* Hirschoff, *supra* note 51, at 918–941, 952–955.

124. *E.g.,* California, see CAL. EDUC. CODE §§51240 and 51550 (West 1978) (Section 51240 is limited to those whose objections relate to their religious beliefs, including "personal moral convictions," but section 51550, which provides a substantively narrower exemption, is available to all objectors); Hawaii, see Medeiros v. Kiyosaki, 52 Hawaii at 440–441, 478 P.2d at 316–317; Illinois, see ILL. ANN. STAT. § 122-27-9.1 (Smith-Hurd) (Supp. 1983); Louisiana, see LA. REV. STAT. ANN. § 17.281D (West 1982); Michigan, see MICH. COMP. LAWS ANN. §§ 380.1506(1), 380.1507(4) (West Supp. 1983); New Jersey, see Smith v. Ricci, 446 A.2d at 504–05. *Cf.* LA. REV. STAT. ANN. § 17:275 (West 1982), providing excusal from required instruction concerning breast examination and Pap smear if such instruction "conflicts with the religious beliefs of the student."

125. Recent Development, *supra* note 5, at 1050, n.5. Michigan law mandates that the course be elective. MICH. COMP. LAWS ANN. § 380.1507(2)(West Supp. 1983).

126. Note, *supra* note 3, at 568.

127. See Davis v. Page, 385 F.Supp. at 398–399, 400, citing Wisconsin v. Yoder, 406 U.S. 205, 245–246 (1972) (Douglas, J., dissenting).

128. Note, *supra* note 3, at 568.

129. See the July 27, 1970, memorandum of the New Jersey Commissioner of Education, quoted in Valent v. New Jersey State Board of Education, 114 N.J. Super. at 68–69, 274 A.2d at 835.

130. Note, *supra* note 3, at 568. The peer pressure to participate, however, will not render an excusal system unconstitutional under the free exercise clause, Smith v. Ricci, 446 A.2d at 505, and, if it did, could require abolition of the entire program as a remedy. See Rice, *supra* note 26, at 863. See also *San Mateo,* 51 Cal. App.3d at 17, 124 Cal.Rptr. at 81 ("[I]ndirect social pressures are not sufficient to cause a violation of the free exercise clause") (citing Abington School District v. Schempp, 374 U.S. at 233). Social pressures may violate the establishment clause. *See generally,* Recent Development, *supra* note 5, at 1056–1057. Indeed, the pressure need not be felt only by nonparticipants. In Davis v. Page, 385 F.Supp at 406, a teacher testified that Apostolic Lutheran children, who objected to the use of audiovisual equipment in the classroom, exerted great pressure on students participating in audiovisual exercises, calling them sinners and thereby arousing emotional conflict. It is not far-fetched to fear the same phenomenon in some sex education excusal situations.

131. Davis v. Page, 385 F.Supp. at 405–406.

132. *Cf. San Mateo,* 51 Cal.3d at 18, 124 Cal.Rptr. at 82, n. 17.

133. *Id.* at 7, 124 Cal.Rptr. at 74–75.

134. 385 F.Supp. at 397. Under the new policy, students were required to stay in the

classroom, but could lay their heads on the desk, turn their chairs away or stand in the rear of the room. *Id.*

135. *Cf.* Spence v. Bailey, 465 F.2d 797, 799, n.2 (6th Cir. 1972) (citing Sherbert v. Verner, 374 U.S. at 407).

136. See, *e.g.*, CAL. EDUC. CODE § 51550 (West 1978); ILL. ANN. STAT. § 122-27-9.1 (Smith-Hurd Supp. 1983); MICH. COMP. LAWS ANN. § 380.1507(3) (West Supp. 1983); Medeiros v. Kiyosaki, 478 P.2d at 316–317; and Smith v. Ricci, 446 A.2d at 504. *Cf.* LA. REV. STAT. ANN. § 17:281C (West 1982), requiring approval of all sex education instructional materials by a "parental review committee."

137. 379 F.Supp. at 580 (E.D. Mich. 1974). *Mercer* was affirmed on appeal, without opinion, by the U.S. Supreme Court. 419 U.S. 1081 (1974). Justices Douglas, Brennan and White would have noted probable jurisdiction and set the case for oral argument. *Id.*

138. See MICH. COMP. LAWS ANN. § 340.782 (West 1976) (Repealed by P.A. 1976, No. 451, § 1851, effective Jan. 13, 1977).
     Michigan now allows "family planning" instruction. See MICH. COMP. LAWS ANN. § 380.1507(1) (West Supp. 1983).

139. 379 F.Supp. at 585.

140. See also Chapter 1, *supra;* and Pratt v. Independent School District, 670 F.2d 771, 776 (8th Cir. 1982).

141. 379 F.Supp. at 585.

142. 417 F.2d 1169 (D.C. Cir. 1969).

143. *Id.* at 1177.

144. See *id.* ("minimal relevance"). The court also noted that the course was a quick language training course, not allowing much spare time. *Id.*

145. *Id.*

146. 393 U.S. 97 (1968).

147.   The overriding fact is that Arkansas' law selects from the body of knowledge a particular segment which it proscribes for the sole reason that it is deemed to conflict with a particular religious doctrine; that is, with a particular interpretation of the Book of Genesis by a particular religious group.
     Id. at 103. *Cf.* Pratt v. Independent School District, 670 F.2d at 773: "The school board cannot constitutionally ban [these] films because a majority of its members object to the films' religious and ideological content and wish to prevent the ideas contained in the material from being expressed in the school."

148. See 393 U.S. at 111, 116 (concurring opinions).

149. "Arkansas did not seek to excise from the curriculum of its schools . . . all discussion of the origin of man." *Id.* at 109.

150. It is interesting to note that *Mercer* itself suggests that birth control may be but a component of a larger area, family planning. The court refers to "acts and words that do not involve the teaching, advising, etc., on birth control but do fall within the overall concept of family planning or sex education." 379 F.Supp. at 587. If family planning may be discussed but, due to its religious sensitivity, birth control (however defined) cannot, an *Epperson* violation seems arguable.

151. 379 F.Supp. at 586.

152. See note 147, *supra.*

153. "No suggestion has been made that Arkansas' law may be justified by considera-

tions of state policy other than the religious views of some of its citizens." 393 U.S. at 107.

154. "[T]here is no reason . . . why a State is without power to withdraw from its curriculum any subject deemed too emotional or controversial for its public schools." 393 U.S. at 113 (concurring opinion).

155. The court states that the teacher's "basic contention is that his First Amendment rights are being infringed. . . . " 379 F.Supp. at 584. It is not clear, therefore, that the teacher pushed the establishment clause argument as opposed to a free speech argument. The former would have more likely prompted a full *Epperson* discussion from the court.

156. Board of Education of Township of Rockaway v. Rockaway Township Educational Association, 120 N.J. Super. 564, 295 A.2d 380 (1972).

157. *Id.* at 567, 295 A.2d at 382.

158. Of course, if the school officials are free to remove any area of discussion from the classroom, the contract's academic freedom provision may be eviscerated. Under the court's ruling, however, the defendants were free to protest the matter to the Commissioner of Education, with an ultimate appeal to the courts. *Id.* at 571, 295 A.2d at 384.

159. *Cf.* LA. REV. STAT. § 17:281F (West 1982), prohibiting any sex education program from counselling or advocating abortion.

160. Even the relatively prudish Soviet Union has introduced sex education into its schools. See "Soviets to introduce sex education," *Chicago Tribune*, August 13, 1983, Sec. 1, p. 5, cols. 4–6. See also Notes 17 and 65, *supra.*

161. For an extended discussion of the "remedies of objecting parents," see Rice, *supra* note 26, at 861–888. Beyond the elimination of sex education from the schools or excusal therefrom, the author discusses the introduction into the schools of nonreligious principles of morality, the formation of voluntary, extracurricular religious clubs and the institution of independent private schools.

Chapter 3

SEX AND THE SCHOOL LIBRARY

INTRODUCTION

In September of 1975, three members of the Board of Education of the Island Trees Union Free School District No. 26, in New York, attended a conference sponsored by a politically conservative group of parents, Parents of New York United (PONYU), concerned about New York law dealing with education.[1] At the conference, they obtained lists of books called "objectionable" by one of these three and "improper fare for school students" by another. As it turned out, nine of the listed books were currently carried by the Island Trees High School library and one by the Island Trees Memorial Junior High School library. The curriculum of a twelfth-grade literature course contained an additional listed book, Bernard Malamud's *The Fixer*.[2] In February of 1976, the Board issued an "unofficial directive" that the listed library books be taken to the Board's offices so that Board members might read them. After the books were removed, the directive became generally known and the Board issued a press release justifying its action and characterizing the books involved as "anti-American, anti-Christian, anti-Semitic, and just plain filthy." The release concluded with a reference to the Board's perceived moral obligation to protect school children from "moral danger."

Shortly thereafter, the Board appointed a committee, made up of four parents and four staff members of the school system, to make recommendations to the Board with regard to the books, in light of their "educational suitability," "good taste," "relevance" and "appropriateness to age and grade level." In its final report, the committee recommended that five of the books be retained and that two be removed. The committee could not agree with regard to two other books, took no position with regard to still another, and urged that the last book be made available to those students whose parents consented. The Board "substantially rejected"[3] the committee's report by removing nine of the contested books from the school libraries and from curricular use. Teachers did remain free to discuss the removed books and their ideas and positions.[4] Students at the two schools then sued the Board of Education and its members, claiming a violation of the students' First Amendment rights.

It is clear that the Board was significantly motivated by the sexual content of the books. Its press release called the works "filthy" and spoke of the Board's "moral" duty to protect the children from "this moral danger."[5] Moreover, the excerpts which prompted the Board to look into the educational suitability of the books contain sexually-explicit language.[6] The *Island Trees* litigation, therefore, raised important questions concerning the power of a school board to control sexual content in public school libraries.

Regrettably, the litigation, despite consideration at three different judicial levels, failed to settle the questions in any definitive way. The U.S. District Court granted summary judgment in favor of the School Board and its members. The U.S. Court of Appeals for the Second Circuit disagreed, finding a trial necessary to resolve whether removal was politically motivated and whether the books were removed because of the ideas they contained. The United States Supreme Court affirmed the need for a trial, on a five-to-four vote, but no clear theory on the merits of the case controlled a majority of the Court.[7] Justice Brennan, joined by Justices Marshall and Stevens, emphasized the student's right to receive information and concluded that a school board may not remove books from school libraries merely because it dislikes the ideas in those books and seeks to prescribe by such removal political, religious or other orthodoxy. Concurring in most of Justice Brennan's approach, but embracing "a somewhat different perspective,"[8] Justice Blackmun observed that the state may not "suppress exposure to ideas—for the sole *purpose* of suppressing exposure to those ideas—absent sufficiently compelling reason."[9] Justice White felt it premature to discuss limits on school board discretion prior to resolution of the factual issues at trial.[10] Justices Burger, Powell, Rehnquist and O'Connor, dissenting, felt that the school board should prevail on the pleadings, without a trial.[11]

The *Island Trees* case posed "difficult first amendment issues in a largely uncharted field."[12] This chapter will examine state control of school library content in light of the nature of the public school library and its impact on the curriculum. An exploration of *whose* rights are implicated will be in order here, as it was in discussing the curriculum.

The issues are especially critical. After all, governmental condemnation of a book "touches the central nervous system of the First Amendment."[13]

Yet, such censorship remains relatively common.[14] Over 1,000 cases of attempted book-bannings in school libraries took place between 1981 and mid-1982.[15] Indeed, one study has shown that attempts to censor books occur annually in a fifth of the nation's schools and, in half the cases, succeed.[16] Moves to censor come mainly from the Right, but also from the Left and involve such classics as John Steinbeck's *Of Mice and Men,* Shakespeare's *The Merchant of Venice,* and *The Diary of Anne Frank.*[17] Occasionally, this serious situation has humorous overtones, such as the attempt to censor *The Adventures of Huckleberry Finn* at the Mark Twain Intermediate School, in Fairfax, Virginia,[18] and the effort in one school system to ban *Making It With Mademoiselle,* which turned out to be a dressmaking book for teenagers.[19]

THE NATURE OF THE SCHOOL LIBRARY

The school library, although typically a small auxiliary facility run on a limited budget,[20] has been called "a storehouse of knowledge,"[21] an "important privilege,"[22] a "mighty resource in the free marketplace of ideas,"[23] a "forum for silent speech,"[24] "a valuable asset to the educational process",[25] and "a place dedicated to quiet, to knowledge, and to beauty."[26] As one court put it:

> There a student can literally explore the unknown, and discover areas of interest and thought not covered by the prescribed curriculum. The student who discovers the magic of the library is on the way to a life-long experience of self-education and enrichment. That student learns that a library is a place to test or expand upon ideas presented to him, in or out of the classroom.[27]

The library's unique aspects, it has been said, make it especially suited for recognition under the protection of the First Amendment.[28]

These praises, however, do not inevitably control the applicability of First Amendment principles. A closer look at the function of the school library is in order, a look revealing two fundamentally different constitutional assessments.

The first of these sees the library as an extension of the classroom. Moreover, since classroom instruction may constitutionally seek to inculcate society's morals and values, so too may the school library—unlike, presumably, the public library. As Justice Blackmun has observed, "[I]f schools may be used to inculcate ideas, surely libraries may play a role in that process."[29] Recognition of the library's inculcative role in turn leads rather naturally to approbation of the school board's right to decide on the retention of library books according to "content-based" criteria.[30]

> [C]ourts that have limited the board's power to remove books have wholly ignored the board's general powers for controlling access to information within the school system. They have ignored powers over teachers, course existence and content, and teaching methods. To view the book on the library shelf as different from all these elements of control—including the right to select the book in the first place—is to make a distinction without justification in first amendment terms. It is to select a single event with the emotional overtones of "book burning" and to view it in the abstract, wholly apart from its context within the public school system.[31]

Indeed, a corollary of this view is that putting a book into the library, or allowing it to remain there, at least implies approval of the worth of the book's content.[32] This perspective emphasizes that the school library, for first amendment purposes, and unlike a street corner or public park,[33] need not offer a smorgasbord of views.

A different emphasis is reflected in Justice Brennan's plurality opinion in *Island Trees*. Unwilling to affirm officialdom's "unfettered" discretion to inculcate societal values, Brennan stressed the differences between the classroom and the library.[34] In the *Island Trees* case, at least, the record indicated that all student use of the school libraries was voluntary. The libraries were therefore a vehicle for optional "self-education" and "individual enrichment."[35]

In truth, each of these views falls short of the mark. Perhaps most school libraries, at least at the junior high and high school levels, seek to be more than a monolithic indoctrinator of establishmentarian values. A library, even more so than the classroom, need not be limited to one viewpoint. At least at the upper levels, a library might well reflect the view that controversy and dissent present golden opportunities for education.[36]

Indeed, the school library may provide a counterbalance to a curriculum representing majoritarian values, since it can afford a diversity of viewpoints with no danger that a child's selection of particular books will in any way impose on other students,[37] or impose a particular teacher's views on him.[38]

Nonetheless, problems remain. Although it is true that a student borrowing from the library a book that is too "mature" or "unappealing" may return it "unread",[39] he may be exposed to a large part of the book before he discovers, if he does, the true extent of its maturity. Too, a child may not choose to stop reading a book that is beyond his years—the book may be too mature for him but remain appealing. Furthermore, a borrowed book may involve material to which the child's parents do not want him exposed.[40]

The typical school library, whether or not its use is optional, will inevitably play a large inculcative role if only because it is likely to contain the most popular and traditional books, that is, books that transmit, overtly or otherwise, traditional values.

Of course, few adherents of either the inculcative model or the "marketplace of ideas" model would suggest an "unfettered" right to control library content. Even those most wedded to value inculcation would balk at a purely partisan stocking or pruning of school libraries.[41] But clearly, the more one emphasizes the value-inculcating role of the school library, the more he will tolerate school board control of which books are acquired for, or removed from, that library.

THE LIBRARY AND THE CLASSROOM

Whatever the situation in the *Island Trees* case, the school library is often an important adjunct of the classroom. Many jurists, in evaluating book removal issues, have therefore looked to the possible impact of the removal on classroom activity. In the Court of Appeals consideration of the *Island Trees* case, for example, Judge Mansfield, dissenting, felt that the school board had the right to remove the books, at least in part because the school's teachers and students remained free to discuss the ideas contained in the books.[42] On the other hand, Justice Brennan noted that although the teachers were free to discuss the books or their ideas,[43] these books could not be assigned or recommended to students in connection with their class work.[44] At least one court has found book removal to impose a more serious burden upon free discussion in the classroom than the prohibition of black armbands censured by the U.S. Supreme Court in the *Tinker* case.[45]

A more subtle but perhaps more insidious connection between book removal and classroom activity attracted the attention of Judge Newman, concurring in the Second Circuit's *Island Trees* result. Recognizing that removal of a book on the basis of its ideas officially informs students and teachers that these ideas are wrong, unacceptable and not to be discussed, Judge Newman concluded that the "symbolic effect . . . will often be more significant than the resulting limitation upon access to [the book].... The impact of burning a book does not depend on whether every copy is on the fire."[46]

Justice Brennan's assertion that library books are "by their nature" optional reading[47] clearly overstates or oversimplifies the situation. Teachers may assign specific books or parts thereof, may allow students to select among books on a reading list or may refer in class to books that certain students will choose to seek out in the school library.[48] Justice Powell sees the school library as "analogous to an assigned reading list within which students may exercise a degree of choice."[49] Indeed, to the extent that library material constitutes optional reading, it may provide less danger of unconstitutional orthodoxy than does required material,[50] and therefore allow for more school board control, not less. Furthermore, even though we still know little about the extent to which a student's conduct is affected by the sexual material he reads,[51] books may transmit ideas more effectively and more permanently than other forms of communication.[52]

Other differences between the library and the curriculum should be noted. Although the recognition of students' or parents' rights in the context of the curriculum presents dangers of wholesale interference with school functions, books on library shelves do not threaten the school's orderly operation.[53] On the other hand, a library's offerings, unlike classroom content, will generally be available to students of a wide range of ages, lending a greater risk that children will be exposed to inappropriate material.

A QUESTION OF RIGHTS

In our discussion of sex and the curriculum, the question of which— and whose—rights are involved loomed large. Much of that analysis[54] pertains here as well, and will not be repeated. To be sure, school library book cases confront the courts with conflicts among the board's authority to regulate the schools, the parents' recognized duty to raise their children and the rights, however limited, of children under the Constitution.[55] After all, there are situations in which the state's interest in the child outweighs the parent's right to determine how the child is to be raised.[56] Moreover, the teacher, though much less directly affected by the library book issue than by the curricular one, may also have rights in such matters.[57] The problem of achieving the "very delicate balance" required is "seemingly unsolvable."[58]

The right of the student to receive information[59] in the school library context received its most prominent boost in Justice Brennan's plurality opinion in *Island Trees*. Recognizing that school boards retain broad discretion in school management,[60] including control over school library content,[61] and that courts should not intervene in school affairs unless "basic constitutional" values are " 'directly and sharply implicate[d]' ",[62] Brennan nonetheless found that school library book removal may indeed thus implicate students' first amendment rights.[63] The right to receive information is crucial to the recipient's own speech, press and political freedoms.[64] The school library, Brennan asserted, is the "principal locus" of the student's freedom to "inquire, to study and to evaluate, to gain new maturity and understanding."[65]

Justice Brennan remarked, however, that the right to receive ideas flows inevitably from the sender's first amendment right to send these ideas.[66] Along the same lines, Judge Mansfield, dissenting from the Court of Appeals result in *Island Trees*, had emphasized that the student right to receive information could be no greater than the speaker's right to give it.[67] The right to receive information, therefore, seems stronger in the classroom context where, after all, the sender—usually the teacher—is directly implicated. In the school library situation, the sender—the book author—is not directly implicated and is typically not asserting a constitutional right to be represented among the school's library books:

> Here no speaker exists claiming a constitutional right to address the students with respect to the text of the removed books unless it is the teachers, who are not prevented from speaking on the subject matter. The publishers and authors of the books do not claim any constitutional right mandating use of their books in the school.[68]

It would indeed seem difficult to posit in the author a constitutional right to have his books purchased for a public school library.[69] After all, an author wishing to say something has no right to insist that the government be the courier,[70] let alone at a specific place.[71] Perhaps, however, precisely because the removal from a school library of an isolated book makes unlikely any claim by the author, "the impact of the government's action on those indirectly affected comes to the forefront."[72] Perhaps no direct connection between the sender and receiver is necessary since, in the school library context, both have first amendment interests at stake, the author in the circulation of his book free of governmental restraint and the student in access to a broad selection of reading material.[73]

Also militating against a right to receive information is the fact that even the wide variety of views made possible by the school library may still fail to satisfy everyone. "[A] mass institution designed to meet the needs of the population at large cannot be reconstructed at the desire of each individual 'customer'."[74]

In any event, any right to receive information cannot be absolute. Surely students do not have a right to obscenity or, for that matter, to "ideas" clearly devoid of merit. "If someone authored a book advocating that the earth was flat, it could hardly be argued that the work could not be removed from the public school library unless it was obscene."[75] This suggests that sexually explicit matter, though not obscene, is not *ipso facto* immune to elimination from school library shelves.

Furthermore, any academic freedom right to receive information ultimately accepted by the courts[76] will probably be limited according to the intellectual level of the elementary and high school (as opposed to college) student[77] and by the recognized fact that primary and secondary schools have, beyond their intellectual goals, a "broad formative role" in inculcating and encouraging the development of fundamental social, political, and moral values seen as necessary for life in American society.[78] These limitations surely make the contours of the academic freedom[79] right in subcollege academic life imprecise, at best.[80]

SCHOOL BOARD POWER

Justice Brennan's plurality opinion in *Island Trees* suggested the limits of school board power in school library book cases. The critical issue, he concluded, was the motivation behind the book removal. If the school board intended to suppress ideas with which the board disagreed, and if this intent constituted the "decisive factor" in the removal decision, the First Amendment has been violated.[81] Due to its procedural posture and the split among the Court, however, *Island Trees* did not provide ultimate guidance concerning the allocation of power in school library cases. A look at lower court pronouncements is therefore in order.

All courts agree with Justice Brennan that school officials have broad discretion to control school operations, including any school library.[82] Presumably, all courts also agree that at some point (for example, removing from the library all literature involving Democrats), the First Amendment voids official action. Two overriding issues, then, arise: how much authority should school officials be deemed to have and, closely related and sometimes overlapping, what criteria of book removal (or selection) are valid under the Constitution?

The traditional view tends strongly to favor the school official's independence in overseeing library content. This view tends to be supported by theories of *in loco parentis,* a vanishing phenomenon, and of indoctrination in majoritarian values and customs, as purportedly required by the school board's representation of the majority. Such a view emphasizes value inculcation, not value neutrality, and assumes that any book selection device will leave some constituents unhappy.[83]

Zykan v. Warsaw Community School Corporation,[84] though a very recent case, represents an accentuated version of the traditional outlook. In *Zykan,* the plaintiffs claimed that the defendant school board violated their First Amendment rights in permanently removing from the high school library a book entitled *Go Ask Alice.*[85] The Seventh Circuit Court of Appeals held that the complaint failed to allege a constitutional violation.[86] Allowing that students had some measure of academic freedom, the court stressed that in light of youth's need for intellectual and moral guidance, states vested in local school boards the primary control over education.[87] The breadth of control which Indiana, the state involved in *Zykan,* had entrusted to local boards reflected the view that educational guidance concerns should predominate over many academic freedom interests.[88] Consequently, concluded the court, it is generally permissible "for local boards to make educational decisions based upon their personal social, political and moral views."[89] Therefore, even ill-advised and imprudent decisions will generally be beyond constitutional complaint.[90] In matters involving library book selection and retention, therefore, courts may interfere only when the board has substituted "rigid and exclusive indoctrination" for the legitimate exercise of its authority to make educational choices concerning matters of legitimate contention.[91] Only a flagrant abuse of discretion by the board, said the court, would justify such court intervention: a cognizable complaint must allege that the school board, in its actions, sought to impose a religious or scientific orthodoxy or to outlaw generally a certain type of inquiry.[92] The court made clear its high threshold of judicial intercession by observing: "This is not to say that an administrator may remove a book from the library as part of a purge of all material offensive to a single, exclusive perception of the way of the world, anymore than he or she may stock the library on this basis."[93] Several other courts share the Seventh Circuit's presumption of board action constitutionality.[94]

The Court of Appeals for the Sixth Circuit, in *Minarcini v. Strongsville City School District*,[95] demonstrated a greater willingness to require school boards to justify their actions in library book removal cases.[96] At issue there was the removal from the high school library of Vonnegut's *Cat's Cradle* and Heller's *Catch 22*. (The board also forbade discussion of these works in class). Although clearly recognizing that discretion in book selection must be lodged somewhere, may be given to elected school board officials, and need not be given to the faculty,[97] the court nonetheless held that, absent some constitutionally neutral explanation, and in light of the evidence suggesting that the removals were due to the board members' view that the books were "objectionable" and "distasteful," the board action was unconstitutional.[98] While the Seventh Circuit in *Zykan* stressed the right of board members to decide educational questions on the basis of their personal social, political and moral views,[99] the Sixth Circuit in *Minarcini* emphasized that neither the State of Ohio nor the local school board "could place conditions on the use of the library . . . related solely to the social or political tastes of school board members."[100] The plaintiffs' case was not hurt by the fact that the parties to the litigation conceded the literary value of the novels and agreed that they were not, under U.S. Supreme Court guidelines, obscene.[101]

GENERAL GUIDELINES

In light of this judicial uncertainty, what may one generally conclude with regard to the power of the school board in library book cases? Clearly, the day-to-day management of school libraries is within the power of school officials.[102] For courts to intervene, constitutional rights must be "directly and sharply" implicated,[103] a standard mandated by *Epperson v. Arkansas*.[104] Once so implicated, the *Tinker*[105] standard may require yielding to first amendment rights absent some strong interest on the part of the schools,[106] this despite the strong feeling in some quarters that the school's reasonable educational judgment should prevail, without recourse to the more demanding *Tinker* standard.[107] It must be recalled that *Tinker* pitted an unobtrusive armband against the school's disciplinary structure—the content of neither the curriculum nor the library was at stake.

Finally, it must be emphasized that the choice between judge and school official cannot wholly depend on the relative educational expertise of each. The U.S. Supreme Court has noted that "we act in these matters not by the authority of our competence but by force of our commission. We cannot, because of modest estimates of our competence in such specialties as public education, withhold the judgment that history authenticates as the function of this Court when liberty is infringed."[108] When courts do intervene, they are exercising their expertise in constitutional matters, not in educational matters. Indeed, when local school boards purport to have the final say on matters of constitutional dimension, it is they who are intruding on the courts' expertise and prerogative. These broad guidelines set the stage for additional considerations in the school library book controversy.

SELECTION VERSUS REMOVAL

Almost all school library cases involve book removal and not book selection although, obviously, the purchase of some books budgetarily precludes the purchase of others.[109] A successful constitutional attack on selection seems unlikely.[110] It would rarely be appropriate to compel school districts, which have limited resources, to acquire a particular book, especially since many books may serve the library's legitimate needs.[111] After all, how does one demonstrate that constitutionally inappropriate reasons governed the nonpurchase of several among presumably thousands of other books not selected for reasons of budget, redundancy or whatever?[112] Perhaps extensive judicial intervention would be needed to deal comprehensively with the selection issue.[113]

Nonetheless, clearly some limit even on purchases must exist. As Justice Blackmun said in *Island Trees*, "It is difficult to see how a school board, consistent with the First Amendment, could refuse for political reasons to buy books written by Democrats or by Negroes, or books that are 'Anti-American' in the broadest sense of that term."[114]

Some have seen the substantial unreviewability of book selection as affirming the same broad discretion of local officials in the removal area. If, the argument goes, a school official can refuse to buy a particular book in the first place, that same official must have the authority to rescind that decision by removing the book.[115] Otherwise, the book receives preferential treatment merely by having once been on the shelves, a concept of book "tenure" specifically resisted by some jurists.[116] Chief Justice Burger has observed: "[I]f the First Amendment commands that certain books cannot be *removed*, does it not equally require that the

same books be *acquired?* Why does the coincidence of timing become the
basis of a constitutional holding?"[117]

Moreover, any more severe limitation on the removal decision than on
the selection decision may assume an unrealistic ability to screen purchases.
Despite one observer's view that the professional responsibility exercised by school librarians makes questionable claims that school libraries
have inappropriate material,[118] a school librarian, pressed for resources
to service the many needs of the library, obviously cannot read every
line of every book.[119] A more severe limitation may also weld a school
board to its own or another board's earlier decisions despite a currently
different pedagogical outlook which could be threatened by the legitimacy cast by the presence in the library of particular books.[120]

There are, however, significant and legitimate differences between
selection and removal, perhaps not so much in the abstract—both removal
and failure to select result in a particular book's absence[121]—but rather
in the practical and evidentiary aspects.

In *Right to Read Defense Committee of Chelsea v. School Committee of City
of Chelsea,*[122] the plaintiffs, including three students, two parents, the
school librarian, the English Chairperson and one English teacher, alleged
that the local school board had violated the first amendment in ordering
removed from the high school library *Male and Female Under 18,* an
anthology of writings by adolescents. The removal had been prompted
by one parent's objection to the language in "The City to a Young Girl,"
a poem included within the book and containing sexual concepts and
several specific sexual slang terms.[123] The school board chairman receiving the parental complaint had concluded after reading the poem that it
should be removed because of its "filthy" and "offensive" language.[124]
Apparently, the school board members themselves did not read any of
the book save the poem itself prior to voting to ban the entire anthology.[125]

The United States District Court concluded that the book had been
banned because of its perceived offensive theme and language, as indicated at the trial itself by the board members' consistent referral to the
poem as "filthy," "obscene" and "disgusting."[126] The removal thus violated the First Amendment rights of students and faculty.[127]

The court thus rejected the school board's argument that since it could
have refused to purchase *Male and Female Under 18* it had an equal right
to remove it from the shelves of the library.[128] Although the school board
may decide which books the library will purchase, there are decided
limits, the court said, to the board's authority to remove. The court

noted the lack of any contention that the book had been improperly procured under local regulations.[129]

The court referred to the "familiar constitutional principle" that a state action, even if not itself compelled, may result in a constitutionally protected interest. Therefore, the school board, free to buy or not to buy *Male and Female Under 18*, was not as free to remove it.[130]

Clearly, the court feared that total discretion to remove would carry with it excessive power to overrule the actions of previous boards:

> The prospect of successive school committees "sanitizing" the school library of views divergent from their own is alarming, whether they do it book by book, or one page at a time.[131]

The net result could, of course, be the reduction of the library's content to the lowest common denominator of blandness acceptable to all boards.

Moreover, not only does the removal decision override a past one, but—at least if the book is disposed of—it preempts future boards from placing that book or, as a practical matter, another copy of it on the shelves. Library budgets cannot keep up with current offerings, let alone restock past acquisitions and, in any event, the book may not currently be available.

Indeed, the removal decision, precisely because it overrides a prior judgment, may give rise to a presumption that improper motivation is at work.[132] The real difference between selection and removal, then, may not be the denial of a particular book to the students and faculty, but rather the extent to which intent to control ideas is telegraphed:

> To refuse to acquire a book merely makes that book one of innumerable others that have not been acquired, unless, because of extraordinary attention already drawn to that book, it has been specifically barred from acquisition. On the other hand, removal singles out that book for disapproval. In addition, removal, more than failure to acquire, is likely to suggest that an impermissible political motivation may be present. There are many reasons why a book is not acquired, the most obvious being limited resources, but there are few legitimate reasons why a book, once acquired, should be removed from a library not filled to capacity.[133]

We do not, after all, usually cast out valuable items.[134]

It should be added that removal, unlike a failure to purchase, sends to faculty and students a signal that the book, its ideas and similar matters should not be discussed.[135]

Because removal may be so much more telling, it has been suggested that the acquisition decision be presumed constitutional, with the burden placed on the person challenging it, and that the removal decision be presumed unconstitutional, with the burden on the remover.[136]

Others would contend that the situation involving the removal of *Male and Female Under 18* confirms the similarity of selection and removal. The book had been purchased when the librarian became interested in a Prentice Hall Publishing Company program offering 1,000 paperbacks[137] at a favorable price. The librarian "had reviewed" all of the books upon their receipt, but could not be expected to read every line and, consequently, had not read the controversial poem.[138] In a very real sense, a close look at the book came only after it had been placed on the shelves.

Given the large number of acquisitions, perhaps the only close analysis of a particular book is likely to come after its acquisition, and perhaps in connection with a controversy surrounding the book.[139] Even teacher tenure does not usually take place until after a period of years—should a book be given a greater right? One commentator, analogizing the book tenure concept to the medieval one of sanctuary, noted that the poem was admitted to the school library quite inadvertently and therefore was not in any real sense "selected." The court's distinction between selection and removal, he continued, "allows the sloppy acquisition somehow to imbue [a] book with a First Amendment right to remain on the shelves."[140] Must a school board, to maintain control over educational matters, read every page of every prospective library book?[141]

REMOVAL FACTORS

The cases do make clear that school library book decisions may be based upon neutral factors, that is, those unconnected with content. Among these are space considerations,[142] financial factors,[143] and the physical condition of the book.[144] School library book decisions presumably may also reflect factors which, though related to content, are politically neutral, such as obsolescence,[145] relevance,[146] psychological or intellectual appropriateness for a particular age group,[147] curricular priorities,[148] duplication of resources,[149] and balance of views.[150]

VULGARITY, OBSCENITY[151] AND SEXUAL EXPLICITNESS

Justice Brennan's plurality opinion in *Island Trees* suggests that school boards may remove school library books on the basis of their "pervasive" vulgarity, but not because the board "dislikes the ideas contained in those books"[152] and seeks through removal to prescribe orthodoxy. Difficult questions flow from this suggestion. First, when does vulgarity become "pervasive"? Second, why can the board decide that the use of vulgar phrases throughout one work makes it inappropriate for the affected children but not that one use or two may? As Justice Burger queried: "[W]hy must vulgarity be 'pervasive' to be offensive? Vulgarity might be concentrated in a single poem or a single chapter or a single page, yet still be inappropriate. Or a school board might reasonably conclude that even 'random' vulgarity is inappropriate for teenage . . . students".[153] The key objection would seem to be the nature of the language, not the incidence of its use, unless the suggestion is that the greater the use the less worthy the work—a presumption not clearly related to reality—or the more likely that children exposed to it will be adversely affected.

Third, where is the line between the idea and its mode of expression? The contours of a concept are surely drawn in part by the harshness or softness of the language. The vulgar phrase conveys something different, else why all the fuss?[154] In a speech case involving use of the phrase "Fuck the Draft," the U.S. Supreme Court said:

> [W]ords are often chosen as much for their emotive as their cognitive force. We cannot sanction the view that the Constitution, while solicitous of the cognitive content of individual speech, has little or no regard for that emotive function which, practically speaking, may often be the more important element of the overall message sought to be communicated.[155]

Justice Rehnquist states that the determination of vulgarity is "based as much on the content of the book as [a determination] that the book espouses political views," but apparently finds some distinction plausible when he says that the *Pico* board merely removed books containing vulgarity and profanity but did not bar discussion of the books or of their themes.[156]

In *Bicknell v. Vergennes Union High School Board of Directors*,[157] which involved the removal of *Dog Day Afternoon* (by Patrick Moran) and *The Wanderer* (by Richard Price), the Court of Appeals for the Second Circuit sought to draw a clear distinction. Noting that the removal was concededly due to vulgarity and inappropriate sexual explicitness, and finding no suggestion that the removal was due to the books' ideas or the Board's political motivation,[158] the court concluded that vulgarity or indecency, even judged by the Board members' own tastes, justified book removal.[159]

Boards may bar works that are obscene,[160] even under the "variable obscenity" standard for children,[161] and therefore at least certain sexually explicit material,[162] and expert testimony may be received regarding the appropriateness of the material for the students involved.[163] Nonetheless, the problem remains: Isn't even a determination that material is too sexually explicit for particular school children a political decision of sorts and, perhaps, among the most political?[164] Indeed, a certain twist can occur if the school board removes a book not for the "content" of the clauses but merely for its "language." In *Right to Read Defense Committee of Chelsea v. School Committee of the City of Chelsea*, the court, persuaded that the school committee had removed the book *Male and Female Under 18* because they thought it filthy and obscene,[165] held the removal unconstitutional, absent a substantial and legitimate governmental interest.[166] Even on the assumption that the mode of expression can be separated from the content, two different emphases, then, emanate from the cases: some say that vulgarity and obscenity may clearly be removed but that ideas cannot, while others suggest that removal merely for offensiveness of language may be unconstitutional.

COMPARISON OF MATERIAL OR AUTHORS

Board action or inaction with regard to material other than the book actually removed may be relevant. In *Island Trees*, Justice Brennan noted that the books actually removed were limited to those on a private group's list, and that the board did not undertake its own examination of other books in the school libraries.[167] Similarly, in *Salvail v. Nashua Board of Education*, the U.S. District Court noted that the dislike of certain school board members for material in *MS* magazine apparently did not extend to comparable material found in other publications in the Nashua High School Library.[168] This led the court to conclude that the political content of the magazine rather than its sexual overtones led to its "arbitrary displacement."[169] As one jurist has commented:

> [T]he bona fides of a school's claim of concern with vulgarity or explicitness may be refuted by evidence that other books with similar passages were not removed. A school's effort to regulate vulgarity is not unconstitutional because it is not completely thorough, but if only isolated examples are condemned, the inference will be strengthened that vulgarity was the excuse, not the reason, for book removal whose principal, or at least partial motivation was political.[170]

Courts may look to the curriculum to note that it too includes candid language concerning the "provocative themes" of homosexuality, drug abuse, sexual experience and ghetto life.[171]

Relevant also may be the relatively high standing of the author in the literary community. When works by such "generally recognized" authors as Swift, Richard Wright and Bernard Malamud are removed, a court might well take notice.[172] Such removals might suggest illegitimate board motivation.[173]

REGULARITY OF PROCEDURES

Courts should, in assessing the lawfulness of any book removal, consider whether the school system has a specified policy providing adequate notice of what speech is prohibited. The criteria set out must be sufficiently objective.[174] The policy should be narrowly drawn so as to promote the state interests justifying it with the least hindrance possible to the exercise of free speech.[175] A complaint that a book is "filthy," "anti-Christian," or "anti-American" paints with too broad a brush,[176] and so too, presumably, would a general policy articulated in such terms. The presence of sensitive decisionmaking tools "naturally" indicates a concern for first amendment rights; their absence suggests a lack of concern.[177]

Moreover, the administration of any policy is as important as the policy's substance.[178] The Second Circuit, in its *Island Trees* opinion, alluded to the "unusual and irregular intervention in the school libraries' operation by persons not routinely concerned with such matters."[179] The school board's "erratic and free-wheeling procedures" left teachers, librarians and students with but a guess at what speech was prohibited and with little opportunity to put forth any defense.[180] Agreeing with this assessment, Justice Brennan observed that "[t]his would be a very different case if the record demonstrated that petitioners had employed established, regular, and facially unbiased procedures for the review of controversial materials."[181] There should be, then, both narrowly specific criteria and sensitive administration.[182]

Not all courts are equally enthusiastic about this notion, however.[183] Indeed, a court might find that even a written policy setting out procedures for voicing public displeasure was not intended to limit the school board's own exercise of its power or that, in any event, "these informal procedures, which presumably do not have the force of law, could [not] achieve the status of a constitutionally enforced due process restraint on the board."[184] Nonetheless, the possibility of arbitrariness or of the exercise of bad faith is greatly reduced when official discretion is controlled and channelled.

PROCEDURES SHORT OF TOTAL SUPPRESSION

Courts have not generally been called upon to deal with procedures which prevent library books from reaching certain but not all children in a school. Regulations might, for example, be developed for deciding at which grade level students generally possess sufficient maturity to deal with particular books.[185] Too, regulations might specify that certain books are available only if the student's parents consent[186] or, as a slight variation, will not be available to students whose parents object. This has the advantage of giving the parent, who knows the child best, control over what the student is exposed to.[187] As a bonus, this process may prevent or diffuse volatile community reaction triggered by an irate parent. The net result may be to make available the greatest variety of materials to the greatest number. Such a system does, however, take away some of the school's authority to decide what the student should have access to and, depending on his age, may impinge on the student's own rights. In some cases, the child most likely to profit from a particular book of a sensitive nature may be the very one whose parents are most likely to object to it.

A further variation is parental notification whenever a student checks out a particular book. Again, more control is thereby given the family, but the process will chill many students' willingness to read more controversial books. Indeed, in some states, parental notification may be illegal.[188]

In some school libraries, whether pursuant to formal rules or not, the librarian puts sensitive materials on a restricted shelf and decides which students should be allowed access to them. This system, while extremely flexible, centers in the librarian usually unreviewed authority to decide two crucial issues: what materials are too sensitive for general circulation and which students are old, mature or sophisticated enough to deal with them. Of course, such determinations may be erroneous and, in any event, rely on the library official's familiarity with every student in the school. The quiet but mature (or immature) student may have escaped the librarian's attention.

Finally, in certain cases, an isolated offending passage or page might be excised from the text,[189] leaving the remainder of the book on the library shelves. In rare cases, perhaps involving an anthology, this might be an appropriate device. This crude form of censorship, however, raises serious constitutional objections[190] and, in any event, risks public outcry and litigation.

Indeed, each of these devices is subject to constitutional scrutiny on the basis of the actual content of the material restricted. In some cases, a less restrictive device may be as intolerable as total suppression. In others, it might be acceptable although total suppression would not be.

ISLAND TREES EPILOGUE

Although the U.S. Supreme Court ruling in *Island Trees* paved the way for a trial to deal with the factual issues presented, no trial ensued. The Island Trees Board of Education decided to restore the banned books to the school library bookshelves. The Board did, however, direct libraries to notify the parent of any child withdrawing any of the controversial books that the book may contain material objectionable to the parents.[191]

The parental notification policy was in turn challenged under a New York state law,[192] similar to those found in other states,[193] making confidential all library circulation records.[194] The State Attorney General's office notified the Board of the statute and asked the Board to resolve the violation within one week. The Board then suspended indefinitely its parental notification procedure.[195] For his part, the most prominent *Island Trees* plaintiff, Steven Pico, was, as of January, 1983, a special assistant to the National Coalition Against Censorship.[196]

CONCLUSION

Because the *Island Trees* litigation ended so inconclusively, it is not yet clear what fundamental constitutional principle with regard to library book selection and removal on the basis of sexual content will ultimately prevail. Will Justice Brennan's conclusion that a student has a right to receive information and that a school board may not remove a book because it dislikes its ideas and seeks by removal to prescribe political, religious or other orthodoxy carry the day? Or, especially as Court membership changes, will the view of the dissenters that school boards have virtually plenary power to select or remove school materials triumph? Whatever the outcome, at least tentative conclusions with regard to such selection or removal are possible even now.

First, student minds must be challenged and exercised, and this is best done through exposure to diverse and sometimes controversial materials, including sexually-oriented ones. Sex is an obviously fundamental aspect of human life and cannot be ignored in any appropriate education.

Second, the constitutional issue deals only with what a school board has the power to do, not with what the wisest course might be. The path of wisdom will often lead away from censorship of a particular book even if the ultimately prevailing constitutional principle might support the board's power to censor.

Third, to the extent school boards seek to control sexual content in the school library, arbitrariness, narrowmindedness, community controversy and litigation[197] are best avoided through the establishment of, and adherence to, written, neutral and narrowly-drawn policies governing book selection,[198] book removal and the resolution of grievances with regard to book content.[199] The policies should provide for a balanced presentation of ideas, a record of proceedings for possible court review, and deference to the views of education experts.[200] Parents and students should have some input into selecting material for school libraries, possibly through service on library selection committees.[201] Perhaps school boards should be required to provide written reasons for book selection and removal decisions.[202]

Constitutionally valid procedures and adherence to them help school libraries to provide students an exciting and diverse educational experience without the necessity for distracting and expensive controversy or litigation.

NOTES

1. Except as otherwise indicated, these and subsequent facts in the case are taken from Board of Education, Island Trees Union Free School District No. 26 v. Pico, 457 U.S.853, 854–861 (1982) (hereafter *Island Trees*).
2. Those in the high school library: *Slaughterhouse-Five* (Kurt Vonnegut, Jr.); *The Naked Ape* (Desmond Morris); *Down These Mean Streets* (Piri Thomas); *Best Short Stories of Negro Writers* (Langston Hughes, ed.); *Go Ask Alice* (anonymous); *Laughing Boy* (Oliver LaFarge); *Black Boy* (Richard Wright); *A Hero Ain't Nothin' But a Sandwich* (Alice Childress); and *Soul on Ice* (Eldridge Cleaver). In the junior high school library: *A Reader for Writers* (Jerome Archer, ed.). See *Island Trees*, 457 U.S. at 856–857, n.3.
3. *Island Trees*, 457 U.S. at 858.
4. See *id.* at 858, n.12.
5. *Id.* at 857.

6. *Island Trees*, 638 F.2d 404, 419–422, n.1 (2d Cir. 1981) (dissenting opinion), *aff'd*, 457 U.S. 853 (1982).

7. *Island Trees*, 457 U.S. at 886, n. 2 (dissenting opinion).

8. *Id.* at 875–876 (concurring opinion).

9. *Id.* at 877 (emphasis in original).

10. *Id.* at 883–884 (concurring opinion).

11. See *id.* at 885, 893, 904 and 921 (dissenting opinions). For later developments in the *Island Trees* saga, see text at notes 191–196, *infra*.

12. *Island Trees*, 457 U.S. at 884 (White J., concurring).

13. *Island Trees*, 638 F.2d at 432 (concurring opinion).

14. See Comment, *Censorship in the Public School Library—State, Parent and Child in the Constitutional Arena*, 27 WAYNE L. REV. 167, n. 1 (1980).

15. Shaman, "Let's ban this ancient tradition," *Chicago Tribune*, July 29, 1982, section 1, p. 19, col. 1.

16. Lauerman, "New censors are emerging, but this time foes are ready," *Chicago Tribune*, March 30, 1982, section 1, p. 13, col. 1.

17. *Id.* at cols. 1 and 3; Shaman, *supra* note 15, at col. 1. See also Kinsella, "Book banning on the rise," *California Lawyer*, pp. 34, 37 (February 1983).

18. Kinsella, *supra* note 17, at 37.

19. Lauerman, *supra* note 16, at col. 3.

20. Zykan v. Warsaw Community School Corporation, 631 F.2d 1300, 1308 (7th Cir. 1980) (citation omitted).

21. Minarcini v. Strongsville City School District, 541 F.2d 577, 581 (6th Cir. 1976).

22. *Id.*

23. *Id.* at 582.

24. *Id.* at 583.

25. Niccolai, *The Right to Read and School Library Censorship*, 10 J. LAW & EDUCATION 23, 32 (1981).

26. *Island Trees*, 457 U.S. at 868, quoting Justice Fortas' opinion in Brown v. Louisiana, 383 U.S. 131, 142 (1966).

27. Right to Read Defense Committee of Chelsea v. School Committee of City of Chelsea, 454 F.Supp. 703, 715 (D. Mass. 1978).

28. *Island Trees*, 457 U.S. at 868.

29. *Id.* at 878 (concurring opinion). See also *id.* at 915 (dissenting opinion), and Diamond, *The First Amendment and Public Schools: The Case Against Judicial Intervention*, 59 TEXAS L. REV. 477, 517–18 (1981).

30. See *Island Trees*, 457 U.S. at 889 (dissenting opinion).

31. See Diamond, *supra* note 29, at 524.

32. See *Island Trees*, 457 U.S. at 890 (dissenting opinion).

33. Diamond, *supra* note 29, at 510.

34. *Island Trees*, 457 U.S. at 869.

35. *Id.*

36. See ALA. CODE § 16-21-2 (1977), providing that the list of books, prepared at the state level, from which school libraries select "shall be as nearly as possible representative of the whole field of literature." In Salvail v. Nashua Board of Education, 469 F.Supp. 1269 (D.N.H. 1979), the court noted that the Nashua, N.H., Board of Education "interim guidelines" required that "a

selection of materials on controversial issues be directed toward maintaining a balanced collection representing various views." *Id.* at 1271.

37. Comment, *supra* note 14, at 179.
38. Comment, *School Library Censorship: First Amendment Guarantees and the Student's Right to Know,* 57 J. URBAN LAW 523, 542 (1980).
39. *Id.*
40. On balancing the "sometime conflicting rights" of child and parent, see Niccolai, *supra* note 25, at 34, and Comment, *supra* note 14, at 173–174, 184–91.
41. See, e.g., *Island Trees,* 457 U.S. at 871, 879–880 (concurring opinion), 907–908 (dissenting opinion).
42. *Island Trees,* 638 F.2d at 419 (dissenting opinion). See also *id.* at 428 (dissenting opinion) and 431 (dissenting opinion); Presidents Council, District 25 v. Community School Board No. 25, 457 F.2d 289, 292 (2d Cir. 1972) ("The action of the Board [in removing the book from the school library] does not even preclude the teacher from discussing *Down These Mean Streets* in class or from assigning it for outside reading").
43. At least one court has assumed that the First Amendment guarantees the teacher's freedom to speak well of a removed book and the students' right to hear the teacher so speak and to seek out the book. *Minarcini v. Strongsville City School District,* 541 F.2d at 582.
44. *Island Trees,* 457 U.S. at 858, n. 12.
45. Minarcini v. Strongsville City School District, 541 F.2d at 582. See Tinker v. Des Moines Independent Community School District, 393 U.S. 503 (1969).
46. *Island Trees,* 638 F.2d at 434 (concurring opinion). See *id.* at 416 (Judge Sifton, for the court): "The very nature of this broad brush approach must inevitably be to suggest that the school officials' concern is . . . to express an official policy with regard to God and country of uncertain and indefinite content which is to be ignored by pupils, librarians and teachers at their peril." In response, Professor Diamond has observed that such "undefined conduct was not at issue in this case, and would have changed the analysis." Diamond, *supra* note 29, at 524.
47. *Island Trees,* 457 U.S. at 862.
48. The regulations of the Commissioner of Education of New York State cite "supplementing the curriculum" as one selection criterion for secondary school library book collections. 8 N.Y. Code, Rules and Regulations (Educ.) §91.1 (b) (1966). Some courts apparently see much of the school library's value in its role as "facilitator of classroom discussion." Comment, *Removal of Public School Library Books: The First Amendment Versus the Local School Board,* 34 VANDERBILT L. REV. 1407, 1429 (1981). See also Zykan v. Warsaw Community School Corporation, 631 F.2d at 1308, suggesting that a school library's function is to provide "materials that properly supplement the basic readings assigned through the standard curriculum."
49. *Island Trees,* 457 U.S. at 896, n.2 (dissenting opinion).
50. *Id.* at 892 (dissenting opinion).
51. "No conclusive data supports the assumption that young persons are harmed by exposure to obscenity." Comment, *supra* note 14, at 176, n. 60, citing *THE REPORT OF THE UNITED STATES COMMISSION ON OBSCENITY AND PORNOGRAPHY* 26, 27, 139–202 (1970) (a report not approved by the full commission); *Effects of the Response to Reading,* 9 J. RESEARCH & DEV. IN

EDUCATION 3 (1976); and Ginsberg v. New York, 390 U.S. 629 (1968). In Ginsberg, the U.S. Supreme Court observed that a causal link between obscenity and impairment of ethical or moral development has been neither proved nor disproved. 390 U.S. at 641–642, quoting Magrath, *The Obscenity Cases: The Grapes of Roth*, 1966 SUP. CT. REV. 7, 75. See also Comment, *supra* note 14, at 175–176.

52. See *Island Trees*, 638 F.2d. at 432 (concurring opinion).
53. *Island Trees*, 457 U.S. at 878, n. 1 (concurring opinion).
54. See Chapter 1, *supra*.
55. Niccolai, *supra* note 25, at 33. Content-based elimination of a library book may violate not only the child's rights but those of the parent wishing the child to have access to that book. Comment, *supra* note 14, at 180. But see Right to Read Defense Committee of Chelsea v. School Committee of City of Chelsea, 454 F. Supp. at 705, n.2, where the U.S. District Court found that the parents of two student-plaintiffs lacked standing in the action. Outside groups generally interested in such matters may also lack the focused right in the particular situation necessary to confer standing. See *id.*, where the court dismissed from the action, for lack of standing, the Massachusetts Library Association. *Id.*
56. See Prince v. Massachusetts, 321 U.S. 158 (1944); Niccolai, *supra* note 25, at 34.
57. See Right to Read Defense Committee of Chelsea v. School Committee of City of Chelsea, 454 F.Supp. at 710.
58. Niccolai, *supra* note 25, at 34.
59. See Chapter 1, *supra*. For a good discussion of the right to receive information in the school library context, see also Comment, *supra* note 48, at 1412–1415; and Comment, *supra* note 38, at 535–537.
60. *Island Trees*, 457 U.S. at 863.
61. *Id.* at 869.
    For statutes setting out local power over selection of school library books, see, *e.g.*, MONT. REV. CODES ANN. §§ 20-3-205(19), 20-4-402(5), and 20-7-204 (1983); and N.C. GEN. STAT. § 115C-98 (1983).
    In many states, in fact, substantial influence over school library collections is exercised at the state level. See, *e.g.*, ALA. CODE § 16-21-2 (1977); MINN. STAT. ANN. § 134.04 (1979) [Renumbered § 121.496 in MINN. STATS. 1984]; and N.D. CENT. CODE § 15-21-13 (1981).
62. *Island Trees*, 457 U.S. at 866, citing Epperson v. Arkansas, 393 U.S. 97, 104 (1968).
63. 457 U.S. at 866. In Right to Read Defense Committee of Chelsea v. School Committee of City of Chelsea, 454 F.Supp. at 714, the U.S. District Court referred to the "right to read and be exposed to controversial thoughts and language" as a "valuable right subject to First Amendment protection."
64. 457 U.S. at 866.
65. *Island Trees*, 457 U.S. at 868–869.
66. *Id.* at 867. Compare Justice Blackmun's view that the state has no affirmative obligation to provide information to students. *Id.* at 878 (concurring opinion).
67. *Island Trees*, 638 F.2d at 429 (dissenting opinion). At least one commentator sees the book itself as the "source of the communication." Niccolai, *supra* note 25, at 28. See also Diamond, *supra* note 29, at 511.

68. *Island Trees*, 638 F.2d at 429 (dissenting opinion).
69. It has been suggested that perhaps the book itself, the author or the publisher could be seen as a "speaker" with a right to be heard from the library shelves. Diamond, *supra* note 29, at 511. The author's right not to have his book *removed* from the library shelves for inappropriate reasons seems more plausible.
70. *Island Trees*, 457 U.S. at 887 (dissenting opinion).
71. *Id.* at 888 (dissenting opinion). See also *id.* at 912 (dissenting opinion) ("Justice Brennan . . . fails to explain the constitutional or logical underpinnings of a right to hear ideas in a place where no speaker has the right to express them.")
72. *Island Trees*, 638 F.2d at 433, n.2 (concurring opinion).
73. Comment, *supra* note 38, at 541.
74. Diamond, *supra* note 29, at 477, n.86. Diamond sees as perhaps still more persuasive the state's interest in the well-being of the children. *Id.*
75. Presidents Council, District 25 v. Community School Board No. 25, 457 F.2d at 293.
76. And courts have begun to be receptive to the concept. See Comment, *supra* note 48, at 1428–1429; Niccolai, *supra* note 25, at 2425 ("This emerging concept"); and especially Justice Brennan's opinion in *Island Trees*, 457 U.S. at 866–867.
77. The traditional approach sees children as different from adults and, consequently, with no "inherent entitlement to rights"—each "right" is evaluated on an *ad hoc* basis. The alternative view presumes children to have all rights enjoyed by adults *except* those which must be limited because of a "special justification" applicable to children. Each of these views finds some support in recent cases. Comment, *supra* note 14, at 171.
78. See Zykan v. Warsaw Community School Corporation, 631 F.2d at 1304.
79. Some see the "freedom to hear" as part of academic freedom, see *id.*, while others see the right to receive information and academic freedom as separate components of the student's right to know, see Niccolai, *supra* note 25, at 25–26.
80. Zykan v. Warsaw Community School Corporation, 631 F.2d at 1304. See Niccolai, *supra* note 25, at 26 ("[A]cademic freedom at the secondary education level has not been widely accepted or consistently applied.")
81. *Island Trees*, 457 U.S. at 871. A "decisive factor" is one "in the absence of which the opposite decision would have been reached." *Id.*, n.22 (citing Mt. Healthy City Board of Education v. Doyle, 429 U.S. 274, 287 (1977)).
82. A school district is presumably free to have no school library whatever. Right to Read Committee of Chelsea v. School Committee of City of Chelsea, 454 F.Supp. at 711.
83. See Presidents Council, District 25 v. Community School Board No. 25, 457 F.2d at 292.
84. 631 F.2d 1300 (7th Cir. 1980).
85. *Id.* at 1302.
86. *Id.* at 1304.
87. *Id.* at 1305.
88. *Id.*
89. *Id.*, citing Cary v. Board of Education, 598 F.2d 535, 544 (10th Cir. 1979).
90. 631 F.2d at 1306.

91. *Id.*

92. *Id.*

93. *Id.* at 1308.

94. *See, e.g.,* Bicknell v. Vergennes, 638 F.2d 438 (2d Cir. 1980); Cary v. Board of Education, 598 F.2d 535, 544 (10th Cir. 1979); and Presidents Council, District 25 v. Community School Board No. 25, 457 F.2d 289 (2d Cir. 1972). See also Seyfried v. Walton, 668 F.2d 214, 218 (3d Cir. 1981), in which the Court of Appeals for the Third Circuit relied upon and echoed *Zykan* in upholding the cancellation of a school play.

95. 541 F.2d 577 (6th Cir. 1976).

96. See also Salvail v. Nashua Board of Education, 469 F.Supp. 1269 (D.N.H. 1979); and Right to Read Defense Committee of Chelsea v. School Committee of City of Chelsea, 454 F.Supp. 703 (D. Mass. 1978). *Cf.* Pratt v. Independent School District No. 831, Forest Lake, Minnesota, 670 F.2d 771, 773 (8th Cir. 1982).

97. 541 F.2d at 579–580.

98. *Id.* at 582.

99. See text accompanying note 89, *supra.*

100. 541 F.2d at 582.

101. *Id.* at 580.

102. See *Island Trees,* 638 F.2d at 414.

103. *Island Trees,* 457 U.S. at 866; *Island Trees,* 638 F.2d at 425 (dissenting opinion); Presidents Council, District 25, v. Community School Board No. 25, 457 F.2d at 292. See also *Island Trees,* 638 F.2d at 434 (concurring opinion); and Zykan v. Warsaw Community School Corporation, 631 F.2d at 1306 ("a relatively high threshold").

104. 393 U.S. at 104.

105. See chapter 1, *supra,* at notes 112–114.

106. Justice Douglas has suggested that *Tinker* allows restriction of First Amendment rights in the school only when a disciplinary problem presents itself. Presidents Council, District 25 v. Community School Board No. 25, 409 U.S. 998 (1972) (dissenting from denial of certiorari).

107. *Cf. Island Trees,* 638 F.2d at 425 (dissenting opinion); Diamond, *supra* note 29, at 477. *But see* Comment, *supra* note 38, at 533 (citing Note, 55 TEX. L. REV. 511, 513 (1977)): "The *Tinker* decision has been seen as a *de facto* rejection of the 'reasonable educational basis' standard for reviewing school board action in favor of a test requiring a 'clear and present danger' to legitimate educational activities."

108. West Virginia State Board of Education v. Barnette, 319 U.S. 624, 640 (1943), quoted in *Island Trees,* 638 F.2d at 412. *Compare* Presidents Council, District 25 v. Community School Board No. 25, 457 F.2d at 292: "Academic freedom is scarcely fostered by the intrusion of three or even nine federal jurists making curriculum or library choices for the community of scholars." See also *Island Trees,* 457 U.S. at 894 (dissenting opinion).

109. *Island Trees,* 457 U.S. at 909 (dissenting opinion).

110. In Minarcini v. Strongsville City School District, 541 F.2d 577 (6th Cir. 1976), both *textbook* selection and *library* book removal were at stake. The court found the selection process constitutional, but the library book removal unconstitutional.

See also Loewen v. Turnipseed, 488 F.Supp. 1138 (N.D. Miss. 1980), where state approval of one book, and disapproval of another, for purchase and for use in ninth grade history classes were held unconstitutional. The situation is distinguishable from ordinary book selection cases, however. First, a particular book was disapproved. Second, racial issues, about which courts are especially sensitive, were involved. Third, the selection *procedure* was found faulty. See M. YUDOF, D. KIRP, T. VON GEEL & B. LEVIN, EDUCATIONAL POLICY AND THE LAW 164–165, 166 (2d ed. 1982). Moreover, the *Loewen* court did not substitute one book for another, but merely placed both books on the approved list. See Comment, *What Johnny Can't Read: School Boards and the First Amendment*, 42 U. PITT. L.REV. 653, 664 (1981).

111. Comment, *supra* note 14, at 180.
112. See Niccolai, *supra* note 25, at 30; Note, *Schoolbooks, School Boards and the Constitution*, 80 COLUMBIA L.REV. 1093, 1117 (1980).
113. Niccolai, *supra* note 25, at 30. The author observes that courts nonetheless have the capacity to distinguish censorship from appropriate selection. *Id.*

   One analogy sees book selection as a legislative function and book removal as an adjudicative one, more conducive to judicial review. Comment, *supra* note 110, at 664.
114. *Island Trees*, 457 U.S. at 878 (concurring opinion) (emphasis added). Justice Rehnquist suggests that a "pall of orthodoxy" could as well be "cast by a well-executed book-acquisition plan." *Id.* at 918 (dissenting opinion).
115. *Island Trees*, 638 F.2d at 431; *Island Trees*, 457 U.S. at 917–918 (dissenting opinion).
116. See Zykan v. Warsaw Community School Corporation, 631 F.2d at 1308; Presidents Council, District 25 v. Community School Board No. 25, 457 F.2d at 293.
117. 457 U.S. at 892 (dissenting opinion) (emphasis in original).
118. Comment, *supra* note 38, at 542.
119. Diamond, *supra* note 29, at 511, n. 145. In Right To Read Defense Committee of Chelsea v. School Committee of Chelsea, for example, the school had purchased a package of 1,000 paperbacks at a special price. Clearly the librarian could not (and did not) read every line of every book. See 454 F.Supp. at 706.
120. Diamond, *supra* note 29, at 514.
121. *Island Trees*, 457 U.S. at 910 (dissenting opinion).
122. 454 F.Supp. 703 (D. Mass. 1978).
123.   THE CITY TO A YOUNG GIRL
   The city is
   One million horney lip-smacking men
   Screaming for my body.
   The streets are long conveyor belts
   Loaded with these suckling pigs
   All begging for
   a lay
   a little pussy
   a bit of tit
   a leg to rub against
   a handful of ass

the connoisseurs of cunt
Every day, every night
Pressing in on me closer and closer.
I swat them off like flies
but they keep coming back.
I'm a good piece of meat.
                    Jody Caravaglia, 15, F.
                    Brooklyn, New York.

Id. at 705, n.1. The defendants did not ultimately contend, however, that the poem was "obscene" under Miller v. California, 413 U.S. 15 (1973). 454 F.Supp. at 705, n.1.

124. 454 F.Supp. at 706.
125. *Id.* at 709.
126. *Id.* at 711.
127. *Id.* at 710.
128. *Id.*
129. *Id.* at 711.
130. *Id.* at 712.
131. *Id.* at 714. See also Minarcini v. Strongsville City School District, 541 F.2d at 581.
132. Note, *supra* note 112, at 1116.
133. *Island Trees*, 638 F.2d at 435–436.
134. Justice Brennan apparently found persuasive the distinction between selection and removal: "[N]othing in our decision today affects in any way the discretion of a local school board to choose books to *add* to the libraries of their schools." *Island Trees*, 457 U.S. at 871–872 (emphasis in original).
135. See Comment, *supra* note 110, at 666. See text accompanying note 46, *supra*.
136. Note, *supra* note 112, at 1116. See also Comment, *supra* note 110, at 666.
137. The books constituted a collection which had been assembled by professional librarians and teachers to stimulate student reading. 454 F.Supp. at 706.
138. *Id.*
139. Comment, *supra* note 110, at 659.
140. Diamond, *supra* note 29, at 511, n. 145. To illustrate the lack of a clear distinction between selection and removal, he asks into which category falls the decision whether to replace a stolen book. *Id.* at 516.
141. This was the concern Chief Justice Burger voiced with regard to the *Island Trees* plurality opinion. 457 U.S. at 892–893, n. 8 (dissenting opinion).
142. *Id.* at 880 (concurring opinion); Minarcini v. Strongsville City School District, 541 F.2d at 581; Presidents Council, District 25 v. Community School Board No. 25, 457 F.2d at 293; Salvail v. Nashua Board of Education, 469 F.Supp. at 1274; and Right to Read Defense Committee of Chelsea v. School Committee of City of Chelsea, 454 F.Supp. at 711.
143. *Island Trees*, 457 U.S. at 880 (concurring opinion); Presidents Council, District 25 v. Community School Board No. 25, 457 F.2d at 293; Right to Read Defense Committee of Chelsea v. School Committee of City of Chelsea, 454 F.Supp. at 711.
144. Minarcini v. Strongsville City School District, 541 F.2d at 581; Salvail v. Nashua Board of Education, 469 F.Supp. at 1275.
145. Minarcini v. Strongsville City School District, 541 F.2d at 577; Presidents

Council, District 25 v. Community School Board No. 25, 457 F.2d at 293; Salvail v. Nashua Board of Education, 469 F.Supp. at 1274; Island Trees, 638 F.2d at 436; and Right to Read Defense Committee of Chelsea v. School Committee of City of Chelsea, 454 F.Supp. at 711.

146. Presidents Council, District 25 v. Community School Board No. 25, 457 F.2d at 293.

147. *Island Trees,* 457 U.S. at 880 (concurring opinion).

148. See Note, *supra* note 112, at 1115.

149. *Id.*

150. Niccolai, *supra* note 25, at 33.

151. Interestingly, states often exempt school libraries from criminal laws dealing with obscenity and related material. See, *e.g.,* GA. CODE ANN. § 26-3504 (Supp. 1984); VA. CODE § 18.2-383 (1) (1982); WASH. REV. CODE § 7.42.070 (1961); *id.* § 9.68.015 (1977); *id.* § 7.48A.060 (Supp. 1985). *Cf.* Chapter 1, n. 158, *supra.*

152. *Island Trees,* 457 U.S. at 872. See also *Island Trees,* 638 F.2d at 425 (dissenting opinion) and at 436 (concurring opinion). To the effect that vulgarity might be protected, see Right to Read Defense Committee of Chelsea v. School Committee of City of Chelsea, 454 F.Supp. at 713.

153. 457 U.S. at 890 (dissenting opinion).

154. The author [of the poem *City*] is writing about her perception of city life in rough but relevant language that gives credibility to the development of a sensitive theme. *City*'s words may shock, but they *communicate.*
Right to Read Defense Committee of Chelsea v. School Committee of City of Chelsea, 454 F.Supp. at 714. (Emphasis added).

155. Cohen v. California, 403 U.S. 15, 26 (1971), quoted in Right to Read Defense Committee of Chelsea v. School Committee of City of Chelsea, 454 F.Supp. at 714. Compare Justice Stevens' statement in FCC v. Pacifica Foundation, 438 U.S. 726, 743, n. 18 (1978), quoted in *Island Trees,* 638 F.2d at 429 (dissenting opinion): "The requirement that indecent language be avoided will have its primary effect on the form, rather than the content, of serious communication. There are few, if any, thoughts that cannot be expressed by the use of less offensive language."

156. *Island Trees,* 457 U.S. at 915 (dissenting opinion).

157. 638 F.2d 438 (2d Cir. 1980).

158. *Id.* at 441.

159. *Id.*

160. *Cf.* Zykan v. Warsaw Community School Corporation, 631 F.2d at 1302, n. 4; and Right to Read Defense Committee of Chelsea v. School Committee of City of Chelsea, 454 F.Supp. at 711.

161. *Cf.* Presidents Council, District 25 v. Community School Board No. 25, 409 U.S. at 999 (Douglas, J., dissenting from denial of certiorari); *Id.,* 457 F.2d at 292.

162. *Cf.* Bicknell v. Vergennes Union High School Board of Directors, 638 F.2d 438 (2d Cir. 1980). That the book contains material offensive to some people, however, is not enough in itself to justify removal. Salvail v. Nashua Board of Education, 469 F.Supp. at 1273.

163. See Salvail v. Nashua Board of Education, 469 F.Supp. at 1272. *Cf.* Pratt v. Independent School District No. 831, Forest Lake, Minnesota, 670 F.2d at 777.

164. Diamond, *supra* note 29, at 522–523.
165. 454 F.Supp. at 711.
166. See Niccolai, *supra* note 25, at 28.
167. *Island Trees,* 457 U.S. at 874–875. *Cf.* Pratt v. Independent School District No. 831, Forest Lake, Minnesota, 670 F.2d at 778.
168. 469 F.Supp. at 1274.
169. *Id.* The student plaintiff testified that sexual issues were "openly discussed" at the high school. *Id.* at 1272.
170. *Island Trees,* 638 F.2d at 437 (concurring opinion).
171. See Right to Read Defense Committee of Chelsea v. School Committee of City of Chelsea, 454 F.Supp. at 706.
172. See *Island Trees,* 638 F.2d at 418.
173. Diamond, *supra* note 29, at 523.
174. *Island Trees,* 638 F.2d at 418, n. 13. Sometimes, however, the adoption of resolutions by a school board may be seen as a mere tactical subterfuge. See Right to Read Defense Committee of Chelsea v. School Committee of City of Chelsea, 454 F.Supp. at 709, n. 10, and at 712.
175. *Island Trees,* 638 F.2d at 415 (citing Eisner v. Stamford Board of Education, 440 F.2d 803, 806 (2d Cir. 1971)). See Presidents Council, District 25 v. Community School Board No. 25, 409 U.S. at 1000 (Douglas, J., dissenting from denial of certiorari).
176. *Island Trees,* 638 F.2d at 416.
177. *Island Trees,* 457 U.S. at 874, n. 26. See also Comment, *supra* note 48, at 1432.
178. *Island Trees,* 638 F.2d at 416.
179. *Id.* at 414.
180. *Id.* at 416–417. See also Salvail v. Nashua Board of Education, 469 F.Supp. at 1275.
181. *Island Trees,* 457 U.S. at 874.
182. *Island Trees,* 638 F.2d at 417 (citing Keyishian v. Board of Regents, 385 U.S. 589, 603–604 (1967)).
183. "[N]othing in the School Board's statutory authority requires it to make its decisions according to some formal procedure and we do not regard the Constitution as imposing such." Zykan v. Warsaw Community School Corporation, 631 F.2d at 1307, n.8.
184. *Id.* at 1306–1307, n. 8. The court noted the lack of any allegation that the board acted inconsistently with or exceeded its statutory powers or improperly delegated its responsibility.

　　See also Bicknell v. Vergennes Union High School Board of Directors, 638 F.2d at 442 ("[S]tate procedural requirements do not create interests entitled to due process protection").

　　But see Salvail v. Nashua Board of Education, 469 F.Supp. at 1273, 1276, holding that the school board was bound by the "interim guidelines" it had adopted.
185. For a discussion of the concept of "zoning" certain books according to student maturity, see Niccolai, *supra* note 25, at 35–36.
186. See *Island Trees,* 457 U.S. at 858; Right to Read Defense Committee of Chelsea v. School Committee of City of Chelsea, 454 F. Supp. at 705, 708; and Comment, *supra* note 14, at 180–191. Check-out of certain books might be available only

to the parents themselves. See Presidents Council, District 25 v. Community School Board No. 25, 457 F.2d at 290; Comment, *supra* note 38, at 538, n. 96.

187. See Note, *supra* note 112, at 1122.

188. See text accompanying notes 192–194, *infra.*

189. See Salvail v. Nashua Board of Education, 469 F.Supp. at 1272; and Right to Read Defense Committee of Chelsea v. School Committee of City of Chelsea, 454 F.Supp. at 708.

190. "It would be no less offensive to First Amendment principles for a School Committee to bowdlerize an anthology by removing one poem, than it would be for it to excise objectionable passages in a novel." Right to Read Defense Committee of Chelsea v. School Committee of City of Chelsea, 454 F.Supp. at 714, n. 18.

191. "Censorship News", No. 11 (National Coalition Against Censorship, October 1982), p. 1.

192. N.Y. CIV. PRAC. LAW § 4509 (McKinney Supp. 1984–85).

193. See, *e.g.*, ILL. ANN. STAT. ch. 81, ¶ 1202, § 1 (Smith-Hurd Supp. 1984–85); NEB. REV. STAT. § 84-712.05(10)(1984) (applies to "publicly funded library"); NEV. REV. STAT. § 239.013 (1981); and WASH. REV. CODE § 42.17.310(1) (Supp. 1985) (applies to "any library record").

Sometimes, the statute seems inapplicable to school libraries. See, *e.g.*, ME. REV. STAT. ANN. tit. 27, § 121 (Supp. 1984–85) ("public municipal library"). Other statutes are more ambiguous. See, *e.g.*, OR. REV. STAT. § 192.500(i)(j) (1981)("public library").

Typically, confidentiality will not apply in the face of a court order. See, *e.g.*, ILL. ANN. STAT. ch. 81, ¶ 1202, § 1 (Smith-Hurd Supp. 1984–85).

194. "Censorship News," No. 11 (National Coalition Against Censorship, October, 1982), p. 1.

195. December 30, 1982, Memo of Leanne Katz, Director, National Coalition Against Censorship, to the Steering Committee, p. 1.

196. "Censorship News," No. 12 (National Coalition Against Censorship, January 1983), p. 1.

197. See Niccolai, *supra* note 25, at 32.

198. State statutes provide guidelines of varying levels of usefulness with regard to substantive criteria for book selection. See, *e.g.*, FLA. STAT. ANN. § 233.165(1) (West Supp. 1985), under which standards for library book selection include the age of the children; the educational purpose; and the degree to which the material will be supplemented and explained by mature classroom instruction. See also ALA. CODE § 16-21-2 (1977) (prescribing that the books included on the approved list "be as nearly as possible representative of the whole field of literature. . . . "); and MINN. STAT. ANN. § 134.04 (1979) [renumbered § 121.496 in MINN. STATS. 1984] (requiring the State Department of Education to furnish a list of books "suitable for school libraries").

Legislation may also exclude broad categories from acceptability, such as pornography or related material. See, *e.g.*, FLA. STAT. ANN. § 233.165(2) (West 1976 and Supp. 1985). For a broad proscription, see NEV. REV. STAT. § 385.240.1 (1979), mandating that the list of approved public school library books issued by the superintendent of public instruction *not* include "books containing . . . any story in prose or poetry the tendency of which would be to influence the minds of children in the formation of ideals not in harmony with truth and morality or the American way of life. . . . "

Book selection guidelines are also helpful in dealing with book donations to school libraries. See Niccolai, *supra* note 25, at 32–33.

199. See N.Y. EDUC. LAW §310(5)–(6) (McKinney 1969 and Supp. 1984) (cited in Presidents Council, District 25 v. Community School Board No. 25, 457 F.2d at 289), providing appeals to the state commissioner of education for persons aggrieved by certain official action with regard to school libraries.
200. Niccolai, *supra* note 25, at 31.
201. *Id.* at 31–32.
202. See Comment, *supra* note 110, at 665.

Chapter 4

THE SEXUAL ORIENTATION
OR ACTIVITY OF TEACHERS

INTRODUCTION

In late 1982, a group of parents in East Hampton, New York, circulated a petition calling for the dismissal of a high school biology and human behavior teacher on the grounds that her unwed, pregnant status made her "immoral" and a bad role model.[1] Although about one hundred people signed that petition, almost five hundred signed a separate petition in her support.[2] An informal public hearing on the matter was held at which speakers represented both sides of the issue.[3] One speaker said that the teacher's conduct "was a slap in the face of every decent teacher in the school" and another that she had "abused her privilege as a teacher." Still other speakers called her "one of the most valuable teachers we are privileged to have . . . ", and argued that the matter did not affect the students' well-being or the quality of their education.[4] The school board ultimately decided to take no action against the tenured teacher.[5]

The intense reaction generated by this case reflects the deep interest which the public has traditionally shown toward the sexual orientation or behavior of teachers. The fact that so many people rose to the teacher's defense[6] and that the board declined to dismiss her may well indicate, however, that the public increasingly regards sexual conduct not directly and substantially affecting one's teaching duties as beyond the legitimate concern of public officials.[7] This chapter will explore the law's treatment of the sexual orientation or conduct of teachers by analyzing the teacher's special role, the substantive limits on state regulation in this area, the kinds of orientation or behavior giving rise to litigation and the factors attending teacher behavior deemed relevant by the courts. Manageable and meaningful criteria for the discipline of teachers for sexual conduct will be suggested.

THE TEACHER AS MODEL

The courts have left no doubt that some aspects of a teacher's life are properly scrutinized by the state.[8] The school, and therefore the teacher, has the recognized duty to inculcate community values[9] in students. In California, for example, legislation makes this duty clear: "Each teacher shall endeavor to impress upon the minds of the pupils [among other things] the principles of morality . . . and to instruct them in . . . morals. . . . "[10] Even aside from such affirmatively-stated duties, it is clear that the teacher heavily influences not only the intellectual life of the child but the moral and psychological life as well.[11] We rightly expect teachers to "foster and elevate" the ideals of the young.[12] Given the impressionable age of schoolchildren and their tendency to look up to their teachers as role models, the likelihood of imitation is considerable.[13]

Since teachers may even unconsciously convey their values to students,[14] an immoral teacher may not be able to shed his outlook upon entering the classroom.[15] Moreover, a school district retaining a teacher who acts in a sexually immoral way, whether in or out of[16] the classroom, may lend an air of approval to that conduct.[17] The delicacy of sexual matters for schoolchildren, who are in the most formative period of their sexual and moral development, only exacerbates the situation.[18]

These points are reflected in *B.R.** u Bathke*,[19] which involved the failure to rehire an unmarried teacher who had become pregnant. Some of her students had suspected the pregnancy. The trial court felt that a teacher developing a good relationship with students becomes a model to them even with regard to personal values. The school board could properly feel, therefore, that students might view her continued employment as condoning pregnancy out of wedlock.[20] (The appellate court ultimately reversed on essentially procedural grounds[21].)

Of course, teachers cannot reflect every quality we seek for our children.[22] Furthermore, students will not directly imitate conduct of which they are unaware or conduct which a teacher once indulged in but now discourages.[23] Indeed, such a teacher might provide the most effective lesson in moral rectitude.[24] Unless the teacher is of good moral character, nonetheless, the future of the children entrusted to his care may be jeopardized.[25] Indeed, we have traditionally expected the teacher not

---

*In the interest of personal privacy, the names of many of the teachers alluded to in this chapter are not provided.

only to be more moral than other citizens but to avoid even the appearance of immorality.[26]

In a statement oft-quoted by courts in teacher-conduct cases,[27] the U.S. Supreme Court observed:

> A teacher works in a sensitive area in a schoolroom. There he shapes the attitudes of young minds toward the society in which they live. In this, the state has a vital concern. It must preserve the integrity of the schools. That the school authorities have the right and the duty to screen the officials, teachers, and employees as to their fitness to maintain the integrity of the schools as a part of ordered society, cannot be doubted.[28]

Accordingly, the state agency sponsoring the school may ensure personnel equal to the task,[29] and states have, at various times in our history, claimed the right to dismiss a teacher even for marriage,[30] for divorce, or for liquor or tobacco use.[31] Nonetheless, among dismissals, those for sex-related immorality are the most sensitive, the most controversial,[32] and perhaps the most frequent.[33]

The situations raising these issues pit against each other two important values. On the one hand, too liberal a policy or practice with regard to retention of teachers jeopardizes the character or psychological well-being of our children. An overzealous or over-reaching personnel policy vis-a-vis the sexual orientation or activity of a teacher, on the other hand, risks the inappropriate loss to the public of the teacher and the inappropriate loss to the teacher of his teaching position. The latter is especially serious in light of the difficulty a teacher dismissed for moral reasons will have securing new employment.[34]

Perhaps the traditional pedestal on which we have insisted that our teachers stand is no longer justified. Decades ago, a student or his parent was much more likely to know about his teacher's off-grounds conduct than is true today.[35] A large proportion of parents, students and teachers today live in large cities or sprawling suburbs in which one tends to know little about even his own neighbors. Automobiles, modern roads and consolidated schools have dispersed teachers and students over large areas.

Too, for better or for worse, people today are less likely to care about the conduct indulged in by others and perhaps, therefore, less likely to learn of it or to emulate it. The teacher's special modeling role traditionally sprang at least in large part from the fact that he was, along with the doctor, lawyer and minister, one of the few professionals in the area and was, therefore, much looked up to.

Today, the student is exposed to many more professionals and others thought to be sophisticated, causing the teacher's influence to be diluted significantly. Moreover, the teacher's own standing and prestige[36] have been hurt by the low pay and poor working conditions associated with teaching. No longer, in short, is the teacher looked up to in the same way.

Finally, the impact of the teacher as role model was more crucial when a student had but one teacher all year long, if not for that student's total elementary education. In such a case, no other teacher provided balance, perspective, and diffusion with regard to the hero image. Today in high school and to a considerable extent in grade school, students are exposed to a large number of teachers with the consequence that no one teacher will likely have the same effect as the one-room schoolhouse teacher did.

Perhaps today, therefore, the view that "teachers in their private lives should exemplify Victorian principles of sexual morality, and in classrooms should subliminally indoctrinate the pupils in such principles is hopelessly unrealistic and atavistic."[37]

VAGUENESS

A key issue in the discipline of teachers for their sexual activity concerns whether the statutory or regulatory provisions under which they work provide sufficient notice that such activity is prohibited, notice required by the due process clause of the Fourteenth Amendment.[38] Personnel decisions in this area are often based on allegations of immoral conduct,[39] conduct unbecoming a teacher,[40] lack of fitness,[41] incompetence[42] or "other good and just cause."[43] Obviously, all of these terms, besides substantially overlapping each other,[44] are extremely broad and leave much, if not everything, to subjective evaluation.[45] The New Mexico Supreme Court, for example, concluded that the words "for any other good and just cause" have no reasonably specific legal definition.[46]

School boards have used such "catch-all" phrases to justify dismissal decisions which too often "reflect idiosyncratic community mores rather than professional standards of conduct."[47] On the other hand, at least one court has found virtue in allowing some variation among school districts with regard to standards of immorality or gross unfitness, reasoning that "what is acceptable in one district may not be in another."[48]

Generality and specificity present a difficult choice.[49] When school officials have almost unbridled discretion to condemn, after the fact, conduct which they object to, the potential for arbitrariness and discrimination looms large.[50] So too, a provision so broad as to defy effective enforcement against most of the group to which it purportedly applies invites capricious application.[51] Moreover, such discretion carries with it the possibility of pretext dismissals, dismissals for which the real reason may be not the alleged immorality, unprofessionalism or unfitness, but personal disagreement with lifestyle, the teacher's exercise of first amendment rights or even the administration's perception that the teacher is teaching badly, but not badly enough to satisfy a hearing board.[52]

Ineligibility for or dismissals from teaching positions based upon broad proscriptions of immorality may fail to recognize changing mores and the ultimate cost to our schools. Referring to the threatened "wastefulness of human resources," one California jurist observed:

> [W]e know that a large proportion of the younger generation do engage in unorthodox sexual activities deemed anathema by some members of the older generation. To what extent will we frustrate highly productive careers of younger persons in order to castigate conduct that is widely practiced by some but regarded by others as abominable? Is the legal standard to be no more definite or precise than that the involved practice is regarded as "immoral" or "unprofessional" or "tasteless" by judges?[53]

Reasonable notice, then, helps to dissipate concerns of arbitrariness, capriciousness, pretext, and wastefulness of resources.

On the other hand, drafting a statute or regulation that specifies all inappropriate teacher conduct is impossible.[54] The varieties of human misbehavior are limitless.[55] Furthermore, as specifics are added to a prohibition, gaps may inevitably appear. Specifying certain forms of prohibited conduct, then, may result in the approval, by implication, of other equally or more serious forms of misconduct. The United States Supreme Court has recognized the problem:

> The root of the vagueness doctrine is a rough idea of fairness. It is not a principle designed to convert into a constitutional dilemma the practical difficulties in drawing. . . . statutes both general enough to take into account a variety of human conduct and sufficiently specific to provide fair warning that certain kinds of conduct are prohibited.[56]

Notice is not equally valuable in all situations. It is especially helpful when the conduct under consideration might be seen as appropriate by some and not by others. In such cases, the notice concept honors both basic fairness and human dignity, and allows for meaningful judicial review.[57] Consequently, laws should give reasonably intelligent people reasonable warning of what is prohibited,[58] at least if the teacher has acquired a property interest in his employment.[59] If, for example, a school district wishes to dismiss a young and single teacher for dancing closely with her date at a high school dance, reasonably specific notice that such conduct is prohibited may be in order. Such notice might come from a statute, regulation, treatment of other persons,[60] specific warnings to the individual,[61] or otherwise. Obviously, notice is too late when the teacher is informed of his error only upon the allocation of a penalty.[62]

On the other hand, certain conduct by teachers is clearly inappropriate, even under broadly worded proscriptions, and the teacher is therefore on notice that he is not to engage in such conduct.[63] A teacher charged with immorality for having fondled a student on school property should not be heard to say that he had no specific forewarning that such conduct was prohibited, for he did not appropriately rely on any perceived gap in the applicable provision. Similarly, even if not criminal or seriously disruptive, conduct may be "sufficiently odd and suggestive" that one should know, in advance, that it falls within a broad prohibition.[64]

The United States Supreme Court has indicated a willingness to tolerate considerable breadth in dismissal criteria for public employment. In *Arnett v. Kennedy*, the Court, through the opinions of six of its justices, found the clause "such cause as will promote the efficiency of the service" sufficiently specific.[65] There, however, the federal employee had available a personnel manual elaborating upon the statute and advice in advance of conduct, if sought, from the agency's general counsel.

The Court of Appeals for the First Circuit, relying on *Arnett*, found constitutionally valid, against a vagueness claim, the application of a prohibition against "conduct unbecoming a teacher" to one who had dressed, undressed and caressed, in a lewd and suggestive manner, and in public view, though on his own property, a dress mannequin.[66] The court found the lack of an elaborating manual in the teacher case not significant since the manual in *Arnett* "added nothing of value to the statutory standard except to give notice of its enormous breadth."[67] The unavailability of counsel to the teacher before the fact, the court added, did not distinguish his case from *Arnett*, since the teacher's conduct was not the sort for which he was likely to seek legal advice.[68]

In constitutional terms, less specific notice is required when neither criminal penalties nor First Amendment freedoms are involved.[69] Nevertheless, other interests as well are protected by procedural due process.[70] The loss of one's livelihood constitutes a serious deprivation and one is therefore entitled to reasonable notice of what conduct on his part jeopardizes his governmental position.[71] Moreover, some teacher conduct cases may implicate such first amendment claims as freedom of association or speech.[72] Therefore, despite the presumption of constitutionality to which statutes are entitled, teachers' complaints alleging overly-vague proscriptions should be carefully considered.

OVERBREADTH

Related to vagueness is the doctrine of overbreadth,[74] the gist of which is the claim that an otherwise clear and precise prohibition includes within it constitutionally protected conduct.[75] Except in limited situations, however, including especially those involving pure speech, a statute must be judged not on its face, that is, not with regard to all hypothetical situations, but on its application to the facts of the particular case before the court.[76]

In *K.I. v. Wright*,[77] a tenured teacher dismissed for immorality, including the making of sexual advances to female students, argued that the statute authorizing dismissal for "immorality" and for "other good and just cause" prohibited protected as well as unprotected conduct and was thus constitutionally overbroad. Noting the United States Supreme Court's emphasis that facial overbreadth adjudication constitutes the exceptional case,[78] the fact that the statute prohibited neither speech nor conduct but merely set out the bases for discharging tenured teachers, the fact that no rights of association were affected and that no regulation of "conduct resulting in unreviewable prior restraints" was provided for, and certain limitations specified in the statute, the U.S. District Court found the overbreadth doctrine inapplicable:[79] "[W]hile a 'fertile legal imagination' can conjure up situations in which application of the statute would infringe on protected activity, this determination is best left to a case-by-case determination rather than the broadsword of the overbreadth doctrine."[80]

AN ILLUSTRATION: "IMMORALITY"

Personnel decisions based on immorality[81] allegations have repeatedly forced courts to determine what constitutes immoral conduct and whether prohibitions, whatever the particular phrase, against immorality are specific enough to pass constitutional or statutory muster.[82] After all, immorality could refer to a wide variety of even nonsexual activity such as alcohol or drug use, smoking, card playing, failure to serve in the military,[83] laziness, gluttony, cowardice and the like.[84] Even with regard to sexual activity, our secular society may present a variety of moralities, among which it may be impossible to choose.[85] When state statutes or regulations fail to define "immorality," the usual principle of statutory interpretation calls for giving the term its "ordinary, common, everyday meaning."[86] In an analogous case, involving the attempted revocation of a teaching certificate on grounds of the teacher's alleged "moral turpitude," the Supreme Court of Iowa emphasized that the revocation power of the board was not a punitive one and could not reflect the exercise of board members' personal moral judgment, a subjective standard contrary to legislative intent.[87]

On the other hand, as suggested earlier, if the teacher misconduct alleged, for example sexual advances to students, falls clearly within an otherwise vague prohibition, the court may not worry about the hypothetical vagueness of the term "immorality."[88]

A LIMITING CONSTRUCTION

The most noteworthy attempt to deal with the vagueness issue in connection with criteria for teacher discipline occurred in *M.S. v. State Board of Education.*[89] For a number of years M.S. had held a California General Secondary Life Diploma and a Life Diploma to Teach Exceptional Children.[90] During these years, the record revealed, the teacher's performance had caused no complaint. His out-of-class activity also had been exemplary, except for one matter. M.S. became friendly with a fellow teacher and his spouse and, indeed, counseled them in connection with their serious marital and financial difficulties. The husband frequently came to M.S.' apartment for counseling. In April of 1963, for a one-week period during which both M.S. and the husband were under considerable stress, "the two men engaged in a limited, non-criminal physical relationship . . . described [by M.S.] as being of a homosexual nature,"[91] one involving neither sodomy nor oral copulation.[92] Although the two men met several times during the spring and summer following this incident, no further conduct of a homosexual nature occurred and, when the husband and his wife separated, M.S. suggested to the husband women he might date.

The husband reported the incident to the School District Superintendent and, in light of that report, M.S. resigned his teaching position on

May 4, 1964. About a year and a half after the report to the Superintendent, the State Board of Education conducted a hearing to explore the revocation for cause of M.S.' life diploma. There, M.S. testified that although he had experienced an unspecified homosexual problem at the age of 13, he had not, except for the April, 1963, incident, had any homosexual urge or inclination for over twelve years. An investigator, called by the board to testify, confirmed that the April, 1963, incident constituted M.S.' only homosexual act.

Some three years after that incident, the State Board of Education revoked M.S.' life diploma, labeling the homosexual incident immoral and unprofessional conduct and an act involving moral turpitude, criteria justifying life diploma revocation under the California Code.[93] As a result, M.S. was barred from employment as a teacher in any California public school.

On review, the California Supreme Court stated that without some reasonable limitation the terms "immoral or unprofessional conduct" or "moral turpitude" could be so broadly applied as to subject virtually any California teacher to potential discipline. Consequently, the terms must be construed to mean conduct indicating unfitness to teach:[94] "Terms such as 'immoral,' 'unprofessional' and 'moral turpitude' constitute only lingual abstractions until applied to a specific occupation and given context by reference to fitness for the performance of that vocation."[95] Noting that the terms at issue were applicable to many other categories of state employees or licenses, the Court asserted that unless the terms were limited according to the particular occupation involved, the "identical standards of probity" would apply to hundreds of thousands of government and professional employees despite greatly different responsibilities and varying extents of public contact. This the legislature could not have intended.[96] Nor, added the Court, should the legislature be presumed to have enacted a standard for teacher conduct that widely varies according to time, location or popular mood.[97]

Conceding that the terms "immoral or unprofessional conduct" and conduct "involving moral turpitude," if restricted to activity indicating unfitness to teach, would be specific enough to be constitutionally applied to M.S.' conduct,[98] the court found no evidence in the record to support a finding that M.S. was unfit to teach.[99]

FITNESS: THE ELUSIVE CONCEPT

Almost all cases have echoed this limiting construction of broadly-phrased criteria of teacher dismissal or certificate revocation.[100] Announcing that immoral or unprofessional conduct or conduct involving moral turpitude justifies a teacher's removal only if it demonstrates a lack of fitness to teach may, however, be easier than applying the new principle.

In light of the teacher's expansive responsibilities, when has fitness been negated? The court in *M.S. v. State Board of Education*, attempting to provide some guidance, stated that lack of fitness is shown only if the teacher's retention "poses a significant danger of harm to either students, school employees, or others who might be affected by his actions as a teacher."[101] Factors relevant to a decision on fitness include the age and maturity of the students,[102] the likelihood of an adverse effect on fellow students or teachers, the extent of any such adversity, the amount of time since the occurrence, any extenuating or aggravating factors, the motivation involved, the likelihood of repetition, and the probability of any chilling effect the potential discipline might cause to the exercise of constitutional rights by that teacher (or others).[103] The type of teaching certificate involved could also be relevant since it might limit the nature of the teacher's relationship with students and the age-level of students the teacher will deal with; a teacher could be disqualified for some activities and qualified for others.[104] These factors are not necessarily exhaustive, since "[h]uman conduct is infinitely various."[105]

A central problem with the purported limitation wrought by the court in *M.S.* relates to the role of teacher as exemplar. To the extent he is given a modeling function, does not *any* immoral or unprofessional conduct or *any* conduct involving moral turpitude affect his fitness to teach? If so, the limitation may be more illusory than real. This problem was suggested by the court's statement that the homosexual incident had not become so notorious that it adversely affected the respect of students and colleagues for M.S. and the confidence they had in him.[106]

This statement suggests that the limitation does add something to the teacher's protection. For example, it makes clear that not every homosexual act, even if considered immoral by school officials, will warrant discipline—only those that affect one's fitness to teach. On the other hand, the clear implication is that if that homosexual conduct became known to many students or colleagues—as it already may have if the teacher's job or certificate is being challenged—school officials may well be able to conclude, after eliciting some expert testimony about the modeling aspects of that conduct, that the teacher's fitness to teach has been adversely affected. Interestingly, even the court in *M.S.* left the State Board of Education free to "reopen its inquiry" if it felt able to demonstrate M.S.' unfitness for teaching.[107]

The difficulty of applying *M.S.* is clear even from the dissent. There, Justice Sullivan, conceding for the sake of argument that the majority's construction of the statutory criteria for revocation was correct, responded: "[T]he plain, hard fact of the matter is that [M.S.'] conduct *did* indicate his unfitness to teach. . . . "[108] Justice Sullivan reached the conclusion in light of the teacher's close relationship with students and his statutory duty to impress the principles of morality upon their minds.[109]

One might nonetheless have hoped that *M.S.* would settle the issue, at least in California, and that henceforth unfitness would present an empirical question,[110] not one of subjective values. Justice Sullivan's dissent, however, should have signaled that the battleground would shift only slightly. Since the *M.S.* case had established that in order to justify credential revocation even immoral or unprofessional conduct must establish unfitness to teach, the major inquiry concerned the concept of unfitness. The substance of the issue—what conduct justifies dismissal or revocation—remained the same, with the result too often dependent upon the personal values of the judges involved.[111]

M.E. v. State Board of Education[112] illustrates how the promise of *M.S.* might go unfulfilled, its letter but not its spirit honored. The evidence in *M.E.* indicated that the teacher had masturbated in public view in a public restroom and had touched the private parts of another male. The California appellate court, requiring no evidence of an impact, real or reasonably likely, on the teacher's school performance, found that conduct "sufficient, in and of itself, to establish unfitness to teach."[113] The distinctions which the court drew between *M.S.* and *M.E.*—that the conduct in *M.S.* occurred in private and did not constitute a crime—may be significant in some respects but do not in themselves mandate a different finding with regard to fitness to teach. For example, the result in *M.E.* would presumably be the same if the conduct had occurred far away from the teacher's school district, yet such conduct might have no effect whatever on the teacher's ability to teach effectively. The crucial nexus is lacking. The *per se* approach wholly undermines *M.S.* by allowing any conduct thought immoral by a court majority to justify dismissal or credential revocation.

That *M.S.* may have been more noise than substance is indicated as well by *P.E. v. State Board of Education*,[114] decided by the Supreme Court of California just four years after it decided *M.S.* In *P.E.*, the State Board of Education had revoked the teacher's elementary school life diploma on the grounds that she had "engaged in immoral and unprofessional conduct, in acts involving moral turpitude, and in acts evidencing her unfitness for service."[115] The specific conduct included joining a "swingers club," engaging in sexual intercourse and oral copulation with men not her husband and appearing on television in disguise to discuss nonconventional sexual behavior. In an evaluation of her classroom work introduced at the hearing, her principal called her teaching satisfactory and noted "her classes' progress and improvement."[116]

Three elementary school superintendents testified that in their opinion her conduct demonstrated a lack of fitness to teach. As summarized by the court, one testified that a teacher has the responsibility not only to teach morality but to practice it and that, given the fact that pupils see teachers as moral models, P.E. "would lose her effectiveness" and "*might* even inject her ideas regarding sexual morals into the classroom."[117] A second testified to his opinion of P.E.'s unfitness and to the effect that "every teacher *should* possess high morals, and that it *would* be difficult to teach morality without practicing it."[118] The third testified that "one who engaged in the sexual conduct performed by the [teacher] would be unfit" to teach young children.[119]

The expert opinion focused on the possible, not the actual. None of the testimony showed any actual harm to the students or to the school. Closest to reflecting any actual impact on the school was the statement of one superintendent that some of P.E.'s colleagues had discussed her televised statements.[120] Nonetheless, the California Supreme Court upheld the credential revocation.

The expert testimony in *P.E.* seems relevant to fitness in only two possible ways. First, the administrators may merely be predicting that the teacher might at some point have an adverse impact on the schools; such speculation, however, seems a flimsy basis for such a devasting penalty to the teacher. Is it asking too much that there be evidence of actual harm, or at least very likely harm,[121] before a career is perhaps ruined? As the Supreme Court of New Mexico said of allegations that a teacher's unmarried pregnancy created the possibility she might not be able to perform her duties, "This is purely speculative."[122] The exercise of state power to dismiss or discipline a teacher in such cases should require a showing that harm to the school community "has or is *likely to* occur."[123] The "likely to" phrase tends to screen out the more speculative cases and, in that respect, seems superior even to a "reasonable possibility" criterion.[124]

Second, in light of the modeling role expected of teachers, the point of the testimony in *P.E.* may be that such a person in fact adversely influences the children but that the influence is too subtle and too intangible to demonstrate directly. Again, a very speculative conclusion is used to justify an enormously important personnel decision.

To be sure, such a teacher is perhaps unlikely to lecture students on the importance of traditional fidelity in marriage or traditional sexual lifestyles. But we do not expect such lectures in most school courses anyway. It is unlikely, on the other hand, that such a teacher will urge students to follow her example.

The *P.E.* court noted that unfitness to teach could be shown by the expert opinion of other teachers or of administrators,[125] even if that evidence reflects their personal moral views.[126] This observation clearly reaffirms the extent to which *P.E.* undermines *M.S.* After all, surely three administrators could be found to make the same speculative observations with regard to M.S. that were made with regard to P.E.[127] Requiring only testimony by an administrator that certain conduct he considers immoral or unprofessional affects the modeling impact of the teacher, thus yielding unfitness, does not significantly narrow the terms "immoral or unprofessional conduct" or "moral turpitude." Similarly, if the connection to fitness is appropriately established through speculation as to whether, for example, a teacher involved in any conduct considered immoral can teach morality effectively, the vagueness of the word "immoral" remains.

Yet *M.S.* required a showing that retention "poses a significant danger of harm to . . . students, school employees or others,"[128] a showing of the likelihood of an adverse impact, past or future, on the educational mission of the school. For example, the *M.S.* court stressed the lack of any evidence that the teacher "had ever committed any act of misconduct whatsoever while teaching."[129] To be sure, the *M.S.* court, in listing the factors relevant to a fitness determination, included "the likelihood that the conduct may have adversely affected students or fellow teachers [and] the degree of such adversity anticipated".[130] The clear implication is that there need not be definite proof that the harm has already occurred, and it has been so held.[131] If a teacher has, for example, exposed himself to children other than children at the teacher's own school, school officials need not wait for him to expose himself to students at his school before moving to dismiss. But the tenor of the *M.S.* opinion seems equally clearly to require more than a *pro forma* and automatic finding of unfitness once some conduct, thought undesirable by an expert, has occurred.

This may be especially true in cases involving homosexuals. For example, in *G.A. v. Tacoma School District No. 10*,[132] the district fired a high school teacher on grounds of "immorality" because he was a known homosexual. The trial court sustained the dismissal, finding that a known homosexual's fitness to teach is impaired. The court found that "fear, confusion, suspicion, parental concern and pressure on the administration" would result if he was not discharged.[133] The Supreme Court of Washington, noting a student's complaint that a homosexual continued to teach at the school,[134] sanctioned the dismissal. The court concluded that substantial evidence supported the trial court's finding that once his homosexual status became known, the teacher's efficiency became impaired. The dissent protested that a finding of detrimental effect should not, even when coupled with a status, be predicated on "conjecture alone."[135]

The *M.S.* court's list of the fatal gaps in the record concerning M.S.' unfitness to teach also suggests that more than some automatic connection between the alleged immoral or unprofessional conduct, or conduct involving moral turpitude, and unfitness is needed for teacher dismissal or revocation of a life diploma. The list bears reciting, at least summarily. There was no evidence that M.S. (1) was likely to repeat the conduct; (2) was more likely than the average person to engage in inappropriate conduct with students; (3) might publicly advocate improper conduct; (4) had even considered any improper relationship with a student; or (5) "had failed to impress upon the minds of his pupils the principles of morality." The court specified that (6) "the board failed to show that [the] conduct in any manner affected his performance as a teacher" or (7) had become "so notorious as to impair [his] ability to command the respect and confidence of students and fellow teachers. . . . "[136]

Which of these gaps are filled in the *P.E.* case? The third, relating to public advocacy of improper conduct, is perhaps the most applicable, given the teacher's television appearance. But although the record indicated that at least some of P.E.'s colleagues knew of the appearance, the teacher did wear a disguise and there seems to have been no general awareness of the identity or, perhaps, even of the occupation of the television speaker. As a result, there was little or no connection between the television appearance and the operation of the school system. With regard to the fifth, there was no showing that P.E. had in fact failed to impress the principles of morality upon her students. With regard to the sixth, which most approaches the modeling role, her conduct had not become "so notorious" that students and fellow teachers had lost respect or confidence in her. The list, although providing anything but a clear direction, suggests that the case made against P.E. was lacking.

P.E.'s infidelity to the spirit of *M.S.* is most dramatically illustrated by the fact that Justice Tobriner, the author of *M.S.*, dissented. In Tobriner's view, P.E.'s thirteen years of competent teaching of mentally retarded children constituted the best evidence of her fitness to teach. The board decided on the basis of "questionable conjecture," he continued, rather than on any showing that her performance had been impaired. He made clear what he suggested in *M.S.*, namely, that such a decision should have been based on "solid and credible evidence that clearly established [P.E.'s] lack of fitness to teach."[137] The experts, he urged, provided no reason for their assertions of unfitness: "None of them know [P.E.]; none considered her 13-year record of competent teaching; none could point to a single instance of past misconduct with students, nor articulate the nature of any possible future misconduct."[138] With regard to her ability to teach morality, he pointed out that her duties did not include teaching sexual rectitude.[139]

As it turns out, the only impact of *M.S.* may be to require the securing of one or more experts to testify that the conduct charged is immoral or unprofessional, or involves moral turpitude. Such experts will almost invariably be prepared to testify that the teacher's modeling role is adversely affected, if all that is meant by that is the *possibility* that the teacher will not adequately convey moral teaching, as opposed to a showing of a substantial adverse impact, real or *likely*, on the students or fellow teachers. As Justice Tobriner lamented, "If 'immoral conduct' *ipso facto* shows inability to model or teach morals, and this in turn shows unfitness to teach, then we are left with the proposition that proof of 'immoral conduct,' whatever it may be, will always justify revocation of a teaching credential."[140]

Fortunately, some cases have been true to the spirit of *M.S.* In *E.R. v. Iowa State Board of Public Instruction*,[141] for example, the Supreme Court of Iowa held the commission of adultery insufficient in itself to establish unfitness to teach. The teacher's conduct outside the classroom may indeed affect fitness to teach, the court acknowledged, but its relevance is limited.[142] In *T.H. v. Southwest School District*,[143] a federal district court held that the teacher's cohabiting with a man to whom she was not married did not, absent evidence of disciplinary problems, a hostile atmosphere undermining her authority, discussion of her conduct with her students, or the like, establish unfitness to teach.[144]

Moreover, Justice Tobriner was again able to write for the majority on this issue in *Board of Education v. M.I.*,[145] in which a school board sought to establish its right to discharge a tenured teacher who had been arrested, but never criminally charged, in connection with an alleged homosexual solicitation in a public restroom. Although some testimony at the trial had suggested that the teacher could no longer provide a "behavioral example" and that the conduct would harm the teacher's dealings with students, parents and staff,[146] the California Supreme Court, recognizing that "trial court findings supported by substantial evidence" must be upheld on appeal,[147] sustained the trial court's conclusion that the teacher was not unfit,[148] a finding based upon the pressure the teacher was under at the time, the fact that the conduct was an isolated act, the unlikelihood of recurrence, especially with regard to children, and the lack of widespread community knowledge of the conduct.[149] Moreover, the Court noted that these factors must be seen in the light of the teacher's "proven 16-year record of competent teaching"[150] and that the board had presented no evidence that the teacher had ever failed "to impress and instruct his students in manners and morals. . . . "[151]

Another way of weakening the *M.S.* principle requiring a nexus between the alleged conduct and one's fitness to teach is reflected in *W.E. v. Board of Education*,[152] in which the Supreme Court of Colorado observed that neither the hearing panel nor the school board had specifically found that the teacher's conduct affected his ability to teach. Nonetheless, said the court, such a finding is necessarily implicit in the teacher's dismissal, especially since the conduct involved students and occurred during a school field trip.[153] In the context of this particular case, in which direct evidence of impact on the school itself was adduced, perhaps no serious problem is presented; in the context of the larger problem, however, the "necessarily implicit" concept may encourage a further dilution of the salutary principle announced in *M.S.*

RIGHT TO PRIVACY

Teachers whose positions or credentials have been attacked on the grounds of inappropriate sexual conduct or the like have relied not only upon vagueness and overbreadth arguments but also upon their right to privacy.[154] In *B.R. v. Bathke*,[155] for example, a school board terminated the contract of a first year probationary teacher on the grounds that she became pregnant while unwed. The teacher ultimately sought relief in federal district court. The trial court recognized her right to personal privacy, but went on to find the intrusion into that right justified in this particular context.[156] (The Court of Appeals ultimately reversed on essentially procedural grounds.)[157]

The right to personal privacy alluded to by the court derives from a series of U.S. Supreme Court cases. In *Roe v. Wade*, that Court, conceding that the U.S. Constitution makes no specific mention of a privacy right, noted nonetheless that for a long period of time the existence of a "right of personal privacy, or a guarantee of certain areas or zones of privacy" had been recognized by the Court.[158] At least the "roots" of such a right could be found in the First,[159] Fourth and Fifth,[160] Ninth,[161] and Fourteenth[162] Amendments and in the penumbras of the Bill of Rights.[163] The Court stressed that the constitutional guarantee of privacy includes only "fundamental" rights, rights "implicit in the concept of ordered liberty".[164] Moreover, added the Court, the right extends to marriage-related activities,[165] procreation,[166] contraception,[167] family relationships,[168] and child rearing and education.[169] Further, the right even in sexual matters cannot be limited to the married couple: "If the right of privacy means anything, it is the right of the *individual,* married or single, to be free from unwarranted governmental instrusion into matters so fundamentally affecting a person as the decision whether to bear or beget a child."[170]

All of the United States Supreme Court cases taken together do not set out the exact contours of the right to privacy generally[171] or, therefore, as it relates to the sexual activity of teachers. It is not surprising that teachers or school administrators whose positions or credentials have been challenged on grounds of sexual or related activity have invoked the right, with varying success.[172] In any event, despite the list of matters presumably within the right to privacy, not everything related to sexual activity is protected. Surely, the private sexual and childbearing activity of married couples is protected.[173] The childbearing activity[174] of single persons is covered. Whether private sexual conduct is generally within the right is not clear, since the United States Supreme Court has yet to so declare,[175] and may be unlikely to do so.[176]

Indeed, in some cases the right to privacy may focus not on one's freedom to indulge in certain conduct without penalty,[177] but on the methodology of enforcement by school officials. In *D.R. v. Covington County Board of Education*[178] the school board terminated on grounds of immorality a teacher who allegedly became pregnant while unmarried. Since all of the evidence relied upon by the board ultimately derived from disclosures secured by the Superintendent, without the teacher's consent, from the teacher's physician, the teacher's constitutional right to privacy had been violated.[179]

It has been held, on the other hand, that homosexual conduct at an adult bookstore "is not of the character afforded constitutional protection."[180] Too, whatever right to privacy might inhere in an extramarital affair, the right does not immunize the neglect of official duties occasioned by the affair.[181] Finally, the right to privacy does not protect conduct carried on in public,[182] matters as to which the right is otherwise waived,[183] or perhaps even matters of which the public is already aware, with or without an explicit or implicit waiver.[184]

Even when one's right to privacy is implicated, the state's hand is not wholly stayed. The right to privacy is not absolute,[185] but rather must be balanced against legitimate state interests which, if weighty enough, will prevail.[186] For rights as fundamental as whether to bear or beget a child, the countervailing state interest must be compelling[187] and any regulation burdening that right narrowly drawn.[188] Moreover, in any balancing, the school board's decision warrants substantial weight.[189] The state will prevail if the conduct involved directly affects the teacher's professional performance,[190] for the state's interest in teacher effectiveness is a strong one.[191] To that extent, then, the privacy issue assumes less importance if the applicable statute prohibiting immorality or the like is interpreted to require a real impact on performance. Indeed, the right to privacy is one factor in favor of construing broad prohibitions to require the fitness-to-teach nexus.[192]

RIGHTS OF ASSOCIATION AND OF CHOICE

The right to association[193] and the right to choice in one's personal life[194] have also been mentioned in teacher personnel cases having sexual implications. These rights have not figured prominently in the law in this area, however, and in any event presumably would, like the right to privacy, yield to legitimate and sufficiently weighty state interests.[195]

FREEDOM OF SPEECH

In relatively rare cases, the First Amendment right to free speech has been mentioned in teacher personnel cases having sexual implications.[196] Teachers in such cases, however, have had little success relying upon that right.

To be sure, a teacher does not lose his free-speech rights upon entering the schoolhouse,[197] let alone upon becoming a teacher.[198] A teacher therefore generally retains full citizenship rights to free speech in matters relating to sex. Moreover, in the absence of a showing of interference with the teacher's professional performance or with the smooth operation otherwise of the school system, a teacher's comments on public issues are protected unless they are knowingly false or uttered with reckless disregard of the truth.[199] So, for example, a statute authorizing the punishment of a teacher for "public homosexual conduct" is unconstitutional if that conduct is defined to include mere advocacy of homosexual activities.[200] Similarly, the television, radio and press interviews of a homosexual teacher focusing on the problems confronting homosexual children and their parents were protected speech since the interviews did not disrupt the school, substantially impair the teacher's teaching capacity or provide a reasonable forecast of such an impact.[201]

Even pure speech, however, may be unprotected if it does not involve a public issue. In *R. W. v. Mad River Local School District, Montgomery County, Ohio,* the Sixth Circuit held that a counselor's communications to other school employees concerning her sexual preferences were not made as a citizen speaking on public issues;[202] consequently, she could not, under the first amendment, maintain a cause of action against the school district for allegedly failing, in part due to the communications, to renew her contract.[203]

Pure speech may also be unprotected if it adversely affects the school system.[204] Thus, a Pennsylvania court held a male teacher properly dismissed for calling a ninth-grade female student a slut and suggesting in statements to her that she was a prostitute.[205] The statute[206] allowing dismissal for "immoral" or "cruel" conduct did not violate the teacher's freedom of speech; the issue was not the teacher's rights as a citizen but as a teacher, and the state could legislate qualifications concerning teachers' moral character. The court concluded that the dismissal, although directly based on speech, really resulted from character shortcomings reflected in language and conduct wholly inappropriate to the teacher-student context. Protecting the students, a vulnerable group, constituted a legitimate state interest.[207]

The state's interest is still stronger when the speech both relates to school matters and urges inappropriate conduct.[208] When a male teacher argued that his comments proposing spanking to two of his female students constituted protected speech, the court was unimpressed: "When speech is likely to incite or produce imminent deleterious effects on the educational process, such speech, like obscenity, is not protected by the first amendment."[209] Sexual discussion, which, especially with children, is particularly sensitive, could, said the court, cause psychological harm, and children could thereby be led to emulate the teacher.[210] In effect, the court treated the speech like conduct.

The United States Supreme Court has long recognized that protected speech need not be verbal.[211] The black armbands worn by students in *Tinker v. Des Moines Independent School District*[212] to protest the war in Vietnam were thus speech within the First Amendment. Nonetheless, the extent to which teacher conduct with sexual implications could ever be found to be such symbolic speech and, if so, immune to state action remains speculative at best. According to *United States v. O'Brien,*[213] even symbolic speech may be regulated if the regulation is within the state's constitutional power, promotes a substantial governmental interest which is unrelated to suppressing speech and occasions an incidental speech restriction no greater than required for the protection of that interest.[214] Indeed, even if the regulation fails this test, it must still be analyzed within general First Amendment principles,[215] including the *Tinker* balancing test, which allows regulation if the conduct at issue "materially and substantially" affects the operation of the schools,[216] a criterion which seems heavily to overlap the *O'Brien* test. Even if conduct with sexual implications may have communication components, then, the state's interest could still prevail. Perhaps the unusual situation of a homosexual teacher holding hands with another homosexual in a gay rights demonstration,[217] or even perhaps the wearing of sexy clothes,[218] could raise the symbolic speech issue, although school officials might still be free to show a substantial and adverse effect on the school system, for example significant community or student hostility adversely affecting the teacher's professional performance.

EQUAL TREATMENT

A teacher against whom adverse personnel action is threatened may also assert unequal treatment in violation of the equal protection clause of the Fourteenth Amendment or of a parallel state constitutional provision. Traditionally, courts in enforcing the federal equal protection clause have assessed disparate treatment of individuals by the state under a two-tiered analysis. A suspect classification (*e.g.*, one on the basis of race) or one impairing a fundamental right (*e.g.*, to bear a child) warrants "strict scrutiny" to determine that a "compelling" state interest justifies the classification;[219] other classifications generally require for justification only a rational basis, that is, that the classification be reasonably related to a legitimate state interest.[220] Of late, a third category has developed,[221] requiring a governmental interest that is substantial, though not necessarily compelling, for certain distinctions, such as those based on gender[222] or those denying educational rights.[223]

Several teacher-personnel cases of a sexual nature which raise the equal treatment issue have involved pregnant teachers. Of course, to dismiss on the basis of pregnancy itself may constitute unlawful gender discrimination.[224] Terminating pregnant blacks while giving maternity leaves to pregnant whites is unconstitutional and illegal racial discrimination.[225]

Even when the termination is based on the fact that the pregnant woman is unmarried, however, unequal treatment issues arise. In *A.N. v. Drew Municipal Separate School District*,[226] the Court of Appeals for the Fifth Circuit held unconstitutional under the equal protection clause a school district rule prohibiting the employment, at least as instructional personnel,[227] of unwed parents.[228] Although the rule discriminated on the basis of gender[229] since, as the court noted, only unwed mothers, not unwed fathers, were adversely affected,[230] the court found that the rule could not even pass the rational basis test.[231] The court asserted that it is not enough that the state objective—here, according to school officials, fostering a moral school environment—be legitimate; the regulation must advance that objective consistently with the equal protection clause.[232] Furthermore, the state had an alternative, reasonable method for advancing its interest, namely, the regular procedure for removal or suspension of teachers for immorality; since all others charged with immoral conduct are given a public hearing, the rule denies equal protection to those automatically terminated for unwed parenthood.[233] Other reasonable alternatives might be a leave of absence, a transfer to a position having less student contact,[234] or perhaps even a request that the teacher marry.[235]

Claims of unequal treatment may arise when school officials seek on immorality grounds to terminate the services of some but not all single persons who become pregnant or bear a child.[236] Indeed, even if the school defends its inaction against other unwed parents by asserting a lack of knowledge of those situations until the current litigation, a court may still find no serious investigative efforts, no good faith intent, therefore, to proceed against the others, and a consequent violation of the equal protection clause.[237] The treatment of homosexuals may also raise equal protection concerns.[238]

DUE PROCESS

The dismissal of a teacher violates substantive due process if it is arbitrary or capricious.[239] In turn, a dismissal is arbitrary and capricious if the reasons given are trivial, unrelated to professional performance or effectiveness or unsupported by a factual basis.[240] In *F.I. v. Snyder*,[241] a middle-aged divorcee on several occasions hosted in her home "young ladies, married couples, and young men, who were friends of her son. . . ."[242] Due to the local scarcity of commercial lodging, she, following the advice of the school board secretary, "allowed these guests to stay overnight at her apartment."[243]

The school board, noting that men unrelated to her had stayed at the apartment, dismissed her on the grounds of "unbecoming conduct." Although the board did not accuse the teacher of immoral conduct, it noted that "the inferences from her social behavior are that there was a strong potential of sexual misconduct" and that her conduct was "not conducive to the maintenance of the integrity of the public school system."[244] The court found much evidence negating inferences of improper conduct, including the lack of any attempt to conceal the guests' presence in her home and the age differential between her and her guests, but no evidence of improper conduct: the presence of guests in her home afforded "no inkling beyond subtle implication and innuendo which would impugn [the teacher's] morality."[245] No harm to her effectiveness as a teacher was shown. At most, concluded the court, she perhaps used bad judgment.[246] The board's inference of impropriety, having no factual basis, was therefore arbitrary and capricious and could not justify the termination of her employment.[247]

Official action may also violate the due process clause by enforcing an irrebuttable presumption,[248] that is, presuming fact A to coincide inevitably with proven fact B, even though in reality the two are not always associated. When one school board sought to justify its rule barring unwed parents from certain school positions on the grounds, in part, that unwed parenthood constituted prima facie evidence of immorality, the Court of Appeals for the Fifth Circuit found the regulation in violation of the due process clause for presuming that present immorality inevitably attends the proven fact of unwed parenthood.[249] After all, said the Court, the rule made no allowance for such matters as a subsequent marriage, how much time has passed since the illegitimate birth, the person's good reputation, whether the conception resulted from force, deception, alcohol or drugs or, in short, any of the "multitudinous circumstances under which illegitimate childbirth may occur and which may have little, if any, bearing on the parent's present moral worth." The presumption of "irredeemable moral disease" from "the single fact of illegitimate birth" was "patently absurd," "mischievous" and "prejudicial".[250] Ironically, as the court noted, the rule ignored extramarital sexual activities and could encourage abortion, strongly felt by some to be immoral.[251]

THE CATEGORIES OF
ALLEGED SEXUAL MISCONDUCT AND RELATED MATTERS

At this juncture, it is instructive to categorize the varieties of alleged sexual misconduct or related matters in teacher personnel cases and, where appropriate, to discuss matters unique to a particular category. Since the earlier discussion of various constitutional concerns common to many or all of these categories will not be repeated, the reader is reminded that a case in any of the following categories may involve a vague[252] or overbroad[253] underlying proscription, or a violation of the teacher's right to privacy,[254] association,[255] choice,[256] speech,[257] equal treatment[258] or due process.[259]

Homosexuals and Homosexual Conduct

Many cases dealing with teacher discipline[260] involve allegations of homosexuality, homosexual conduct or related matters.[261] The most heavily litigated issue in this area concerns whether homosexuality or related activity adversely affects fitness to teach. In 1967, in *S.A. v. State Board of Education*,[262] a California appeals court upheld the revocation of a teacher's credential on grounds of immoral and unprofessional conduct in connection with an alleged homosexual act by a teacher on a public beach. Said the court:

> Homosexual behavior has long been contrary and abhorrent to the social mores and moral standards of the people of California as it has been since antiquity to those of many other peoples. It is clearly, therefore, immoral conduct. . . . It may also constitute unprofessional conduct . . . as such conduct is not limited to classroom misconduct or misconduct with children. It certainly constitutes evident unfitness for service in the public school system. . . . [263]

This language suggests that any teacher whose homosexual activity becomes known to public school officials is as a matter of law subject to credential revocation or dismissal, even if no significant impact on professional performance is demonstrated.[264] *M.S.*,[265] however, decided shortly after *S.A.*, seemed to temper *S.A.* by stressing that homosexual (or other) activity relied upon for credential revocation must be shown to reflect unfitness to teach.[266] Contrary to the suggestion in *S.A.*, then, homosexual activity does not automatically establish unfitness to teach; some significant impact on job performance, real or potential, must be demonstrated.[267]

Although, as we have seen, the promise of *M.S.* was not wholly fulfilled,[268] in 1977 the Supreme Court of California did reaffirm its point. In *Board of Education v. M.I.*,[269] the school board sued to establish its right to discharge a tenured teacher who had been arrested for, but never charged with, an alleged homosexual solicitation.[270] The Court rejected the school board's argument that the conduct itself demonstrated unfitness to teach.[271] In sexual misconduct cases, there is no rule of unfitness *per se;* the teacher must be shown to be unfit to teach.[272]

G.A. v. Tacoma School District No. 10,[273] perhaps the most prominent case dealing with homosexual teachers, involved a certificated high school teacher with an outstanding record.[274] His homosexuality became known to school officials when, in October of 1972, a former student at the high school informed the vice-principal that he thought G.A. to be a homosexual. G.A. admitted this when confronted with the accusation. After a hearing, the school board discharged G.A. for immorality.[275] The Washington Supreme Court, which ultimately reviewed the case, nodded toward the *M.S.* reasoning in finding that immorality, to justify dismissal, must be coupled with "resulting actual or prospective adverse perform-ance as a teacher."[276]

To the court, there were two basic issues. First, was the trial court's conclusion that G.A. was guilty of immorality justified? The court, after lengthy quotes merely describing homosexuality, noted that homosexu-ality was widely condemned as immoral in both biblical and current times[277] and, further, that G.A. had admitted being a homosexual. From this admission the lower court had inferred sexual gratification and, therefore, sodomy and lewdness,[278] even though there was no direct evidence of such acts[279] or of "any overt act."[280] (To be sure, there was evidence that G.A. had been a homosexual for 20 years and he testified that he had actively sought the company of other male homosexuals, had been an active member of a homosexual society and had responded to advertisements for homosexual company carried by the society's news-paper.)[281] The Washington Supreme Court impliedly approved this find-ing despite the fact that the description of homosexuality it quoted clearly allowed for homosexuality without overt activity.[282] The court thus put much of the burden on the teacher:[283] he admitted being a homosexual, stated the court, and the traditional rule of construction, when the meaning of a term is in doubt, calls for the interpretation least favorable to the one using the term.[284] Moreover, the court added, if he meant anything other than the ordinary sense of the word, or wished to avoid an adverse inference, he could have explained that he was not an overt homosexual and did not commit the acts attributed to him by the court.[285] (Ironically, the court said that G.A. must have known what homosexuality could mean because he was a "competent and intelligent teacher."[286])

The second issue, according to the Washington Supreme Court, was whether the evidence justified the trial court's conclusion that G.A.'s known homosexuality impaired his fitness to teach. The Court noted that at least one student objected to G.A.'s teaching at the school; three teachers objected, both as teachers and as parents, to his remaining a teacher at the school; and school officials testified his continued pres-ence on the faculty would cause problems. The trial court had found that failure to dismiss G.A. once his homosexuality became known would have resulted in "fear, confusion, suspicion, parental concern and pres-sure on the administration by students, parents and other teachers."[287] Although most of the concern seemed speculative,[288] the Washington

Supreme Court found justified the trial court's conclusion that G.A.'s effectiveness had been impaired.[289]

The result is questionable on several grounds. First, the opinion, while ambiguous on the point, suggests that homosexuality with or without any overt conduct will, at least when publicly known, disqualify a teacher. After all, there was no evidence of any overt act by G.A., and the Washington Supreme Court specified that school officials need not "wait for prior specific overt expression of homosexual conduct before they act."[290]

Second, the problem was not, apparently, the teacher's homosexuality, for the trial court found that until it was publicly known, his effectiveness was not impaired.[291] Presumably, therefore, there was no subtle but adverse impact during the many years of teaching in which his homosexuality remained unknown. The real concerns were other people's inability to cope with the presence of a homosexual on the faculty, including objections by teachers, parents and students, and perhaps the approval of homosexuality inferred by students from G.A.'s retention.

Third, the treatment of G.A. reflects a real inequality when compared with what likely would have befallen a heterosexual in an otherwise essentially parallel situation. Would the school board, with no evidence of any overt act, have dismissed a teacher with an outstanding record for being a known heterosexual, even if he had been a heterosexual for a long time, had actively sought out the company of female heterosexuals and had responded to an advertisement from a female seeking male companionship? It is highly doubtful. It certainly is hard to believe that a court would presume that a single, male teacher professing his heterosexualty had engaged in illegal or immoral conduct,[292] let alone to the extent that teaching fitness had been impaired.

What then should a sane public policy have to say about the dismissal or the credential revocation of a homosexual teacher? First, no harm to students should be presumed from the mere fact of the teacher's homosexuality.[293] The fact that many homosexuals have taught for years without their homosexuality even being discovered[294] suggests there is little to fear from their presence in the classroom. The litigated cases suggest no more reason to believe that a male homosexual teacher will accost a young male student than that a male heterosexual teacher will accost a young female student.[295]

Second, even if school officials should learn of a teacher's homosexuality or of homosexual activity, no action should be taken against that teacher on the basis of undifferentiated fear, speculation as to what could happen, vague concerns about modelling roles or even the possible inference of school board approval to which retention of the teacher might give rise. Any action taken against the teacher should be based on actual and significant harm to the school system or the real likelihood of such harm. Surely, the objections of a few teachers, students or parents, especially in light of the likelihood that the real problem is theirs, not the teacher's, should not suffice.

Moreover, to the extent that the reaction of the public is relevant, protest against the teacher must be balanced against possible protest in favor of the teacher, which is increasingly likely, the increased acceptance of homosexuality and the increased visibility of homosexuals generally, especially in communities with large homosexual populations.[296] When official action is being considered against a homosexual teacher, or a teacher involved in homosexual activity, the best check against possible bias is to ask whether a heterosexual teacher, or a teacher involved in heterosexual activity, would, in an essentially parallel situation, be subject to the same official action.[297] Under this test, homosexuals, like heterosexuals, would remain subject to discipline for making advances to students, for inciting students to illegal or immoral conduct, for disrupting classes or for neglecting their duties. They would not be subject to dismissal for their sexual preference, for their private sexual conduct, or for their public statements not impairing their professional performance.

Heterosexuality and Related Activity

The principal categories of heterosexual conduct and related matters involve cohabitation, unmarried pregnancy and childbearing, and adultery. Although many cases have dealt with alleged teacher misconduct with students, such cases, despite their heterosexual features, are better discussed later.[298]

Cohabitation

Relying in part on the modelling notion,[299] school officials have attempted to terminate teachers allegedly living (or staying overnight) with members of the opposite sex without the benefit of marriage. In *Y.N. v. School District No. 23, Lake County, Montana,*[300] the Supreme Court of Montana sustained nonrenewal of the contract of a tenured teacher for living with[301] a woman to whom he was not married.[302] Finding sufficient evidence that the living arrangement had become a matter of public knowledge, had negatively affected the moral formation of his students and had generated "numerous parental complaints,"[303] and noting the teacher's concession that the conduct adversely affected his classroom work, the court found the conclusion that the teacher lacked fitness to teach supported by the record.[304] In another case, the Court of Appeals for the Eighth Circuit avoided deciding whether a female teacher had a constitutional right to live unmarried with a male; since the school board had, in dismissing her, acted in good faith,[305] no monetary damages (the only issue remaining) were appropriate.[306] Of course, even if cohabitation or the like implicates the right to privacy, the teacher's privacy interest must be balanced against legitimate governmental interests.[307]

Other such cases have been more favorable to the teacher. One concluded that a preliminary injunction prohibiting the suspension or termination of the teacher should issue, due in part to the lack of evidence that the alleged immoral conduct—living with a man to whom she was not married—had adversely affected teaching performance.[308] Another case found even the implication of sexual misconduct from the fact that males stayed temporarily at a female teacher's home unjustified due to the disparity in age between the female teacher and the males, and the "openness of the association" involved.[309] Termination of the teacher in these circumstances was arbitrary and capricious, and violated the teacher's substantive due process rights.[310]

Cohabitation out of wedlock does not itself make a teacher unfit.[311] Especially in light of the reduced modelling role of teachers nowadays,[312] the increased acceptance of unwed cohabitation and our enhanced respect for the right of privacy, cohabitation should rarely justify the termination or credential revocation of a teacher. When such action against a teacher is undertaken, school officials must bear the burden of proving that the teacher cohabited, including, of course, the fact that sexual misconduct occurred, and that the cohabitation caused or is very likely to cause a direct and substantial impact on the smooth functioning of the school system. Such an impact, requiring more than a few complaints over a short period of time,[313] could be indicated, for example, by evidence that the teacher urged her lifestyle upon students[314] or ridiculed the traditional ban on extramarital sex. Finally, whatever policy is settled upon must be enforced without regard to gender.[315]

Unmarried Pregnancy or Childbearing

Pregnancy and childbearing yield a relatively long-term visibility of the implication of sexual activity and unsurprisingly, therefore, have been the basis of many teacher discipline cases.[316] The same school board concerns that might generate action against teachers cohabiting with members of the opposite sex outside of marriage, including role modelling,[317] loss of respect,[318] the implied condonation of misconduct possibly signaled through retention of the teacher,[319] and the conservation of marital values,[320] are obviously at work here too.

The most thorough and the soundest treatment of the unwed mother situation is that of the Fifth Circuit Court of Appeals in *A.N. v. Drew Municipal Separate School District.*[321] There, two unwed mothers sued under federal civil rights statutes to have declared unconstitutional an unwritten rule of the district making unwed parents ineligible for employment in instructional positions.[322] The court concluded that the rule yielded an irrational classification in violation of the equal protection clause. The school district urged three justifications for the rule: (1) unwed parenthood is *prima facie* proof of immorality; (2) unwed parents constitute inappropriate role models; and (3) unwed parents employed in a scholastic context aggravate the schoolgirl pregnancy problem. The first of these, besides violating equal protection, violates due process because it creates an irrebuttable presumption that present immorality necessarily flows from the fact of unwed parenthood.[323] The second rationale advanced by the district also fails, said the court. There was no evidence that the unwed mothers proselytized their students; indeed, since these mothers, along with their illegitimate children, lived with their parents and siblings, students would be hard-pressed even to know of the unwed status of the mothers. Even if the students discovered the fact of unwed parenthood, they were unlikely to infer that it was a desirable status, one to be emulated.[324] Finally, in response to the third rationale advanced by the district, the court found nothing but speculation to support the notion that the presence of unwed parents in the scholastic environment aggravates the problem of schoolgirl pregnancies.[325]

The decided cases do not justify an unqualified statement that school boards may never deny employment to teachers who are unwed parents, but it is clear that the courts will scrutinize such situations, and the school district may need a compelling state interest to countervail the teacher's rights.[326] In any event, sound public policy would rarely justify action against a teacher for unwed pregnancy or childbearing. Increased tolerance for such situations, the reduced modelling role of teachers nowadays, the unlikelihood of a significant impact on the school system and the likelihood of significant adverse community response to such action argue against it.

Adultery and Related Conduct

In cases of adultery or related conduct, the crucial issue again concerns impact on fitness. If a teacher's adulterous relationship or related activity causes absenteeism or other neglect of duty, the adverse impact on fitness to teach is obvious.[327] Even without such an obvious connection, however, an adverse impact might be found. In *P.E. v. State Board of Education*,[328] the California Supreme Court let stand a conclusion that a female teacher's joining a "swingers" club, engaging in acts of sexual intercourse and oral copulation with men other than her husband at club parties and appearing in disguise on television to discuss unconventional sexual behavior demonstrated unfitness to teach. Whether or not *P.E.* is correctly decided,[329] a relatively private adulterous relationship is insufficient in itself to establish one's unfitness to teach.[330] The wise school board (and court) will scrutinize such situations to ascertain, as a precondition to any action adverse to the teacher, the existence (or great likelihood) of a direct and substantial impact on the teacher's professional performance. The Supreme Court of Iowa did just that in overturning the revocation of a teaching certificate when there was no substantial evidence that the teacher's adultery, an isolated occurrence in an otherwise spotless record, adversely affected teaching fitness.[331]

Miscellaneous Situations

Other situations with sexual implications have gained the attention of school officials and the courts. Courts have upheld the dismissal of teachers for lewd and suggestive conduct in public (though on private property), involving a dress mannequin,[332] and for sexual misconduct with a stepchild.[333] One court upheld the nonrenewal of a nontenured teacher despite her allegations that the real reason for termination was the shortness of her dresses.[334] Finally, one teacher was dismissed for "just cause due to incapacity" following sex reassignment surgery. The Superior Court of New Jersey affirmed the dismissal,[335] but held her entitled to a pension due to her physical incapacitation.[336]

FACTORS SURROUNDING THE CONDUCT

In assessing whether alleged misconduct with sexual implications by teachers justifies adverse personnel action, the courts have discussed many contextual factors of the conduct, including the involvement of students, the publicness or notoriety of the conduct, parental or other complaints, the nature of the community, the criminal ramifications of the conduct, remoteness in time, duration, and the likelihood of repetition of the conduct, the need to balance the bad against the good, and remediability.

Involvement of Students

Adverse personnel action against a teacher for conduct with sexual implications is most likely to occur and be upheld when the conduct involves minor students.[337] In such cases, school boards and courts will likely consider the impact on fitness to be obvious[338] and any adverse personnel action substantively justified.[339] In *W.E. v. Board of Education of Jefferson County School District*,[340] a tenured high school teacher on a school field trip had engaged in "good-natured horseplay" with several female students. In addition to the "horseplay," which involved "touching and tickling the girls on various parts of their bodies and occasionally between the legs in proximity of the genital areas," there had been some "reciprocal" conduct by the girls and a dialogue between the teacher and the girls that was occasionally vulgar and suggestive.[341] For these and other reasons,[342] the school board dismissed the teacher. Upholding the dismissal, the Supreme Court of Colorado stated that "whenever a male teacher engages in sexually provocative or exploitive conduct with his minor female students a strong presumption of unfitness arises against the teacher."[343] The same court indulged the same presumption[344] in a later case in which the hearing panel had found that the teacher "hugged, touched or kissed five female students," sometimes in a "sexually charged setting."[345] The court again let stand the dismissal.[346]

Other cases have upheld against various objections discharges of male teachers for "inappropriate physical contact with young female students;"[347] for being in a parked car with a minor female, both teacher and student either naked or partially dressed;[348] for making advances to female students;[349] for proposing a spanking to female high school students;[350] for making sexually exploitive statements to female students during school hours;[351] for calling a 14-year-old female student a "slut" and implying in statements to her that she was a prostitute;[352] and for tolerating and tacitly encouraging "explicit and grotesque sexual harassment" of a female student by male students.[353]

Publicness or Notoriety

A factor often alluded to in the cases,[354] an overrated one at that, is the extent to which the public is aware of or has access to the conduct involved.[355] At times the suggestion is that notoriety is proof of adverse impact on fitness[356] or perhaps that public knowledge will, maybe inevitably, yield a negative impact on the school's operation[357] through impairment of the teacher's role model capacity;[358] other harm to the teacher's relationships within the school system;[359] or parental or other complaints to school officials.[360] School boards and courts in such cases should look beyond the fact of the notoriety, especially when the teacher tried to avoid[361] or at least did not cause the publicness or notoriety,[362] to see what real impact on the schools has occurred or is likely to occur.[363] Knowledge of the matter by parents and students does not in itself adversely influence the teacher's effectiveness, at least unless accompanied by a "hostile atmosphere" or the like, undermining the teacher's classroom authority.[364] Perhaps widespread knowledge among the students will cause the most damaging or long-lived impact. Here as well, however, a substantial impact that has in fact occurred or is imminent should be the only basis for removal or revocation of credentials. Teachers should not lose their livelihoods on the basis of whispering in the halls.

Moreover, even if publicness or notoriety is relevant, it should be discounted by the extent to which it was caused by school officials.[365] Such officials should not be allowed to create the notoriety by filing and processing the charge and then rely on that same notoriety to establish the unfitness needed to discharge or revoke the credentials of a teacher.[366] As one court said: "It would seem to be unfair that . . . the board should seek to publicize the conduct . . . through its actions and thus conclude that [the teacher] is unfit based upon its speculation of unfavorable community reaction. . . ."[367]

Parental or Other Complaints

Related to publicness and notoriety, and subject also to being over-emphasized, is the extent to which school officials have received complaints about a teacher's alleged misconduct. To be sure, courts often allude to this factor,[368] the suggestion perhaps being that the presence of complaints demonstrates the impact of the misconduct on the teacher's professional performance and the absence the opposite, or, more narrowly, that the number and intensity of any complaints reflect the extent to which the teacher's relationships with students, parents or other teachers have been injured. But surely, even several parental complaints do not significantly impede the operation of the school or the performance of the teacher.[369] Indeed, the presence of complaints may suggest that the school board's action against the teacher was intended to placate those complaining rather than to remove a real threat to the schools. School boards and courts should require a direct and substantial impact before depriving a teacher of a livelihood. As one court noted, "The mere fact that some parents may have an adverse attitude towards [the teacher] is not sufficient evidence . . . to demonstrate that an attitude would prevail *in the classroom* that would undermine the learning environment."[370] Conversely, the absence of complaints does not always tell much about the impact of the teacher's conduct on performance. In any event, to the extent that complaints against the teacher are considered, any protestation in favor of the teacher, or other community support, real or likely, should also be put into the balance.[371]

The Nature of the Community

The nature of the community, including its size and whether it is rural or urban, has also gotten attention from school officials or courts.[372] Here, the suggestion has been either that the notoriety of the situation would travel better in a small or rural community[373] or that people in such communities would be more affected by — if not less tolerant of — the conduct complained of.[374]

Criminal Ramifications

The substantive implications of any criminal aspects of the alleged misconduct deserve mention. In some jurisdictions, conviction of certain sexual offenses has carried automatic dismissal or credential revocation.[375] This is an undesirable approach, however.[376] A teacher, before his service is terminated or his credentials revoked, surely deserves a hearing on his current fitness which takes into account the full picture. No more defensible is the suggestion that if the conduct alleged in the dismissal or credential revocation proceedings is of a criminal nature, unfitness is thereby established,[377] whether or not the teacher has been convicted. A third possibility is to consider that the criminal conviction or, in the absence of a conviction, the criminal nature of the conduct is one factor to be considered in assessing whether, under the applicable standard, the teacher is fit.[378] After all, the criminal prosecution might have created such notoriety as to have significantly undermined the professional performance of the teacher[379] or the commission of conduct defined as a crime may reflect disrespect for the law, a factor perhaps to be considered in the fitness formula.[380] To be sure, conduct that is not criminal may still indicate unfitness to teach.[381]

Remoteness in Time, Duration and Likelihood of Repetition

In assessing a teacher's fitness for service, school officials and courts look to the time elapsed since the alleged misconduct.[382] Presumably, the more time passing since the delict, the more irrelevant the conduct to an assessment of current fitness.[383] Further, school boards should not be allowed "to dredge up indiscretions from years past to dismiss a teacher."[384]

The persistence of the alleged misconduct is also relevant.[385] Obviously, all other things being equal, an isolated piece of misconduct gives less concern than a pattern or practice.

The likelihood of repetition of the alleged misconduct, a factor related to its persistence,[386] also counts.[387] With regard to this point, courts may heavily rely on the expert testimony of psychologists and psychiatrists.[388] An unlikelihood of repetition is, of course, not dispositive, especially if the board or court feels that the real threat to the school is not repetition but the teacher's damaged relations with students or others, or the inability to provide good example and moral guidance.[389]

Balancing the Good Against the Bad

School boards and courts must, in evaluating fitness, take into account not only the alleged misconduct but also the entire service of the teacher.[390]

Surely an isolated indiscretion means less in the context of an otherwise impeccable life and a long career of fine service.[391] To be sure, neither good nor bad is easily quantifiable for such offsetting; nonetheless an effort must be made, especially in light of the fact that a current controversy can direct an undue emphasis upon the alleged misconduct. As part of this balancing, of course, decisionmakers should look to any extenuating circumstances, including any praiseworthiness (or at least lack of blame-worthiness) of the motives prompting the alleged misconduct.[392] Remorse should also be considered.[393]

Remediability

In some jurisdictions, including Illinois and Minnesota, immediate discharge on certain grounds, even with a hearing, is proper only if the conduct is not remediable.[394] If the conduct is remediable, the teacher must be given an opportunity to correct the problem prior to any discharge. A dismissal cause is irremediable when there is harm[395] to the students, faculty or the school and the conduct could not have been corrected through the warnings of superiors.[396] In Minnesota, at least, the remediability concept includes an examination of the teacher's entire record[397] and allows discharge for a single incident only when it is "so outrageous that it cannot be remedied in light of the danger the teacher's presence in the classroom would present."[398]

PROCEDURES

A full treatment of the procedures appropriate to a teacher dismissal or credential revocation is beyond the scope of this volume. An outline, however, with special mention of points particularly relevant to our subject, is desirable.[399]

Prohibitions in statutes, regulations and other rules should be as specific as their subject matter permits and should be promulgated to all personnel subject to them. When suspicion of transgressions justifying dismissal or credential revocation arises, the appropriate person or board should order an investigation by a person or panel who will not be directly involved in any ultimate decisionmaking.[400] In emergency situations, for example, when the charges involve assaultive conduct against students, barring the teacher from all school activities pending more formal procedures may be appropriate.[401] The teacher should be given specific written notice of the misconduct charged[402] and of the prohibition allegedly violated,[403] and the right to a timely pretermination[404] or prerevocation hearing[405] before an impartial tribunal.[406] The scheduling of the hearing should allow enough time for the teacher to employ counsel and prepare a defense.

At the hearing, school officials have the burden of proof. The teacher should be allowed to have counsel present, cross-examine adverse witnesses,[407] examine documents, and present witnesses and documents in defense. The school system should do all in its power[408] to secure the attendance of witnesses[409] for each side and to prevent adverse publicity which could prejudice the case.[410] The hearing should be recorded and should result in written findings of fact and conclusions.[411] Administrative and judicial appeal should be provided for. If one of the reasons for dismissal or credential revocation is unconstitutional, the personnel action might still stand if the same result would have been reached on other grounds.[412] The teacher's pay should continue until any final negative resolution of the case.[413]

The situation is more complicated if criminal proceedings based on the same conduct are ongoing or threatened. The fact of criminal proceedings in connection with the alleged misconduct does not bar civil proceedings for dismissal or credential revocation. Moreover, dismissal or revocation proceedings need not await termination of the criminal proceedings.[414] In some cases, however, a school board may wish to put off its hearing for a reasonable time pending completion of the criminal process,[415] perhaps, in emergency situations, suspending the teacher,[416] with pay, from classroom activities in the interim.[417] A conviction should be admissible at the civil proceeding to establish the facts inevitably required for that conviction, sparing school officials the relitigation of that part of the case.[418] As indicated earlier, however, current fitness is a larger issue and should be independently resolved at the hearing.

In part because different burdens of proof apply to criminal and civil processes, the civil proceedings may go forward even if the teacher was acquitted at the trial.[419] The criminal acquittal means only that the factfinder had at least a reasonable doubt; a reasonable person might still find the evidence sufficient in a civil procedure to establish the misconduct.[420] Again because of the different burdens of proof, the fact of acquittal may not be admissible at the civil hearing, unless the criminal charge was referred to in connection with that hearing.[421] Finally, evidence held inadmissible at the criminal trial—for example, under the exclusionary rule—may nonetheless be admissible at the civil hearing.[422]

It should be emphasized that dismissal or credential revocation should be considered devices of last resort, to be used only when absolutely crucial to the well-being of the school system. Accordingly, even while a dismissal or credential revocation hearing is in progress, school officials should pursue any hope of a less drastic resolution.[423]

CONCLUSION

For generations, we have expected teachers to serve as models of morality to their students. Today, that modeling role is much less justified. Although state proscriptions related to teacher misconduct have been construed to require a nexus between the alleged misconduct and fitness to teach, in practice that nexus has been trivialized. Adverse official action against teachers, whatever their sexual preference, because of sexual conduct or related matters should require proof of significant harm to school interests or of the real likelihood of such harm. Carefully-written procedures, carefully adhered to, are necessary to protect both the rights of teachers and the interests of school districts.

NOTES

1. South Bend Tribune, Dec. 22, 1982, at 28, col. 1.
2. *Id.*
3. *Id.* at cols. 1 and 2.
4. *Id.* at col. 2.
5. *Id.,* Jan. 19, 1983, at 2, col. 1. See also Chicago Tribune, Oct. 24, 1982, sec. 3, p. 1, cols. 1 and 2.
6. See also New Mexico State Board of Education v. S.T., 571 P.2d 1186, 1188 (N.M. 1977), where 208 persons signed a petition requesting the reinstatement of a teacher dismissed for her unwed pregnancy.
7. See Board of Education of Alamo-Gordo Public School District No. 1 v. J.N., 651 P.2d 1037, 1042 (N.M. App. 1982), where the court found not unreasonable, "in this day and age," a State Board's conclusion that a private adulterous affair did not constitute "good and just cause" to fire an assistant principal.
8. See, *e.g.,* Adler v. Board of Education, 342 U.S. 485, 493 (1952); F.I. v. Snyder, 476 F.2d 375, 377 (8th Cir. 1973); J.E. v. Board of Education, 294 F.2d 260, 261 (U.S. App. D.C. 1961).
9. See Chapter 1, *supra.*
10. Governing Board of Mountain View School District of Los Angeles County v. M.T.; P.E. v. State Board of Education, 10 Cal.3d 29, 42, 109 Cal.Rptr. 665, 674,

513 P.2d 889, 898 (1973); 36 Cal. App.3d 546, 550, 111 Cal.Rptr. 724, 727 (1974) (quoting CAL. EDUC. CODE § 13556.5).

Until as recently as 1982, Florida law provided that teachers "must embrace every opportunity to inculcate, by precept and example, the principle of truth, honesty and patriotism and the practice of every Christian virtue." FLA. STAT. ANN. § 231.09(2) (West 1977) [rewritten by Laws 1982, c.82-242, § 8]. See also R.I. GEN. LAWS § 16-12-3 (1981): "Every teacher shall aim to implant and cultivate in the minds of all children committed to his care the principles of morality and virtue." See also VA. CODE § 22.1-208 (1980).

11. Penn-Delco School District v. U.R., 382 A.2d 162, 168 (Comm. Ct. Pa. 1978).

12. See B.O. v. Board of School Directors of Indiana Area School District, 377 A.2d 1284, 1288 (Comm.Ct. Pa. 1977) (citing Horosko v. Mount Pleasant Township School District, 335 Pa. 369, 372, 6 A.2d 866, 868 (1939)).

13. See Penn-Delco School District v. U.R., 382 A.2d at 168; Governing Board of Mountain View School District of Los Angeles County v. M.T., 36 Cal.App. 3d. at 550, 111 Cal.Rptr. at 727. "The best type of instruction is by personal example." *Id.* See W.I. v. McDonald, 500 F.2d 1110, 1115 (1st Cir. 1974). See expert testimony summarized in S.U. v. Meade Independent School District, 530 F.2d 799, 804 (8th Cir. 1976) ("[T]eachers teach by example as well as by lecture"); in T.H. v. Southwest School District, 483 F.Supp. 1170, 1176 (W.D. Mo. 1980) (e.g., "[W]hat one *is* is as important as what one knows") (emphasis in original); and in W.E. v. Board of Education of Jefferson County School District No. R-1, 547 P.2d 1267, 1273, n.1 (S.Ct. Colo. 1976). The teacher may be seen as *in loco parentis,* the surrogate parent to whom the child looks for both explicit guidance and moral example. M.S. v. State Board of Education, 1 Cal.3d 214, 247, 82 Cal.Rptr. 175, 200 (1969).

The student's tendency to emulate may increase with with his affection for the particular teacher. S.U. v. Meade Independent School District No. 101, 530 F.2d at 804.

14. W.E. v. Board of Education of Jefferson County School District No. R-1, 190 Colo. 414, 421, 547 P.2d 1267, 1273, n.1 (S.Ct. Colo. 1976).

15. G.I. v. Board of Education of Borough of Paramus, Bergen County, 145 N.J. Super. 96, 105, 366 A.2d 1337, 1342 (1976). *Cf.* Board of Education of Long Beach Unified School District of Los Angeles County v. M.I., 62 Cal. App.3d at 614, 133 Cal.Rptr. 275, 278 (1976), *opinion vacated,* 19 Cal.3d at 691, 139 Cal.Rptr. 700, 566 P.2d 602 (1977); R.O. v. Springfield School District No. 19, 657 P.2d 188, 193 (Oregon, 1982).

16. "No one seriously suggests that a teacher's classroom conduct be the sole basis for determining his fitness." G.O. v. Board of Education of Central School District No. 1, Towns of Brookhaven and Smithtown, 35 N.Y.2d 534, 543, 364 N.Y.S.2d 440, 446 (N.Y. App. 1974) (citing Beilan v. Board of Education, 357 U.S. 399 (1958)). See also E.R. v. Iowa State Board of Public Instruction, 216 N.W.2d 339, 343 (S.Ct. Iowa 1974).

17. *Cf.* G.A. v. Tacoma School District No. 10, 88 Wash.2d 186, 559 P.2d 1340, 1347 (1977).

18. Clay, *The Dismissal of Public Schoolteachers for Aberrant Behavior,* 64 KENTUCKY L.J. 911, 911–912 (1976).

19. 416 F.Supp. 1194 (D.Neb. 1976), *rev'd on procedural grounds,* 566 F.2d 588 (8th Cir. 1977).

20. *Id.* at 1198.
21. 566 F.2d 588 (8th Cir. 1977).
22. Board of Education of Long Beach Unified School District of Los Angeles County v. M.I., 139 Cal.Rptr.700, 704, 566 P.2d 602, 606, n.4 (1977).
23. *Id.*
24. *Id.*
25. See T.O. v. Dade County School Board, 318 So.2d 159, 160 (Fla. App. 1975). See also M.S. v. State Board of Education, 1 Cal.3d at 222, 82 Cal.Rptr. at 181, 461 P.2d at 380–381, n.12.
26. Winks, *Legal Implications of Sexual Contact Between Teacher and Student,* 11 J. LAW. & EDUC. 437, 452 (1982).
27. See, *e.g.,* K.I. v. Wright, 437 F.Supp. 397, 398–399 (M.D. Ala. 1977); Y.N. v. School District No. 23, Lake County, Montana, 641 P.2d 431, 440 (Mont. 1982); G.I. v. Board of Education of Borough of Paramus, Bergen County, 145 N.J. Super. at 105, 366 A.2d at 1342.
28. Adler v. Board of Education, 342 U.S. 485, 493 (1952). *Cf.* K.I. v. Wright, 437 F.Supp. at 398 ("Teachers occupy a singularly important position in society.") The recital of one jurist, however, is perhaps extravagant:

     > [T]he teacher is intrusted with the custody of children and their high preparation for useful life. His habits, his speech, his good name, his cleanliness, the wisdom and propriety of his unofficial utterances, his associations, all are involved. His ability to inspire children and to govern them, his power as a teacher, and the character for which he stands are matters of major concern in a teacher's selection and retention.

     Goldsmith v. Board of Education, 66 Cal.App. 157, 168, 225 P. 783, 787 (1924); See D.R. v. Covington County Board of Education, 371 F.Supp. 974, 983 (M.D. Ala. 1974) (dissenting opinion).
29. See A.N. v. Drew Municipal Separate School District, 507 F.2d 611, 614 (5th Cir. 1975).

     Many states now specifically prohibit employment discrimination on the ground of marital status. See, *e.g.,* CONN. GEN. STAT. ANN. § 10-153 (West Supp. 1985); IND. CODE ANN. § 20-6.1-6.11 (Burns 1978); and MASS. ANN. LAWS ch. 71, § 42 (Mich. Law. Co-op 1978).
30. H. HUDGINS & R. VACCA, LAW AND EDUCATION: CONTEMPORARY ISSUES AND COURT DECISIONS 186 (1979).
31. G.A. v. Tacoma School District No. 10, 559 P.2d at 1350 (citing H. BEALE, A HISTORY OF FREEDOM OF TEACHING IN AMERICAN SCHOOLS (1966 ed.) and F. DELON, SUBSTANTIVE LEGAL ASPECTS OF TEACHING DISCIPLINE (1972)).
32. Fleming, *Teacher Dismissal for Cause: Public and Private Morality,* 7 J. LAW AND EDUCATION 423 (1978).
33. See *id.* at 425 (citing Davis, *Teacher Dismissals on Grounds of Immorality,* 46 CLEARINGHOUSE 418 (1972)). Presumably there is, besides those reflected in the many court actions involving sexual activity, a large number of unchallenged dismissals, voluntary resignations and, for less serious infractions, less drastic disciplinary results. Fleming, *supra* note 32, at 430.
34. Clay, *supra* note 18, at 931. See also M.S. v. State Board of Education, 1 Cal.3d at 239, 82 Cal.Rptr. at 194, 461 P.2d at 394.
35. *Cf.* A.N. v. Drew Municipal Separate School District, 371 F.Supp. 27, 35 (N.D. Miss. 1973), *aff'd,* 507 F.2d 611 (5th Cir. 1975): "We are not at all persuaded

by . . . suggestions, quite implausible in our view, that students are apt to seek out knowledge of the personal and private family life-styles of teachers or other adults within a school system. . . . "

36. See USA Today, Dec. 26, 1984, at ID, col. 5, reporting on a survey in which only 1 percent of teachers and 19 percent of the public regard teaching as a "high-prestige occupation" (citing PHI DELTA KAPPA, January, 1985).

37. P.E. v. State Board of Education, 10 Cal.3d at 44, 109 Cal.Rptr. at 675, 513 P.2d at 899–900 (dissenting opinion).

38. See K.I. v. Wright, 437 F.Supp. at 399–400.

39. See, *e.g.*, J.E. v. Board of Education of District of Columbia, 294 F.2d at 261; T.H. v. Southwest School District, 483 F.Supp. at 1178 (citing MO. REV. STAT. §168.114 1(2); S.E. v. Capital School District, 425 F.Supp. 552, 556 (D.Del. 1976), *aff'd*, 565 F.2d 153 (3rd Cir. 1977); B.U. v. Cascade School District Union High School No. 5, 353 F.Supp. 254, 255 (D. Oregon 1973), *aff'd on different grounds*, 512 F.2d 850 (9th Cir. 1975); Board of Education of Long Beach Unified School District of Los Angeles County v. M.I., 19 Cal.3d at 694, 139 Cal.Rptr. at 701, 566 P.2d at 603; P.E. v. State Board of Education, 10 Cal. 3d at 31, 109 Cal.Rptr. at 666, 513 P.2d at 890 ("moral turpitude"); M.S. v. State Board of Education, 1 Cal.3d at 217, 82 Cal.Rptr. at 177, 461 P.2d at 377 ("immoral and unprofessional conduct and acts involving moral turpitude"); R.I. v. Davis, 627 P.2d 1111, 1114, n.1 (S.Ct. Colo. 1981) (citing COLO. REV. STAT. § 22-63-116 (1973)); W.E. v. Board of Education of Jefferson County School District No. R-1, 190 Colo. at 419, 547 P.2d at 1271; R.S. v. Board of Education of School District No. 1, Denver Public Schools, 677 P.2d 348, 349 (Colo. App.1983); E.R. v. Iowa State Board of Public Instruction, 216 N.W.2d at 341 ("moral turpitude"); R.R. v. Robb, 662 S.W.2d 257, 258 (S.Ct. Mo. 1983); Y.N. v. School District No. 23, Lake County Montana, 641 P.2d at 434 (allegation of "a lack of moral values"); R.O. v. Springfield School District No. 19, 657 P.2d at 189; Penn-Delco School District v. U.R., 382 A.2d at 164; B.O. v. Board of School Directors of Indiana Area School District, 377 A.2d at 1287; G.A. v. Tacoma School District No. 10, 559 P.2d at 1341.

Less vague is a provision allowing dismissal of a tenured teacher *convicted of a crime* "involving moral turpitude." See T.H. v. Southwest School District, 483 F.Supp. at 1178 (citing MO. REV. STAT. §168.114 1(6)). "Moral turpitude" itself may be a redundancy. See *M.S.* v. State Board of Education, 1 Cal.3d at 220, 82 Cal. Rptr. at 179, 461 P.2d at 379, n.9 (quoting Jordan v. DeGeorge, 341 U.S. 223, 234 (1951) (dissenting opinion)).

40. See, *e.g.*, W.I. v. McDonald, 500 F.2d 1110, 1111 (1st Cir. 1974); F.I. v. Snyder, 476 F.2d at 376; C.R. v. Board of Education, City of Chicago, 46 Ill. App. 33, 35, 360 N.E.2d 536, 538 (1977).

See, *e.g.*, N.J. STAT ANN. § 18A:28-5 (West, 1968; West Supp. 1985).

41. See, *e.g.*, Board of Education of Long Beach Unified School District of Los Angeles County v. M.I., 19 Cal.3d at 692, 139 Cal.Rptr. at 701, 566 P.2d at 603; Y.N. v. School District No. 23, Lake County, Montana, 641 P.2d at 434 (The school board there also alleged "a lack of moral values." *Id.*).

42. S.U. v. Meade Independent School District No. 101, 530 F.2d 799 (8th Cir. 1976).

43. See, *e.g.*, R.I. v. Davis, 627 P.2d at 1114. The court in R.I. affirmed the teacher's

dismissal on immorality grounds, and thus did not have to pass on whether the phrase "other good and just cause" was unconstitutionally vague. *Id.* at 1121; W.E. v. Board of Education of Jefferson County School District No. R-1, 190 Colo. at 419, 547 P.2d at 1271; New Mexico State Board of Education v. S.T., 571 P.2d at 1188.

See, *e.g.,* N.J. STAT. ANN. § 18A:28-5 (West, 1968; West. Supp. 1985); WIS. STAT. ANN. § 118.23(3) (West 1973).

See also D.E. v. South Kitsap School District No. 402, 516 P.2d 1080, 1081 (Wash. App. 1973) ("sufficient cause"); ILL. ANN. STAT. ch. 122, ¶ 10-22.4 (West Supp. 1984–85) ("other sufficient cause").

44. See M.S. v. State Board of Education, 1 Cal.3d at 220, 82 Cal.Rptr. at 179, 461 P.2d at 378–79, n.9.

45. "Terms such as 'immoral or unprofessional conduct' or 'moral turpitude' stretch over so wide a range that they embrace an unlimited area of conduct." M.S. v. State Board of Education, *id.* at 224, 82 Cal.Rptr. at 182, 461 P.2d at 382.

The Court of Appeals for the D.C. Circuit has noted that "a pronouncement of 'immorality' tends to discourage careful analysis because it unavoidably connotes a violation of divine, Olympian, or otherwise universal standards of rectitude." Norton v. Macy, 417 F.2d 1161, 1165 (D.C.Cir. 1961) (quoted in M.S. v. State Board of Education, 1 Cal.3d at 220, 82 Cal.Rptr. at 179, 461 P.2d at 379, n.9).

46. New Mexico State Board of Education v. S.T., 571 P.2d at 1189.

47. Winks, *supra* note 26, at 451. See also Clay, *supra* note 18, at 931 ("There is no uniformly consistent view of morality in America today.").

48. R.O. v. Springfield School District No. 19, 56 Or.App. 197, 204, 641 P.2d 600, 605 (1982), *rev'd,* 294 Or. at 357, 657 P.2d at 188.

49. W.I. v. McDonald, 500 F.2d at 1110.

50. T.H. v. Southwest School District, 483 F.Supp. at 1178; M.S. v. State Board of Education, 1 Cal.3d at 231, 82 Cal.Rptr. at 187, 461 P.2d at 387, n.30.

See M.R. v. Board of Education of Chidester School District No. 59, 448 F.2d 709, 713 (8th Cir. 1971). ("[W]e find it difficult to recognize the validity of the moral standards used to evaluate . . . because the board, prior to integration, had never established and announced that it would use such subjective standards in determining whether to employ or dismiss teachers"); *Cf.* Y.N. v. School District No. 23, Lake County, Montana, 641 P.2d at 448 (dissenting opinion) ("[T]he Court is countenancing a 'witch hunt' in this case"); See *id.* at 713.

51. M.S. v. State Board of Education, 1 Cal.3d at 225, 82 Cal.Rptr. at 175, 461 P.2d at 383.

52. See Clay, *supra* note 18, at 930.

53. P.E. v. State Board of Education, 10 Cal.3d at 39, 109 Cal.Rptr. at 672, 513 P.2d at 896 (dissenting opinion). The jurist noted that 95% of males and a large percentage of females have had orgasms in illegal ways and that perhaps up to 80% of women of the plaintiff's age and education engage in oral sex. *Id.* at 40, 109 Cal.Rptr. at 673, 513 P.2d at 897 (citations omitted). See also *id.* at 43, 109 Cal.Rptr. at 675, 513 P.2d at 899, n.7. *Cf.* M.S. v. State Board of Education, 1 Cal.3d at 225, 82 Cal.Rptr. at 183, 461 P.2d at 383, n. 15.

54. T.O. v. Dade County School Board, 318 So.2d at 160.

55. But see *Report of the Subcommittee on Personnel Problems of the Assembly Interim*

Committee on Education, 2 JOURNAL OF THE [CALIFORNIA] ASSEMBLY 26 (Appendix 1965): "No cases were brought to the committee's attention which clearly required the use of an undefined category such as 'unprofessional conduct'." (Quoted in M.S. v. State Board of Education, 1 Cal.3d at 221, 82 Cal.Rptr. at 179, 461 P.2d at 379, n.9).

56. Colten v. Kentucky, 407 U.S. 104, 110 (1972), quoted in W.E. v. Board of Education of Jefferson County School District. No. R-1, 190 Colo. at 423, 547 P.2d at 1274.

57. Whisenhunt v. Spradlin, 104 S.Ct. 404, 407 (1983) (Brennan, J., dissenting from denial of certiorari in police officer discipline case.).

58. T.H. v. Southwest School District, 483 F.Supp. at 1179; B.O. v. Board of School Directors of Indiana Area School District, 377 A.2d at 1288.

59. T.H. v. Southwest School District, 483 F.Supp. at 1179. In *T.H.,* the court stated that since the statute providing for termination for "immoral conduct" of teachers on indefinite contract was penal in nature, it should be assessed by vagueness standards applicable to criminal and First Amendment areas rather than those applying to statutes controlling economic or commercial conduct. *Id.*

60. *Cf.* Shawgo v. Spradlin, 701 F.2d 470, 478 (1983), *cert. denied,* 104 S.Ct. 404 (1983).

61. A lack of notice claim may be nullified if the teacher was specifically warned that his conduct, unless changed, would lead to dismissal. S.U. v. Meade, 530 F.2d at 808, n.12. Of course, persistent failure to obey specific orders may bring the teacher within some other prohibition, *e.g.,* one against insubordination. *Cf.* W.I. v. McDonald, 500 F.2d at 1116.

62. M.S. v. State Board of Education, 1 Cal.3d at 231, 82 Cal.Rptr. at 187–188, 461 P.2d at 387.

63. In W.E. v. Board of Education of Jefferson County School District No. R-1, 190 Colo. at 424, 547 P.2d at 1275, the Supreme Court of Colorado observed:

> Appellant may in good faith have considered his conduct on the Santa Fe [school] trip entirely moral. But statutes cannot be drawn from the point of view of the idiosyncratic few. Most persons of ordinary intelligence would have noticed, even from the broad wording of [our statute], that certain acts are prohibited, including *inter alia* the intimate touching of minor female students by a male high school teacher. And, as Mr. Justice Holmes noted in *Nash v. United States,* 229 U.S. 373, 377 (1913), "the law is full of instances where a man's fate depends on his estimating rightly ... some matter of degree."

See T.O. v. Dade County School Board, 318 So.2d at 160. *Cf.* Shawgo v. Spradlin, 701 F.2d at 478, *cert. denied,* 104 S.Ct. 404 (1983): "The actual conduct for which he [a police officer] was punished—dating and spending the night with a co-employee—is not self-evidently within the ambit of the regulations and thus does not carry with it its own warning of wrong-doing, as does illegal conduct. . . . "

64. See W.I. v. McDonald, 500 F.2d at 1110, where the Sixth Circuit found "conduct unbecoming a teacher" not unconstitutionally vague as it applies to a teacher dismissed for having carried, "in public view on his property located in the town where he taught, in a lewd and suggestive manner, a dress mannequin that he had dressed, undressed and caressed." *Id.* at 1111, 1116; K.I. v. Wright, 437 F.Supp. at 399.

65. Arnett v. Kennedy, 416 U.S. 134 (1974).

66. W.I. v. McDonald, 500 F.2d at 1116.

67. *Id.* The manual in *Arnett* included the following: "Basically a 'cause' for disciplinary action is a recognizable offense against the employer-employee relationship. Cause for adverse action runs the gamut of offenses against the employer-employee relationship, including inadequate performance of duties and improper conduct on or off the job." Arnett v. Kennedy, 416 U.S. at 160, quoted in W.I. v. McDonald, 500 F.2d at 1116.

68. 500 F.2d at 1116.

69. Kolender v. Lawson, 103 S.Ct. 1855, 1858 and n.7 (1983); Parker v. Levy, 417 U.S. 733, 756 (1974); Arnett v. Kennedy, 416 U.S. 134, 159 (1974); Smith v. Goguen, 415 U.S. 566, 573, n.10 (1974); Winters v. New York, 333 U.S. 507, 515 (1948); Shawgo v. Spradlin, 701 F.2d at 477–478, 479; S.U. v. Meade Independent School District No. 101, 530 F.2d at 808, n.12; T.H. v. Southwest School District, 483 F.Supp. at 1179; R.R. v. Robb, 662 S.W.2d at 259. See W.I. v. McDonald, 500 F.2d at 1116, n.7; W.E. v. Board of Education of Jefferson County School District No. R-1, 190 Colo. at 420–421, 547 P.2d at 1272.

70. Whisenhunt v. Spradlin, 104 S.Ct at 408 (Brennan, J., dissenting from denial of certiorari) (citing Village of Hoffman Estates v. Flipside, 455 U.S. 489, 497–505 (1982); Joseph E. Seagram & Sons, Inc. v. Hostetler, 384 U.S. 35, 48–49 (1966); Barsky v. Board of Regents, 347 U.S. 442, 443, 448 (1954); Neblett v. Carpenter, 305 U.S. 297, 302–303 (1938)).

71. T.H. v. Southwest School District, 483 F.Supp. at 1179.

72. See *id.;* B.O. v. Board of School Directors of Indiana Area School District, 377 A.2d at 1288. *Cf.* National Gay Task Force v. Board of Education of City of Oklahoma City, 729 F.2d 1270 (10th Cir. 1984), *aff'd by evenly divided court,* 105 S.Ct. 1161 (1985).

73. W.E. v. Board of Education of Jefferson County School District No. R-1, 190 Colo. at 420, 547 P.2d at 1272.

74. See generally Members of City Council of City of Los Angeles v. Taxpayers for Vincent, 104 S.Ct. 2118, 2125–2127 (1984).

75. K.I. v. Wright, 437 F.Supp. at 400 (citing Grayned v. City of Rockford, 408 U.S. 104, 114–121 (1972); and Zwickler v. Koota, 389 U.S. 241, 249–250 (1967)).

76. K.I. v. Wright, 437 F.Supp. at 400, 401 (citing Broadrick v. Oklahoma, 413 U.S. 601, 610, 615 (1973)).

77. 437 F.Supp. 397 (M.D. Ala. 1977).

78. See National Gay Task Force v. Board of Education of City of Oklahoma City, 729 F.2d at 1273–1274: "[F]acial challenges based on First Amendment overbreadth are 'strong medicine' and should be used 'sparingly and only as a last resort.' " (Citing Broadrick v. Oklahoma, 413 U.S. 601, 613 (1973)).

79. *Id.* at 400–401 (citing Broadrick v. Oklahoma, 413 U.S. at 615).

80. *Id.* at 401 (citing Broadrick v. Oklahoma, 413 U.S. 601 (1973); Hobbs v. Thompson, 448 F.2d 456 (5th Cir. 1971); 437 F.Supp. at 401 (citing Broadrick v. Oklahoma, 413 U.S. 601 (1973); and D.R. v. Covington County Board of Education, 371 F.Supp. 974 (M.D. Ala. 1974)). See also National Gay Task Force v. Board of Education of City of Oklahoma City, 729 F.2d 1270 (10th Cir. 1984), *aff'd by an evenly divided court,* 105 S.Ct. 1161 (1985), holding unconstitutionally overbroad a statute authorizing punishment for "public homosexual conduct," defined as "advocating, soliciting, imposing, encouraging or promoting public or private homosexual activity in a manner that creates a substantial risk that such conduct will come to the attention of school children or school employees."

81. The statutes of thirty-four states list immorality as cause for dismissal. S. GOLDSTEIN and E. GEE, LAW AND PUBLIC EDUCATION: CASES AND MATERIALS 586 (2d ed. 1980).

    For statutes listing immorality as grounds for dismissal of teachers or for denial or revocation of their credentials, see *e.g.*, CAL. EDUC. CODE § 44434 (West 1978); *id* § 44932(1) (West Supp. 1985); FLA. STAT. ANN. § 231.36(4)(c) (West Supp. 1985); ILL ANN. STAT. ch. 122, ¶ 10-22.4 (Smith-Hurd Supp. 1984–85); OKLA. STAT. ANN. tit. 70, § 6-103(A) (West Supp. 1984–85); TEX. EDUC. CODE ANN. § 13.109(1) (Vernon 1972); *id.* § 13.110 (Vernon Supp. 1985); and WIS. STAT. ANN. §§ 118.23(3) and 118.19(5) (West 1973).

82. See, *e.g.*, B.U. v. Cascade School District Union High School No. 5, 512 F.2d 850 (9th Cir. 1975); K.I. v. Wright, 437 F.Supp. 397 (M.D. Ala. 1977); M.S. v. State Board of Education, 1 Cal.3d 214, 82 Cal.Rptr. 175, 461 P.2d 375 (S.Ct. Cal. 1969); W.E. v. Board of Education of Jefferson County School District No. R-1, 547 P.2d 1267 (S.Ct. Colo. 1976); and G.A. v. Tacoma School District, 88 Wash.2d 286, 559 P.2d 1340 (S.Ct.Wash. 1977).

83. P.E. v. State Board of Education, 10 Cal.3d at 43, 109 Cal.Rptr. at 675, 513 P.2d at 899.

84. M.S. v. State Board of Education, 1 Cal.3d at 225, 82 Cal.Rptr. at 183, 461 P.2d at 383 (citing Note, *Private Consensual Adult Behavior: the Requirement of Harm to Others in the Enforcement of Morality*, 14 U.C.L.A. L.REV. 581, 582 (1967)). See also B.U. v. Cascade School District Union High School No. 5, 353 F.Supp. at 255.

85. See M.S. v. State Board of Education, 1 Cal.3d at 227, 82 Cal.Rptr. at 184, 461 P.2d at 383–384, n.9 (quoting Note, *supra* note 84, at 582).

86. G.A. v. Tacoma School District No. 10, 559 P.2d at 1343 (citation omitted).

87. E.R. v. Iowa State Board of Public Instruction, 216 N.W.2d at 343–344. See M.S. v. State Board of Education, 1 Cal.3d at 222, 82 Cal.Rptr. at 180, 461 P.2d at 380–381 (quoting Yankow v. Board of [Medical] Examiners, 68 Cal.2d 67, 73, 64 Cal.Rptr. 785, 790, 435 P.2d 553, 558, n.6 (1968)).

88. K.I. v. Wright, 437 F.Supp. at 399.

89. 1 Cal.3d 214, 82 Cal.Rptr. 175, 461 P.2d 375 (1969).

90. These and subsequent facts are taken from M.S. v. State Board of Education, 1 Cal.3d at 217–220, 82 Cal.Rptr. at 176–179, 461 P.2d at 376–379.

91. *Id.* at 218–219, 82 Cal.Rptr. at 177–178, 461 P.2d at 377–378.

92. See *id.* at 218, 82 Cal.Rptr. at 177, 461 P.2d at 377, n. 4. Conviction of these or other crimes would have called for mandatory revocation of all diplomas and life certificates. See *id.*

93. See CAL. EDUC. CODE §§ 13202, 13129(e).

94. M.S. v. State Board of Education, 1 Cal.3d at 225, 82 Cal.Rptr. at 182–183, 461 P.2d at 382.

95. *Id.* at 239, 82 Cal.Rptr. at 194, 461 P.2d at 394; see E.R. v. Iowa State Board of Public Instruction, 216 N.W.2d at 343.

96. M.S. v. State Board of Education, 1 Cal.3d at 228, 82 Cal.Rptr. at 185–186, 461 P.2d at 383. The Court noted that some prohibitions applicable to other professions did not apply to teachers. *Id.* at 227, 82 Cal.Rptr. at 185, 461 P.2d at 385, n. 21.

97. *Id.* at 226, 82 Cal.Rptr. at 183, 461 P.2d at 383.

98. *Id.* at 230, 82 Cal.Rptr. at 187, 461 P.2d at 387.

Although the Court's gloss eliminates some of the problems presented by vague prohibitions, for example the potential for arbitrary or discriminatory application, it cannot provide appropriate notice to M.S. since it arrives too late to influence his conduct. See Winters v. New York, 333 U.S. 507 (1948), where the United States Supreme Court observed: "We assume that the defendant [convicted of possession of prohibited magazines], *at the time he acted,* was chargeable with knowledge of the scope of *subsequent* interpretation." *Id.* at 514–515 (emphasis added). Compare Bouie v. City of Columbia, 378 U.S. 347 (1964).

The *M.S.* court apparently recognized the problem: "The construction does not mean that the statute will always be constitutional as applied. There may be borderline conduct which would justify a finding of unfitness to teach but about which a teacher would not have a sufficiently definite warning as to the possibility of suspension or revocation." 1 Cal.3d at 233, 82 Cal.Rptr. at 189, 461 P.2d at 389, n. 36. (citing Jordan v. De George, 341 U.S. 223, 231–232 (1951)).

99. 1 Cal.3d at 235, 82 Cal.Rptr. at 191, 461 P.2d at 391.
100. See, *e.g.*, S.U. v. Meade Independent School District No. 101, 530 F.2d at 807; F.I. v. Snyder, 476 F.2d at 377 (a teacher dismissal is arbitrary or capricious if the conduct involved is unrelated to the educational process) (citing McEnteggart v. Cataldo, 451 F.2d 1109, 1111 (1st Cir. 1971), cert. denied, 408 U.S. 943 (1972)); T.H. v. Southwest School District, 483 F.Supp. at 400; B.U. v. Cascade School District Union High School, 353 F.Supp. at 254, 255, n. 1; Board of Education of Long Beach Unified School District of Los Angeles County v. M.I., 139 Cal.Rptr. at 696–697, 566 P.2d at 604; P.E. v. State Board of Education, 10 Cal.3d at 34, 109 Cal.Rptr. at 668, 513 P.2d at 892; R.R. v. Robb, 662 S.W.2d at 259; W.E. v. Board of Education of Jefferson County School District No. R-1, 190 Colo. at 420–421, 547 P.2d at 1272; T.O. v. Dade County School Board, 318 So.2d at 160; R.E. v. Board of Education of Alton Community School District No. 11, Madison and Jersey Counties, 19 Ill. App.3d 481, 484–485, 311 N.E.2d 710, 712 (1974); Y.N. v. School District No. 23, Lake County, Montana, 641 P.2d at 441; G.A. v. Tacoma School District No. 10, 559 P.2d at 1342–1343; S.H. v. Salem School District 24J, Marion County, 669 P.2d 1172, 1174 (Or. App. 1983). Cf. A.C. v. Board of Education of Montgomery County, 491 F.2d 498, 500–501 (4th Cir. 1974), cert. denied, 419 U.S. 836 (1974).

This nexus may be required through statutory interpretation, by the due process clause or even, apparently, by the equal protection clause. See R.O. v. Springfield School District No. 19, 56 Or. App. 197, 209, 641 P.2d 600, 608, *rev'd on other grounds,* 294 Or. 357, 657 P.2d 188 (1982).

Compare Penn-Delco School District v. U.R., 382 A.2d at 167 (Pa. Commw. Ct. 1978), defining immorality as conduct offending community morals and constituting a bad example to the young.

101. 1 Cal.3d at 235, 82 Cal.Rptr. at 191, 461 P.2d at 391.
102. W.E. v. Board of Education of Jefferson County School District No. R-1, 190 Colo. at 421, 547 P.2d at 1273.
103. T.H. v. Southwest School District, 483 F.Supp. at 1182; M.S. v. State Board of Education, 1 Cal.3d at 229, 82 Cal.Rptr. at 186, 461 P.2d at 386; W.E. v. Board of Education of Jefferson County School District No. R-1, 190 Colo. at 421, 547 P.2d at 1273; E.R. v. Iowa State Board of Public Instruction, 216 N.W.2d at 344; P.O. v. Kalama Public School District, No. 402, 644 P.2d 1229, 1230 (1982).

104. 1 Cal.3d at 229, 82 Cal.Rptr. at 186, 461 P.2d at 396, n. 25. See P.E. v. State Board of Education, 10 Cal.3d at 41, 109 Cal.Rptr. at 674, 513 P.2d at 897–898.

105. W.E. v. Board of Education of Jefferson County School District No. R-1, 190 Colo. at 421, 547 P.2d at 1273.

106. 1 Cal.3d at 237, 82 Cal.Rptr. at 192, 461 P.2d at 392.

107. *Id.* at 239, 82 Cal.Rptr. at 194, 461 P.2d at 394.

108. *Id.* at 248, 82 Cal.Rptr. at 200–201, 461 P.2d at 401 (emphasis in original).

109. *Id.* at 243–244, 250, 82 Cal.Rptr. at 197, 202, 461 P.2d at 397, 398 (quoting S.A. v. State Board of Education, 249 Cal. App.2d 58, 63–64, 57 Cal.Rptr. 69, 72 (1967). See CAL. EDUC. CODE. § 7851.

110. M. Willemsen, *Justice Tobriner and the Tolerance of Evolving Lifestyles: Adapting the Law to Social Change,* 29 HASTINGS L.J. 73, 84 (1977).

111. R. Clay, *supra* note 18, at 928.

112. 22 Cal.App.3d 988, 101 Cal.Rptr. 86 (1972).

113. *Id.* at 990, 101 Cal.Rptr. at 87. See also W.L. v. Board of Education of Chandler Unified School District No. 80 of Maricopa County, 667 P.2d 746, 749 (Ariz. App. 1983): "There may be conduct which by itself gives rise to reasonable inferences of unfitness to teach or from which an adverse impact on students can reasonably be assumed." *Compare* D.E. v. South Kitsap School District No. 402, in which the court found the *M.S.* nexus inapplicable to a teacher's sexual relations with a student in the *district,* though not currently a student in the teacher's school, and never a student of that teacher. School officials may deem such conduct "inherently harmful to the teacher-student relation, and thus to the school district." 516 P.2d at 1082. Could not this situation be deemed sufficient even under a strict application of *M.S.?* What is the appropriate concern under *M.S.?* The classroom? School? District?

114. 10 Cal.3d 29, 109 Cal.Rptr. 665, 513 P.2d 889 (1973).

115. *Id.* at 32, 109 Cal.Rptr. at 667, 513 P.2d at 891 (findings of hearing examiner, accepted "in toto" by the board.)

116. *Id.* at 30–32, 109 Cal.Rptr. at 665–667, 513 P.2d at 889–891.

117. *Id.* at 31, 109 Cal.Rptr. at 666, 513 P.2d at 890, n. 1 (emphasis added).

118. *Id.* at 31, 109 Cal.Rptr. at 666, 513 P.2d at 890, n. 1 (emphasis added).

119. *Id.* at 31, 109 Cal.Rptr. at 666, 513 P.2d at 890, n. 1.

120. *Id.* at 31, 109 Cal.Rptr. at 666, 513 P.2d at 890.

121. See W.L. v. Board of Education of Chandler Unified School District No. 80 of Maricopa County, 667 P.2d at 749 (a requirement of proof of actual harm would preclude administrators from acting to prevent predictable future harm).

122. New Mexico State Board of Education v. S.T., 571 P.2d at 1189. The findings of the State Board of Education had a compound speculation: "[Her] unwed pregnancy *could have* a *potentially* adverse effect. . . . " *Id.* (first emphasis added). See the dissenting opinion in D.R. v. Covington County Board of Education, 371 F.Supp. at 983: "The Board of Education must have known that [she] would have encountered grave problems."

123. W.E. v. Board of Education of Jefferson County School District No. R-1, 190 Colo. at 421, 547 P.2d at 1273, (emphasis added).

124. See G.I. v. Board of Education of Borough of Paramus, Bergen County, 145 N.J. Super. 96, 105, 366 A.2d at 1342.

125. 10 Cal.3d at 35, 109 Cal.Rptr. at 669, 513 P.2d at 893. The nexus between act and unfitness may not even require expert testimony but be established by opera-

tion of law. See Board of Education of Long Beach Unified School District of Los Angeles County v. M.I., 62 Cal.App.3d at 614, see: 19 Cal.3d 691, 133 Cal.Rptr. at 279.

126. 10 Cal.3d at 35, 109 Cal.Rptr. at 669, 513 P.2d at 893.

127. Perhaps the only significant difference between *M.S.* and *P.E.* was the court membership at the time of decision. See Willemsen, *supra* note 110, at 86.

128. 1 Cal.3d at 235, 82 Cal.Rptr. at 191, 461 P.2d at 391.

129. *Id.* at 220, 82 Cal.Rptr. at 178, 461 P.2d at 378.

130. *Id.* at 229, 82 Cal.Rptr. at 186, 461 P.2d at 386.

131. G.I. v. Board of Education of Borough of Paramus, 145 N.J. Super. at 104–105, 366 A.2d at 1342.

132. G.A. v. Tacoma School District No. 10, 88 Wash.2d 186, 559 P.2d 1340 (1977).

133. *Id.* at 1341–42.

134. *Id.* at at 1346.

135. *Id.* at 1350 (dissenting opinion). See also F.I. v. Snyder, 346 F.Supp. 396, 401 (D.Neb. 1972), *aff'd,* 476 F.2d 375 (8th Cir. 1973) (undifferentiated fear or apprehension not enough for termination).

136. 1 Cal.3d at 236–237, 82 Cal.Rptr. at 191–192, 461 P.2d at 391–393.

137. 10 Cal.3d at 37, 109 Cal.Rptr. at 670, 513 P.2d at 894 (dissenting opinion).

138. *Id.* at 43, 109 Cal.Rptr. at 675, 513 P.2d at 899 (dissenting opinion).

139. *Id.* at 41–42, 109 Cal.Rptr. at 674, 513 P.2d at 898 (dissenting opinion).

140. *Id.* at 43, 109 Cal.Rptr. at 675, 513 P.2d at 899 (dissenting opinion).

141. 216 N.W. 2d 339 (S.Ct. Iowa 1974).

142. *Id.* at 343.

143. 483 F.Supp. 1170 (W.D.Mo. 1980).

144. *Id.* at 1182. Compare the dissenting opinion in D.R. v. Covington County Board of Education, 371 F.Supp. at 983: "The loss by a teacher of the respect of her students associated with her known pregnancy without marriage is, in my judgment, so obviously a detriment to the teaching ability of such a teacher as to be within the judicial knowledge of this Court."

145. 19 Cal.3d 691, 139 Cal.Rptr. 700, 566 P.2d 602 (1977).

146. *Id.* at 695–696, 139 Cal.Rptr. at 702, 566 P.2d at 604.

147. *Id.* at 694, 139 Cal. Rptr. at 701, 566 P.2d at 603. To escape this principle of appellate review, the school board had argued that the teacher's conduct demonstrated unfitness *per se.* The argument was rejected, since "neither statute nor decisional authority has applied a rule of *per se* unfitness to persons who were not convicted of specified sex offenses." *Id.*

148. *Id.* at 694, 139 Cal.Rptr. at 701, 566 P.2d at 603.

149. *Id.* at 698, 139 Cal.Rptr. at 703, 566 P.2d at 605.

150. *Id.* at 698, 139 Cal.Rptr. at 703, 566 P.2d at 605.

151. *Id.* at 700, 139 Cal.Rptr. at 705, 566 P.2d at 607. Interestingly, the California Supreme Court thus rejected the conclusion of the intermediate appellate court, based largely on *P.E.,* that the sexual conduct involved itself demonstrated unfitness and therefore constituted a *per se* cause for dismissal. See Board of Education of Long Beach Unified School District of Los Angeles County v. M.I., 62 Cal.App.3d at 614, 133 Cal.Rptr. at 279–280.

152. 190 Colo. 414, 547 P.2d 1267 (S.Ct. Colo. 1976).

153. *Id.* at 1273. See also R.I. v. Davis, 627 P.2d at 1120.

154. On the right to privacy, *see generally* J. NOWAK, R. ROTUNDA & J. YOUNG, CONSTITUTIONAL LAW 734–735, 758–760 (1983).
155. 416 F.Supp. 1194 (D.Neb. 1976).
156. *Id.* at 1196, 1199–1200.
157. 566 F.2d 588 (8th Cir. 1977).
158. 410 U.S. 113, 152–53 (1973).
159. Citing Stanley v. Georgia, 394 U.S. 557, 564 (1969).
160. Citing Terry v. Ohio, 392 U.S. 1, 8–9 (1968); Katz v. United States, 389 U.S. 347, 350 (1967); Olmstead v. United States, 277 U.S. 438, 478 (1928) (Brandeis, J., dissenting); Boyd v. United States, 116 U.S. 616 (1886).
161. Citing Griswold v. Connecticut, 381 U.S. 479, 486 (1965).
162. Citing Meyer v. Nebraska, 262 U.S. 390, 399 (1923).
163. Citing Griswold v. Connecticut, 381 U.S. at 484–485.
164. Citing Palko v. Connecticut, 302 U.S. 319, 325 (1937).
165. Citing Loving v. Virginia, 388 U.S. 1, 12 (1967).
166. Citing Skinner v. Oklahoma, 316 U.S. 535, 541–542 (1942).
167. Citing Eisenstadt v. Baird, 405 U.S. 438, 453–454 (1972); *id.* at 460, 463–465 (White J., concurring).
168. Citing Prince v. Massachusetts, 321 U.S. 158, 166 (1944).
169. Citing Pierce v. Society of Sisters, 268 U.S. 510, 535 (1925); and Meyer v. Nebraska, 262 U.S. 390 (1923).
170. Eisenstadt v. Baird, 405 U.S. at 453 (emphasis in original). See generally D.R. v. Covington County Board of Education, 371 F.Supp. at 978–979.
171. S.U. v. Meade Independent School District No. 101, 530 F.2d at 806; S.E. v. Capital School District, 425 F.Supp. at 558.
172. Generally successful: B.C. v. Coyle Public School System, 476 F.2d 92, 96 (10th Cir. 1973) (summary judgment for defendant school system reversed); L.E. v. Delaware State College, 455 F.Supp. 239, 252 (S.D.N.Y. 1978) (teacher entitled to preliminary injunctive relief reinstating her as director of residence halls at state college); D.R. v. Covington County Board of Education, 371 F.Supp. at 976–977.

   Generally unsuccessful: G.R. v. Duganne, 581 F.2d 222, 224 (9th Cir. 1978); W.I. v. McDonald, 500 F.2d at 1113–1114; S.E. v. Capital School District, 425 F.Supp. at 558; B.R. v. Bathke, 416 F.Supp. at 1199–1200; M.S. v. State Board of Education, 1 Cal.3d at 233–234, 82 Cal.Rptr. at 190–191, 461 P.2d at 390–391 (teacher prevails on separate grounds); G.O. v. Board of Education of Central School District No. 1, Towns of Brookhaven and Smithtown, 35 N.Y.2d at 543, 364 N.Y.S.2d at 446; R.O. v. Springfield School District No. 19, 56 Or.App. at 209, 641 P.2d at 608.
173. See Griswold v. Connecticut, 381 U.S. at 485–486; Roe v. Wade, 410 U.S. at 152–153; Eisenstadt v. Baird, 405 U.S. at 453.
174. Eisenstadt v. Baird, 405 U.S. at 453. See L.E. v. Delaware State College, 455 F.Supp. at 248, 252. *Cf.* D.R. v. Covington County Board of Education, 371 F.Supp. at 976–977.
175. J. NOWAK, R. ROTUNDA & J. YOUNG, *supra* note 154, at 735. But see S.U. v. Meade Independent School District No. 101, 530 F.2d at 806; see generally R. Clay, *supra* note 18, at 920–927.

   That the right to privacy does not encompass all private, adult, consensual sexual conduct is indicated by the United States Supreme Court's memorandum affirmance of the constitutionality of Virginia's sodomy statute, VA. CODE ANN. § 18.1-361 (1975). Doe v. Commonwealth's Attorney for City of Richmond, 425U.S. 901 (1976), *aff'g* 403 F.Supp. 1199 (E.D.Va. 1975). Moreover, the court later refused to review a sodomy conviction involving a private act between consenting adults, Enslin v. Bean, 436 U.S. 912 (1978), and the suspension of a patrolwoman and a police sergeant, and the demotion of the latter, for dating and cohabitation, Whisenhunt v. Spradlin, 104 S.Ct. 404 (1983). See also the denials of certiorari in Hollenbaugh v. Carnegie Free Library, 436 F.Supp. 1328 (W.D. Pa. 1977), 578 F.2d 1374 (3d Cir. 1978), *cert. denied,* 439 U.S. 1052 (1978); and Jarrett v. Jarrett, 78 Ill.2d 337, 400 N.E.2d 421 (1979), *cert. denied,* 449 U.S. 927 (1980).

176. J. NOWAK, R. ROTUNDA & J. YOUNG, supra note 154, at 758.

177. See B.C. v. Coyle Public School System, 476 F.2d at 96 ("The classification here is at least susceptible to the charge . . . that it invades plaintiff's privacy by requiring her to choose between employment and pregnancy. . . . "); D.R. v. Covington County Board of Education, 371 F.Supp. at 981, n. 4 (concurring opinion) ("The constitutional right to privacy does not involve the right to keep secret matters that are of an intimate or personal nature. Rather this right involves the creation of a zone of protected activities free from governmental intrusion.")

178. 371 F.Supp. 974 (M.D.Ala. 1974).

179. *Id.* at 978. *Cf.* M.S. v. State Board of Education, 1 Cal.3d at 233–234, 82 Cal.Rptr. at 190, 461 P.2d at 390–391, where the court stated that unless construed to require a showing of unfitness, a proscription of immorality might cause school officials to pry unduly into the private lives of teachers in search of "telltale signs" of immoral conduct (citing Griswold v. Connecticut, 381 U.S. at 485). See also A.N. v. Drew Municipal Separate School District, 507 F.2d at 615.

180. R.O. v. Springfield School District No. 19, 56 Or. at 209, 641 P.2d at 608 (citing Doe v. Commonwealth's Attorney for City of Richmond, 403 F.Supp. 1199 (E.D. Va. 1975), *aff'd,* 425 U.S. 901 (1976)). *Cf.* M.S. v. State Board of Education, 1 Cal.3d at 233–234, 82 Cal. Rptr. at 190–191, 461 P.2d at 390–391.

181. S.E. v. Capital School District, 425 F.Supp. at 558: "[E]ven if the court accepts [the school administrator's] contention that his affair . . . was private, its public impact in terms of job performance took it from behind any protective shield that the right to privacy may have constructed around the underlying conduct."

182. W.I. v. McDonald, 500 F.2d at 1113–1114 (conduct "on private property" is not necessarily "in private").

183. See D.R. v. Covington County Board of Education, 371 F.Supp. at 978: "The evidence fails to show that [the teacher] consented for her doctor to disclose to the Board her private communications with him." See R.O. v. Springfield School District No. 19, 56 Or. at 209, 641 P.2d at 608: "If petitioner's privacy was invaded at all, it was the result of his indiscretion in failing to protect his privacy."

Of course, a person should not be held to waive the right to privacy by bringing the matter to public attention by prosecuting a lawsuit, D.R. v. Covington County Board of Education, 371 F.Supp. at 980, n. 3 (concurring opinion), or by discussing the matter at a private school board hearing. *Id.* at 981 (concurring opinion).

Some would stress a distinction between the constitutional right to privacy and the right to privacy sounding in tort, the latter being a creation of state law and not constitutionally based. D.R. v. Covington County Board of Education, 371 F.Supp. at 980 (concurring opinion). The waiver of the tort right may be easier to establish. *Id.*

184. See D.R. v. Covington County Board of Education, 371 F.Supp. at 981, 983–984 (dissenting opinion).

185. G.O. v. Board of Education of Central School District No. 1, Towns of Brookhaven and Smithtown, 35 N.Y.2d at 543, 364 N.Y.S.2d at 446.

186. S.U. v. Meade Independent School District No. 101, 530 F.2d at 806 (citing Pickering v. Board of Education, 391 U.S. 563 (1968)); B.R. v. Bathke, 416 F.Supp. at 1199 (also citing *Pickering*); D.R. v. Covington County Board of Education, 371 F.Supp. at 979; G.O. v. Board of Education of Central School District No. 1, Towns of Brookhaven and Smithtown, 35 N.Y.2d at 543, 364 N.Y.S. 2d at 446.

187. Carey v. Population Services International, 431 U.S. 678, 686 (1977); B.C. v. Coyle Public School System, 476 F.2d at 96; L.E. v. Delaware State College, 455 F.Supp. at 249, 252; D.R. v. Covington County Board of Education, 371 F.Supp. at 979.

In Whisenhunt v. Spradlin, 104 S.Ct. 404 (1983), a police department suspended a patrolwoman and a police sergeant, and demoted the latter, for dating and cohabiting with one another. After the Court of Appeals upheld the department's action, 701 F.2d 470 (5th Cir. 1983), the United States Supreme Court denied certiorari. Dissenting from this denial on several grounds, Justice Brennan, joined by Justices Marshall and Blackmun, noted that "because petitioners' conduct involved fundamental rights, it could only be abridged to the extent necessary to achieve strong, clearly articulated state interests." 104 S.Ct. at 409 (opinion dissenting from denial of certiorari).

188. Carey v. Population Services International, 431 U.S. at 684–685.

189. B.R. v. Bathke, 416 F.Supp. at 1200 (citing Drake v. North Texas State University, 469 F.2d 829 (5th Cir. 1972)).

190. G.O. v. Board of Education of Central School District No. 1, Towns of Brookhaven and Smithtown, 35 N.Y.2d at 543–544, 364 N.Y.S.2d at 446.

191. D.R. v. Covington County Board of Education, 371 F.Supp. at 983 (dissenting opinion).

192. See M.S. v. State Board of Education, 1 Cal.3d at 233–234, 82 Cal.Rptr. at 190, 461 P.2d at 389–390.

193. See, *e.g.*, G.R. v. Duganne, 581 F.2d at 223; S.U. v. Meade Independent School District, 530 F.2d at 801; F.I. v. Snyder, 476 F.2d at 376; K.I. v. Wright, 437 F.Supp. at 401; B.R. v. Bathke, 416 F.Supp. at 1199; G.I. v. Board of Education of Borough of Paramus, Bergen County, 145 N.J. Super. at 102, 366 A.2d at 1340.

Associational freedom and privacy fall within the "penumbra" of First Amendment rights. Winks, *supra* note 26, at 464 (citing Griswold v. Connecticut, 381 U.S. 479 (1965)).

194. See T.A. v. Quinn, 545 F.2d 761 (1st Cir. 1976).

This right is related to the right of privacy. *Cf.* J. NOWAK, R. ROTUNDA & J. YOUNG, *supra*, note 154, at 735 (2d ed. 1983).

195. See B.R. v. Bathke, 416 F.Supp. at 1199.

196. See, *e.g.*, T.A. v. Quinn, 545 F.2d at 763, n. 3; A.C. v. Board of Education of Montgomery County, 491 F.2d at 499–501; G.I. v. Board of Education of Borough of Paramus, Bergen County, 145 N.J. Super. at 103–104, 366 A.2d at 1341; Penn-Delco School District v. U.R., 382 A.2d at 167 (Pa. Commw. Ct. 1978); B.O. v. Board of School Directors of Indiana Area School District, 377 A.2d at 1289 (Pa. Commw. Ct. 1978).
197. Tinker v. Des Moines Independent School District, 393 U.S. 503, 506 (1969).
198. Pickering v. Board of Education of Township High School District 205, Will County, Illinois, 391 U.S. 563, 568 (1968).
199. *Id.* at 574.
200. National Gay Task Force v. Board of Education of City of Oklahoma City, 729 F.2d 1271 (10th Cir. 1984), *aff'd* by an evenly divided court, 105 S. Ct. 1161 (1985).
201. A.C. v. Board of Education of Montgomery County, 491 F.2d at 501. That the teacher's media statements were protected did not immunize him from dismissal for other matters. The teacher's application form failed to disclose, in response to a request for information about his extracurricular activities, his membership and official position in the Homophiles of Penn State. The teacher had feared that such disclosure would harm his chances for the teaching position. Indeed, the school officials conceded that they would not have hired him had they known of his affiliation with the Homophiles. Ironically, the Court of Appeals for the Fourth Circuit held that his deliberate withholding of such information barred his suit for reinstatement. *Id.* at 499.

  But under certain circumstances, even protected speech may justify compelling a teacher to undergo a psychiatric examination. See G.I. v. Board of Education of Borough of Paramus, Bergen County, 145 N.J. Super. 96, 366 A.2d 1337 (1976), discussed in note 207, *infra.*
202. R.W. v. Mad River Local School District, Montgomery County, Ohio, 730 F.2d 444 (6th Cir. 1984), *cert. denied,* 105 S.Ct. 1373 (1985). The Sixth Circuit relied heavily on Connick v. Myers, 461 U.S. 138 (1983). In the *R.W.* case, Justice Brennan vigorously dissented from the denial of certiorari, arguing that the speech did involve public issues and that in any event *Connick* left open whether nondisruptive speech may ever be the basis for termination under the First Amendment. 105 S.Ct. at 1375–1376.
203. *But see* R.W. v. Mad River Local School District, Montgomery County, Ohio, 730 F.2d 444, 453 (6th Cir. 1984), *cert. denied,* 105 S. Ct. 1373 (1985).
204. See National Gay Task Force v. Board of Education of City of Oklahoma City, 729 F.2d at 1274.
205. B.O. v. Board of School Directors of Indiana Area School District, 377 A.2d 1284 (Pa. Comm. Ct. 1977).
206. Act of March 10, 1949, P.L. 30, *as amended,* 24 P.S. § 1-101 *et seq.* See *id.* at 1286, n. 1.
207. B.O. v. Board of Directors of Indiana Area School District, 377 A.2d at 1289.
208. Of course, the First Amendment generally "protects 'advocacy' even of illegal conduct" if the advocacy is not directed to producing *imminent* lawless action. National Gay Task Force v. Board of Education of City of Oklahoma City, 729 F.2d at 1274. Presumably, this principle does not apply to classroom speech of a teacher. Cf. *id.*
209. Penn-Delco School District v. U.R., 382 A.2d at 167 (citing A.C. v. Board of

Education of Montgomery County, 359 F.Supp. 843 (D.Md. 1973), *aff'd,* 491 F.2d 498 (4th Cir.), *cert. denied,* 419 U.S. 836 (1974)).

210. *Id.* at 167–168.

211. J. NOWAK, R. ROTUNDA & J. YOUNG, *supra* note 154, at 988 (citing Stromberg v. California, 283 U.S. 359 (1931)).

212. 393 U.S. 503 (1969).

213. 391 U.S. 367 (1968).

214. 391 U.S. at 377. See generally J. NOWAK, R. ROTUNDA & J. YOUNG, *supra* note 154, at 989–991.

215. J. NOWAK, R. ROTUNDA & J. YOUNG, *supra* note 154, at 991.

216. Tinker v. Des Moines Independent School District, 393 U.S. at 509. Of course, "many adverse effects are not material and substantial disruptions." National Gay Task Force v. Board of Education of City of Oklahoma City, 729 F.2d at 1275.

217. *Cf.* G.I. v. Board of Education of Borough of Paramus, Bergen County, 145 N.J.Super. at 103, 366 A.2d at 1341.

218. *Cf.* T.A. v. Quinn, 545 F.2d 761 (1st Cir. 1976), in which the court upheld the termination of a nontenured female teacher who alleged that the real reason for her dismissal was her wearing of short dresses: "There is no claim that the length of plaintiff's skirts was intended as a form of symbolic expression, and thus protected by the First Amendment." *Id.* at 763, n. 3.

219. See, *e.g.,* Plyler v. Doe, 457 U.S. 202, 216–17 (1982); *id.* at 217, n. 15; San Antonio Independent School District v. Rodriguez, 411 U.S. 1, 17 (1972).

 For an argument that adverse treatment of homosexuals warrants strict or heightened scrutiny, see R.W. v. Mad River Local School District, Montgomery County, Ohio, 105 S.Ct. 1373, 1377–1378 (1985) (Brennan, J., dissenting from denial of certiorari).

220. San Antonio Independent School District v. Rodriguez, 411 U.S. at 17; Plyler v. Doe, 457 U.S. at 216. See generally K. ALEXANDER, SCHOOL LAW 428–429 (1980).

221. See generally J. NOWAK, R. ROTUNDA & J. YOUNG, *supra* note 154, at 590–599.

222. Craig v. Boren, 429 U.S. 190, 197 (1976). See also Michael M. v. Superior Court of Sonoma County, 450 U.S. 464 (1981); Wengler v. Druggists Mutual Insurance Co., 446 U.S. 142 (1980).

223. Plyler v. Doe, 457 U.S. at 221–224. *Cf.* San Antonio Independent School District v. Rodriguez, 411 U.S. at 23–24.

224. See B.C. v. Coyle Public School System, 476 F.2d 92, 96 (10th Cir. 1973) (citing Shapiro v. Thompson, 394 U.S. 618 (1969); and Williams v. San Francisco Unified School District, 340 F.Supp. 438, 442–43 (N.D. Cal. 1972)).

225. See B.C. v. Coyle Public School System, 476 F.2d at 96–97.

 See also M.R. v. Board of Education of Chidester School District No. 59, Chidester, Arkansas, 448 F.2d at 714, where the court held that the dismissal, following school integration, of a black teacher on "moral influence" grounds, based in part upon her pregnancy, unlawfully discriminated; the underlying situation had existed, and was known by school officials, while she had taught at a black school, but they had taken no action. If she was moral enough to teach at the black school, the court suggested, she was moral enough to teach at an integrated school. In any event, added the court, the school board's decision to dismiss was based on insufficient evidence.

226. 507 F.2d 611 (5th Cir. 1975).
227. There was some confusion as to the scope of the rule. *Id.* at 613, n. 2.
228. *Accord:* A.V. v. Homewood City Board of Education, 674 F.2d 337, 341 (5th Cir. 1982).
229. See Winks, *supra* note 26, at 454–455: "There are no recorded cases in the last ten years of male teachers dismissed for unwed fatherhood or for living with a person of the opposite sex outside of marriage. . . . The brunt of the undefined 'morality' standard's application appears to fall on the female gender." (Citing B.R. v. Bathke, 566 F.2d 588, 593 (8th Cir. 1977) (concurring opinion)).
230. 507 F.2d at 613. The United States District Court had specified gender discrimination as an alternative basis for declaring the rule unconstitutional. *Id.*, citing A.N. v. Drew Municipal Separate School District, 371 F.Supp. at 35.
231. 507 F.2d at 614. For further discussion, see text accompanying notes 321–325, *infra*.
232. 507 F.2d at 614 (Citing Reed v. Reed, 404 U.S. 71, 76 (1971)).
233. 507 F.2d at 615–616.
234. See B.R. v. Bathke, 566 F.2d at 592.
235. See *id.* at 594 (concurring opinion); *cf. id.* at 592–593.
236. See L.E. v. Delaware State College, 455 F.Supp. 250. *Cf.* B.R. v. Bathke, 566 F.2d at 592, n. 1; and New Mexico State Board of Education v. S.T., 571 P.2d at 1190 (Although noting that there were "other unwed mothers who remained employed as teachers in the Taos Municipal Schools and no action had been taken against them," the court did not decide on equal protection grounds, but found the termination "arbitrary, unreasonable and not supported by substantial evidence"); See *id.* at 593 (concurring opinion). For an argument that the school board should be able to assess each situation in context rather than follow an inflexible rule, see *id.* at 594 (dissenting opinion).
237. *See* L.E. v. Delaware State College, 455 F.Supp. at 250. The court noted that although the college sought to dismiss the plaintiff on the grounds of her unwed pregnancy, it had taken no action against the child's father, himself an assistant coach and assistant director of the student center at the college. *Id.* at 243, 250.
238. See R.W. v. Mad River Local School District, Montgomery County, Ohio, 730 F.2d at 449–452; *id.* at 453 (dissenting opinion); and *id.*, 105 S.Ct. at 1376–1379 (Brennan, J., dissenting from denial of certiorari). See also text accompanying note 292 *et seq.*, *infra*.
239. F.I. v. Snyder, 476 F.2d 375 (8th Cir. 1973); L.E. v. Delaware State College, 455 F.Supp. at 247–248; and New Mexico State Board of Education v. S.T., 571 P.2d at 1190.
240. F.I. v. Snyder, 476 F.2d at 377 (citing McEnteggart v. Cataldo, 451 F.2d 1109, 1111 (1st Cir. 1971), *cert. denied*, 408 U.S. 943 (1972)). See L.E. v. Delaware State College, 455 F.Supp. at 247, 252; and New Mexico State Board of Education v. S.T., 571 P.2d at 1190.
241. 476 F.2d 375 (8th Cir. 1973).
242. *Id.* at 376.
243. *Id.*
244. *Id.* at 377.
245. *Id.* at 377–378.
246. *Id.* at 378.
247. *Id.*
248. A.N. v. Drew Municipal Separate School District, 507 F.2d at 614 (citing Cleveland Board of Education v. LaFleur, 414 U.S. 632 (1974); Vlandis v.

Kline, 412 U.S. 441 (1973); and Stanley v. Illinois, 405 U.S. 645 (1972)); L.E. v. Delaware State College, 455 F.Supp. at 247–248.

249. A.N. v. Drew Municipal Separate School District, 507 F.2d at 614–615.

250. *Id.* at 615.

251. *Id.*

252. See text accompanying notes 38–73, *supra.*

253. See text accompanying notes 74–80, *supra.*

254. See text accompanying notes 154–192, *supra.*

255. See text accompanying notes 193–195, *supra.*

256. See text accompanying notes 194–195, *supra.*

257. See text accompanying notes 196–218, *supra.*

258. See text accompanying notes 219–238, *supra.*

259. See text accompanying notes 239–251, *supra.*

260. Statutes (or the like), by specifying grounds such as immorality and unfitness, limit the right of school officials to terminate teachers or revoke their credentials. Since no statute—or a different statute—might apply to hirings, as opposed to terminations or credential revocations, it is not clear whether a school board's refusal to hire a homosexual would violate constitutional rights. See B.U. v. Cascade School District Union High School No. 5, 512 F.2d at 854, n. 5: "We do not address the question whether the school district could refuse to rehire appellant, or whether any other school system could refuse to give her a teaching position, solely on the basis of her homosexual inclination." One thing seems clear: it will usually be more difficult to isolate the reason for a nonhire than for a dismissal, since specific reasons and a hearing must be given for dismissal of tenured teachers and midcontract termination of nontenured teachers. Compare the book selection versus book removal issue, Chapter 3, *supra.*

261. See *e.g.,* A.C. v. Board of Education of Montgomery County, 491 F.2d 498 (4th Cir. 1974); B.U. v. Cascade School District Union High School No. 5, 353 F.Supp. 254 (D.Oregon 1973), *aff'd on different grounds,* 512 F.2d 850 (9th Cir. 1975); Board of Education of Long Beach Unified School District of Los Angeles County v. M.I., 19 Cal.3d 691, 139 Cal.Rptr. 700, 566 P.2d 602 (S.Ct. Cal. 1977); M.S. v. State Board of Education, 1 Cal.3d 214, 82 Cal.Rptr. 175, 461 P.2d 375 (S.Ct. Cal. 1969); Board of Education of El Monte School District of Los Angeles County v. C.A., 35 Cal. App.3d 490, 110 Cal.Rptr. 916 (1974); M.E. v. State Board of Education, 22 Cal. App. 3d 988, 101 Cal.Rptr. 86 (1972); S.A. v. State Board of Education, 249 Cal. App.2d 58, 57 Cal.Rptr. 69 (1967); Board of Education of St. Charles Community Unit School District, No. 303 v. Adelman, 97 Ill. App.3d 530, 53 Ill. Dec. 62, 423 N.E.2d 254 (1981); R.O. v. Springfield School District No. 19, 294 Or. 357, 657 P.2d 188 (1982); G.A. v. Tacoma School District No. 10, 88 Wash.2d 286, 559 P.2d 1340 (1977); *Cf.* G.I. v. Board of Education of Borough of Paramus, Bergen County, 145 N.J. Super. 96, 366 A.2d 1337 (1976).

Homosexuals may constitute up to 15 percent of the population. See R.W. v. Mad River Local School District, Montgomery County, Ohio, 730 F.2d at 455–456 (dissenting opinion) (citing MARMOR, HOMOSEXUAL BEHAVIOR: A MODERN REAPRAISAL (1980)). If bisexual behavior is considered, these figures may double. *Id.*

262. 249 Cal. App.2d 58, 57 Cal.Rptr. 69 (1967).

263. *Id.* at 63, 57 Cal.Rptr. at 72.

264. See Fleming, *supra* note 32, at 426: "Undoubtedly, [*S.A.*] represented the strictest

interpretation of . . . evident unfitness . . . and implied that homosexual conduct, even where unrelated to employment effectiveness, warranted dismissal." See also M.E. v. State Board of Education, 22 Cal. App.3d 988, 101 Cal.Rptr. 86 (1972) (public homosexual conduct establishes unfitness to teach).

265. See the discussion of *M.S.* at text accompanying notes 89–111, *supra.*

266. See B.U. v. Cascade School District Union High School No. 5, 353 F.Supp. at 255, n.1. See also R.O. v. Springfield School District No. 19, 657 P.2d at 195, in which the Supreme Court of Oregon held a teacher's participation in sexual deviate acts insufficient in itself to support the conclusion that the teacher's conduct was immoral.

267. The court in *M.S.* did end on an ambiguous if not mysterious note by stating that "we do not, of course, hold that homosexuals must be permitted to teach in the public schools of California. . . . [T]he relevant statutes, as well as the applicable principles of constitutional law, require only that the board properly find . . . that an individual is not fit to teach." M.S. v. State Board of Education, 1 Cal.3d at 239–240, 82 Cal.Rptr. at 194, 461 P.2d at 394–395. See also Fleming, *Teacher Dismissal for Cause, supra* note 32, at 427. Was the court suggesting that a differently-worded statute might validly exclude all homosexuals from the schools? Was the court suggesting that a link between homosexuality and unfitness could easily be established by school officials stressing the modelling role of teachers? The court noted that even M.S. himself might be shown unfit in subsequent proceedings. 1 Cal.3d at 239, 82 Cal.Rptr. 194, 461 P.2d at 394.

268. See text accompanying notes 110–140, *supra.* See also M.E. v. State Board of Education, 22 Cal.App.3d 988, 101 Cal.Rptr. 86 (1972), decided more than two years after *M.S.,* holding that homosexual conduct in a public place, at least when the conduct involved is criminal, constitutes in and of itself unfitness to teach. *Cf.* Governing Board of Mountain View School District of Los Angeles County v. M.T., 36 Cal.App.3d at 551–552, 111 Cal.Rptr. at 727.

269. 139 Cal.Rptr. 700, 566 P.2d 602 (1977). For more on this case, see text accompanying notes 145–151, *supra.*

270. Although *M.S.* involved credential revocation, the court in *M.I.* found its reasoning to be applicable as well to dismissals of permanent teachers. *Id.* at 702, 566 P.2d at 604, n.2.

271. The intermediate appellate court, in an opinion vacated by the California Supreme Court, had held that even after *M.S.,* "evidence of homosexual behavior in a public place constitutes sufficient proof of unfitness for service in the public school system." Board of Education of Long Beach Unified School District of Los Angeles County v. M.I., 62 Cal. App.3d at 614, 133 Cal.Rptr. at 277, *vacated,* 19 Cal.3d 691, 139 Cal.Rptr. 700, 566 P.2d 602 (1977).

272. 139 Cal.Rptr. at 701, 566 P.2d at 603. In California, prior to 1977, persons *convicted* of *certain* offenses were statutorily subject to automatic sanctions. See *id.* at 705, 566 P.2d at 607 (citing CAL. EDUC. CODE §§ 12912; 13175; 13207; 13220.16; 13255; 13403(h)). As the Court noted, the new legislation, granting a fitness hearing in some situations to those convicted of certain sex offenses, would be meaningless if the offense carried with it an unfitness *per se* designation. Board of Education of Long Beach Unified School District v. M.I., 19 Cal.3d at 703, 139 Cal.Rptr. at 707, 566 P.2d at 609.

For the legislative situation following January 1, 1977, see Board of Education of Long Beach Unified School District of Los Angeles County v. M.I., 19 Cal.3d at 7083, 139 Cal.Rptr. at 707, 566 P.2d at 609, and CAL. EDUC. CODE § 12910.

273. 559 P.2d 1340 (Wash. 1977).

274. *Id.* at 1347 (dissenting opinion).

275. *Id.* at 1341–42.

276. *Id.* at 1342.

277. *Id.* at 1345. Homosexuality, said the court, is not usually a disease—if it were, no moral responsibility would ensue. *Id.*

278. *Id.*

279. See *id.* at 1348 (dissenting opinion) ("There is not a shred of evidence in the record that [G.A.] participated in any ... acts [of sodomy or lewdness].")

280. *Id.* at 1344.

281. *Id.* at 1344.

282. See *id.* at 1343–1344. See also *id.* at 1348 (dissenting opinion): "Undoubtedly there are individuals with a homosexual identity[,] as there are individuals with a heterosexual identity, who are not sexually active."

283. *Cf. id.* at 1348 (dissenting opinion) ("[T]he ... school board did not meet its burden of proof.") See also *id.* at 1349, 1351 (dissenting opinion and opinion concurring in the dissent).

284. *Id.* at 1344.

285. *Id.* "The court has placed upon [G.A.] the burden to negate what it asserts are the implications that may be drawn from his testimony[,] although he never was accused of participating in acts of sodomy or lewdness." *Id.* at 1348 (dissenting opinion).

286. *Id.* at 1345.

287. *Id.* at 1342.

288. See *id.* at 1349–1350 (dissenting opinion).

289. *Id.* at 1346–1347.

290. *Id.* at 1347.

291. *Id.* at 1346. See *id.* at 1349 (dissenting opinion) (G.A.'s "homosexuality did not impair his performance as a teacher. In other words, homosexuality *per se* does not preclude competence.") (Citing A.C. v. Board of Education of Montgomery County, 359 F.Supp. 843 (D.Md. 1973), *aff'd*, 491 F.2d 498 (4th Cir. 1974)).

292. See *id.* at 1349 (dissenting opinion): "Presumably under [the court's] reasoning, an unmarried male who declares himself to be heterosexual will be held to have engaged in 'illegal or immoral acts.' The opportunities for industrious school districts seem unlimited."

293. See Fleming, *supra* note 32, at 427; and A.C. v. Board of Education of Montgomery County, 359 F.Supp. at 856.

294. The homosexual teacher seeking employment may to some extent confront a "Catch-22." If on his application form he discloses directly or indirectly his homosexuality, he may not be hired. If he fails to disclose it (directly or indirectly), even in response to questions that should not be asked, he may be subject to later dismissal for a deliberate withholding of information. See A.C. v. Board of Education of Montgomery County, 491 F.2d 498 (4th Cir. 1974), discussed in note 201, *supra.*

295. See *e.g.,* cases cited in notes 337–353, *infra.*

296. See Willemsen, *supra* note 110, at 74.

297. For an argument that adverse official treatment of homosexuals warrants "strict, or at least heightened, scrutiny" and implicates fundamental rights, thus requiring, to prevail under the equal protection clause, a compelling state interest, see R.W. v. Mad River Local School District, Montgomery County, Ohio, 105 S.Ct. at 1379-1378 (Brennan, J., dissenting from denial of certiorari). But see National Gay Task Force v. Board of Education of City of Oklahoma City, 729 F.2d at 1273.

298. See text accompanying notes 337–353, *infra.*

299. See, *e.g.*, S.U. v. Meade Independent School District No. 101, 530 F.2d at 803.

300. 641 P.2d 431 (Mont. 1982).

301. There was considerable disagreement over whether the record supported even the conclusion that they had lived together. See *id.* at 447 (dissenting opinion).

302. Other charges were also made. See *id.* at 434.

303. See *id.* at 435, 445.

304. *Id.* at 442, 445.

305. See Wood v. Strickland, 420 U.S. 308 (1975).

306. S.U. v. Meade Independent School District No. 101, 530 F.2d 799 (8th Cir. 1976). The teacher's request for reinstatement had been withdrawn. *Id.* at 808.

307. *Id.* at 806. *Cf.* G.O. v. Board of Education of Central School District No. 1, Towns of Brookhaven and Smithtown, 35 N.Y.2d at 543–544, 364 N.Y.S.2d at 446. See also text accompanying notes 185–192, *supra.*

308. T.H. v. Southwest School District, 483 F.Supp. 1170 (W.D. Mo. 1980). See also S.R. v. School Board of Suwannee County, 455 So.2d 1057 (Fla. App. 1 Dist. 1984) (evidence of living with a member of the opposite sex did not constitute good cause to deny a teacher a continuing contract).

309. F.I. v. Snyder, 476 F.2d at 378. See also S.R. v. School Board of Suwannee County, 455 So.2d at 1061.

310. *Id.*

311. Y.N. v. School District No. 23, Lake County, Montana, 641 P.2d at 447, 448 (dissenting opinion).

312. See text accompanying note 35, *supra.*

313. *Cf.* T.H. v. Southwest School District, 483 F.Supp. at 1183: "The mere fact that some parents may have an adverse attitude towards [the teacher] is not sufficient evidence . . . to demonstrate that an attitude would prevail *in the classroom* that would undermine the learning environment." (Emphasis in original).

314. See *id.* at 1182: "There is no evidence here that [the teacher] ever discussed her conduct with her second grade students. Nor is there any evidence that [she] tried to persuade any students, teachers or other associates of the rightness of her conduct."

315. See Winks, *supra* note 26, at 454: "There are no recorded cases in the last ten years of male teachers dismissed for . . . living with a person of the opposite sex outside of marriage."

316. See A.V. v. Homewood City Board of Education, 674 F.2d 337 (5th Cir. 1982); B.R. v. Bathke, 566 F.2d 588 (8th Cir. 1977); A.N. v. Drew Municipal Separate School District, 507 F.2d 611 (5th Cir. 1975); D.R. v. Covington County Board of Education, 371 F.Supp. 974 (N.D.Ala. 1974); R.E. v. Board of Education of Alton Community Unit School District No. 11, Madison and Jersey Counties, 19 Ill. App.3d 481, 311 N.E.2d 710 (1974); New Mexico State Board of Education v. S.T., 91 N.M. 183, 571 P.2d 1186 (1977).

See L.E. v. Delaware State College, 455 F.Supp. 239 (D.Del. 1978). *Cf.* M.R. v. Board of Education of Chidester School District No. 59, Chidester, Arkansas, 448 F.2d at 714.

The same issues seem present whether the situation involves unwed conception, unwed pregnancy or delivery out of wedlock. *Cf.* A.V. v. Homewood City Board of Education, 674 F.2d at 339, n. 1.

Interestingly, at least one school system has had a policy of dismissing teachers at the end of the sixth month of pregnancy, whether or not married. See B.C. v. Coyle School System, 476 F.2d 92 (10th Cir. 1973).

317. See, *e.g.,* B.R. v. Bathke, 566 F.2d at 590, 591; A.N. v. Drew Municipal Separate School District, 507 F.2d at 614.

318. See D.R. v. Covington County Board of Education, 371 F.Supp. at 983 (dissenting opinion).

319. B.R. v. Bathke, 416 F.Supp. at 1198.

320. *Id.*

321. 507 F.2d 611 (5th Cir. 1975).

322. And perhaps others. See note 227, *supra.*

323. See text at notes 248–250, *supra;* L.E. v. Delaware State College, 455 F.Supp. at 247–248.

324. A.N. v. Drew Municipal Separate School District, 507 F.2d at 616–617.

325. *Id.* at 617. The Court of Appeals for the Fifth Circuit reaffirmed this reasoning in A.V. v. Homewood City Board of Education, 674 F.2d at 341–342. See R.E. v. Board of Education of Alton Community Unit School District No. 11, Madison and Jersey Counties, 19 Ill. App. 3d at 484, 311 N.E.2d at 712, involving the discharge of a teacher who, though married but one month, was eight-and-a-half months pregnant:

> The record . . . discloses no injury to the students, faculty or school. No parents of children in her classroom complained. No students complained. There is no evidence of any breakdown in her relationships with other teachers, nor evidence that her teaching ability was affected in any manner, and no evidence that the standards of the school as an education [sic] institution was in any manner affected by [the teacher's] actions.

Cf. New Mexico State Board of Education v. S.T., 571 P.2d at 1189, noting that the possibility of the teacher's inability "to perform her duties" was "purely speculative."

326. L.E. v. Delaware State College, 455 F.Supp. at 249, 252. See text at notes 185–192, *supra;* B.R. v. Bathke, 416 F.Supp. at 1200; D.R. v. Covington County Board of Education, 371 F.Supp. at 979; *id.* at 983 (dissenting opinion).

327. *Cf.* S.E. v. Capital School District, 425 F.Supp. 552 (D.Del. 1976), *aff'd,* 565 F.2d 153 (3d Cir. 1977), *cert. denied,* 434 U.S. 1039 (1978).

328. 10 Cal.3d 29, 109 Cal.Rptr. 665, 513 P.2d 889 (1973). See discussion in text accompanying notes 114–131, *supra.*

329. See discussion in text accompanying notes 114–131, *supra.*

330. E.R. v. Iowa State Board of Public Instruction, 216 N.W.2d 339 (S.Ct.Iowa 1974). But see S.E. v. Capital School District, 425 F.Supp. at 558: "Because an adequate alternative ground for dismissal was offered, the Court deems it unnecessary to probe into the issue of whether a continuing course of adultery could constitute a basis for dismissal from public employment."

331. E.R. v. Iowa State Board of Public Instruction, 216 N.W.2d at 342–344.

332. W.I. v. McDonald, 500 F.2d 1110 (1st Cir. 1974).

333. T.O. v. Dade County School Board, 318 So.2d 159 (Fla. App. 1975).
334. T.A. v. Quinn, 545 F.2d 761 (1st Cir. 1976). Even if the termination was due to dress length, said the court, school officials' concerns about that matter were not, in the school context, necessarily irrational, and did not reflect bad faith.
335. In re Tenure Hearing of G.S., 127 N.J.Super. 13, 316 A.2d 39 (App. Div. 1974).
336. In the Matter of G.S., 157 N.J.Super. 165, 384 A.2d 855 (App. Div. 1978).
337. See F.S. v. Independent School District No. 622, North St. Paul/Maplewood, 357 N.W.2d 152 (Minn. App. 1984); and D.E. v. South Kitsap School District No. 402, 516 P.2d at 1081: "Indeed, it is difficult to conceive of circumstances which would more clearly justify [discharge] than the sexual misconduct of a teacher with a minor student. . . . " See also Clay, *supra* note 18, at 932. The *D.E.* court's allusion to a "minor" student suggests that student status usually carries a double significance: the status of student constitutes the nexus between the conduct and the effect on the teacher's performance and, in elementary, junior high and senior high school, implies an impressionable age which warrants extra protection. See Clay, *supra* note 18, at 932. See also Winks, *supra* note 26, at 447.

For an argument that sexual relations between a teacher and student, however discreet, adversely affects not only the parties but also other teachers and students, see Winks, *supra* note 26, at 458–460. For possible remedies of a student against victimizing teachers, see *id.* at 451 *et seq.*

The person need not be a student at the teacher's school for the student status to be deemed relevant. In *D.E.*, the Court of Appeals of Washington found that sexual relations with a minor female, a student of the district—but no longer a student of the school in which the teacher taught—justified the teacher's discharge.

Indeed, even if the person involved is not currently, but recently was, a student, an inference of prior association during that person's student status might arise. See G.O. v. Board of Education of Central School District No. 1, Towns of Brookhaven and Smithtown, 35 N.Y.2d at 544–545, 364 N.Y.S.2d at 446–447.

Situations involving students can lead to dismissal on separate grounds. In W.L. v. Board of Education of Chandler Unified School District No. 80 of Maricopa County, 136 Ariz. 552, 667 P.2d 746 (1983), the Arizona Court of Appeals upheld the dismissal of a teacher for failure to cooperate (including allegedly lying) in the investigation of a relationship between the teacher and a student which led to marriage.

Some states specifically criminalize a teacher's sexual activity with a student. See, *e.g.*, D.C. CODE ENCYCL. § 22-3002 (1967); ME. REV. STAT. ANN. tit. 17-A, §§ 253(2)(F) and 255(1)(F) (West Supp. 1984–85); and MISS. CODE ANN. § 97-29-3 (Supp. 1984).
338. See, *e.g.*, D.E. v. South Kitsap School District No. 402, 516 P.2d at 1082: "[T]he school board may properly conclude in such a situation that the conduct is inherently harmful to the teacher-student relation, and thus to the school district."
339. See also C.L. v. Ann Arbor School District, 344 N.W.2d 48 (Mich. App. 1983); and K.A. v. Ambach, 472 N.Y.S.2d 492 (N.Y.A.D. 1984).

Perhaps this or the fear of additional publicity accounts for the apparently low number of appeals from adverse decisions of school officials in such cases when "strong evidence for initial dismissal exists. . . . " Fleming, *supra* note 32, at 427.

340. 547 P.2d 1267 (S.Ct. Colo. 1976).
341. *Id.* at 1270.
342. See *id.* at 1270–1271.
343. *Id.* at 1273.
344. R.I. v. Davis, 627 P.2d at 1120.
345. *Id.* at 1119–1120.
346. *Id.* at 1115, 1121.
347. P.O. v. Kalama Public School District, 644 P.2d at 1230. See also C.R. v. Board of Education, City of Chicago, 46 Ill. App.3d 33, 4 Ill. Dec. 600, 360 N.E.2d 536 (1977); L.O. v. Board of Education of School District No. 27, 100 Ill. App.2d 108, 241 N.E.2d 495 (1968).
348. Y.A. v. Special Charter School District No. 150, Peoria County, 11 Ill. App.3d 239, 296 N.E.2d 74 (1973).
349. K.I. v. Wright, 437 F.Supp. 397 (M.D. Ala. 1977). "Unprofessional conduct like that committed by plaintiff clearly relates to the fitness of plaintiff to discharge his duties as a teacher." *Id.* at 400.
350. Penn-Delco School District v. U.R., 382 A.2d 162 (1978).
351. P.R. v. Yakima School District No. 7, 30 Wash. App.16, 632 P.2d 60 (1981).
352. B.O. v. Board of School Directors of Indiana Area School District, 377 A.2d 1284 (Comm.Ct. Pa. 1977).
353. R.R. v. Robb, 662 S.W.2d at 260.
354. See S.U. v. Meade Independent School District No. 101, 530 F.2d at 801–802; W.I. v. McDonald, 500 F.2d at 1112, 1113; D.R. v. Covington County Board of Education, 371 F.Supp. at 981, 984 (dissenting opinion); Board of Education of Long Beach Unified School District of Los Angeles County v. M.I., 19 Cal.3d at 701, 139 Cal.Rptr. at 706, 566 P.2d at 608, n. 5; P.E. v. State Board of Education, 10 Cal.3d at 35, 109 Cal. Rptr. at 669, 513 P.2d at 893; M.S. v. State Board of Education, 1 Cal.3d at 229, 82 Cal.Rptr. at 186–187, 461 P.2d at 386, n. 28; M.E. v. State Board of Education, 22 Cal. App.3d at 990, 101 Cal.Rptr. at 87–88; S.A. v. State Board of Education, 249 Cal. App.2d at 60–61, 57 Cal.Rptr. at 71; E.R. v. Iowa State Board of Public Instruction, 216 N.W.2d at 344; Y.N. v. School District No. 23, Lake County, Montana, 641 P.2d at 441 (quoting G.O. v. Board of Education of Central School District No. 1, Towns of Brookhaven and Smithtown, 35 N.Y.2d at 543–544, 364 N.Y.S.2d at 446, 324 N.E.2d at 111), and at 441–442; R.O. v. Springfield School District No. 19, 657 P.2d at 192, 193, 194–195; G.A. v. Tacoma School District No. 10, 559 P.2d at 1342, 1346; *Cf.* A.C. v. Board of Education of Montgomery County, 491 F.2d at 499–500.
355. The openness of certain conduct may inure to the teacher's benefit by dispelling any inference of impropriety. See F.I. v. Snyder, 476 F.2d at 378. Whether a place or conduct is public may itself be the subject of debate. In one case, involving conduct at a "swingers club" party in a private home, the court's opinion treated the conduct as "semi-public," P.E. v. State Board of Education, 10 Cal.3d at 34–35, 109 Cal.Rptr. at 669, 513 P.2d at 893, while the dissent labeled the conduct essentially private. *Id.* at 40–41, 109 Cal.Rptr. at 673, 513 P.2d at 897.
356. See D.R. v. Covington County Board of Education, 371 F.Supp. at 984 (dissenting opinion); Y.N. v. School District No. 23, Lake County, Montana, 641 P.2d at 441

(quoting G.O. v. Board of Education of Central School District No. 1, Towns of Brookhaven and Smithtown, 35 N.Y.2d at 543–544, 364 N.Y.S.2d at 446, 324 N.E.2d at 111).

357. See generally Clay, *supra* note 18, at 933–934.

358. See W.I. v. McDonald, 500 F.2d at 1115; D.R. v. Covington County Board of Education, 371 F.Supp. at 984 (dissenting opinion); R.O. v. Springfield School District No. 19, 657 P.2d at 193.

359. S.U. v. Meade Independent School District No. 101, 530 F.2d at 803, 804. See M.S. v. State Board of Education, 1 Cal.3d at 229, 82 Cal.Rptr. at 186, 461 P.2d at 386–387, n. 28; M.E. v. State Board of Education, 22 Cal.App.3d at 990–991, 101 Cal.Rptr. at 87–88 (quoting Board of Trustees v. Stubblefield, 16 Cal. App.3d 820, 826, 94 Cal.Rptr. 318, 322 (1971)); Y.N. v. School District No. 23, Lake County, Montana, 641 P.2d at 435; R.O. v. Springfield School District No. 19, 657 P.2d at 193; G.A. v. Tacoma School District No. 10, 559 P.2d at 1342, 1346.

360. See G.A. v. Tacoma School District No. 10, 559 P.2d at 1342, 1346. One court suggested that the publicness of the conduct involved in the case before the court reflected "a serious defect of moral character, normal prudence and good common sense." P.E. v. State Board of Education, 10 Cal.3d at 35, 109 Cal.Rptr. at 669, 513 P.2d at 893.

361. See P.E. v. State Board of Education, 10 Cal.3d at 41, 109 Cal.Rptr. at 673, 513 P.2d at 897 (dissenting opinion). For a suggestion that "teachers have not only a right but a duty to privacy," see Fleming, *supra* note 32, at 430.

362. *Cf.* S.U. v. Meade Independent School District No. 101, 530 F.2d at 804: "[She] did not seek to hide her relationship [with a man to whom she was not married], but neither did she flaunt it." See also E.R. v. Iowa State Board of Public Instruction, 216 N.W.2d at 344.

363. See Y.N. v. School District No. 23, Lake County, Montana, 641 P.2d at 442, where the teacher apparently agreed that his conduct adversely affected his teaching.

364. See the expert testimony summarized in T.H. v. Southwest School District, 483 F.Supp. at 1176–1177.

365. See G.O. v. Board of Education of Central School District No. 1, Towns of Brookhaven and Smithtown, 35 N.Y.2d at 543–544, 364 N.Y.S.2d at 446; Winks, *supra* note 26, at 453.

It has been suggested that teachers should not be disciplined merely because the public learned of private conduct through the indiscretion of any third party, especially if the third party is a school official. See M.S. v. State Board of Education, 1 Cal.3d at 229, 82 Cal.Rptr. at 186–187, 461 P.2d at 386, n. 28. For a suggestion that the means through which the conduct becomes known are irrelevant, see D.R. v. Covington County Board of Education, 371 F.Supp. at 984 (dissenting opinion).

Teachers allegedly injured by the notoriety caused by the charges may seek damages from the school district. See the complaint filed in A.U. v. Board of Education of Georgetown Community Unit School District No. 3 of Vermilion County, Illinois, 562 F.2d 446, 448 (7th Cir. 1977).

366. *But see* W.I. v. McDonald, 367 F.Supp. 530, 535 (D. Mass. 1973), *aff'd*, 500 F.2d 1110 (1st Cir. 1974); and G.A. v. Tacoma School District No. 10, 559 P.2d at 1346. In *G.A.*, the court rejected the teacher's argument that the school had

made the situation known, in part on the theory that "by seeking out homosexual company he took the risk his homosexuality would be discovered," *id.*, a point not wholly responsive to the argument.

367. T.H. v. Southwest School District, 483 F.Supp. at 1183.
368. See M.C. v. Draper, 564 F.2d at 906–908; S.U. v. Meade Independent School District, 530 F.2d at 802, 803; T.H. v. Southwest School District, 483 F.Supp. at 1174; R.E. v. Board of Education of Alton Community Unit School District No. 11, Madison and Jersey Counties, 19 Ill. App.3d at 484, 311 N.E.2d at 712; Y.N. v. School District No. 23, Lake County, Montana, 641 P.2d at 435; R.O. v. Springfield School District, 56 Or. App. at 201, 641 P.2d at 603; G.A. v. Tacoma School District No. 10, 559 P.2d at 1346–1347. *Cf.* S.E. v. Capital School District, 425 F.Supp. at 559; P.O. v. Kalama Public School District, No. 402, 644 P.2d at 1231.
369. Of course, if the teacher's conduct is constitutionally protected, *a fortiori* complaints (or the likelihood thereof) do not justify disciplinary action. L.E. v. Delaware State College, 455 F.Supp. at 248, 251. See also B.U. v. Cascade School District Union High School No. 5, 512 F.2d at 855.
370. T.H. v. Southwest School District, 483 F.Supp. at 1183 (emphasis in original).
371. *Cf.* M.C. v. Draper, 564 F.2d at 908; T.H. v. Southwest School District, 483 F.Supp. at 1175; W.E. v. Board of Education of Jefferson County School District No. R-1, 190 Colo. at 419–421, 547 P.2d at 1271, 1272; R.E. v. Board of Education of Alton Community Unit School District No. 11, Madison and Jersey Counties, 19 Ill. App.3d at 484–485, 311 N.E.2d at 712; E.R. v. Iowa State Board of Public Instruction, 216 N.W.2d at 339; New Mexico State Board of Education v. S.T., 571 P.2d at 1188.
372. See S.U. v. Meade Independent School District No. 101, 530 F.2d at 803; W.I. v. McDonald, 500 F.2d at 1115; D.R. v. Covington County Board of Education, 371 F.Supp. at 981 (dissenting opinion). See Winks, *supra*, note 26, at 453.
373. D.R. v. Covington County Board of Education, 371 F.Supp. at 981 (dissenting opinion). See T.H. v. Southwest School District, 483 F.Supp. at 1175; Winks, *supra* note 26, at 453.
374. See W.I. v. McDonald, 500 F.2d at 1115; D.R. v. Covington County Board of Education, 371 F.Supp. at 981 (dissenting opinion); Clay, *supra* note 18, at 931.
375. Under such a statute, actual conviction in a criminal court is required. See Long Beach Unified School District of Los Angeles County v. M.I., 19 Cal.3d at 703, 139 Cal.Rptr. at 707, 566 P.2d at 608.

For statutes authorizing or requiring dismissal or certificate revocation or denial upon conviction of specified offenses, see, *e.g.*, CAL. EDUC. CODE §§ 44345(i), 44346, 44436, and 44932(8) (West Supp. 1985); FLA. STAT. ANN. § 231.36(1)(a) and (4)(c) (West Supp. 1985); ILL. REV. STAT. ch. 122, ¶ 34–84b and ¶ 21–23a (West Supp. 1984–85); OR. REV. STAT. § 342.175(1)(a) and (2) (1981); S.D. CODIFIED LAWS ANN. § 13-42-10 (Supp. 1984); and TEX. EDUC. CODE ANN. §§ 13.109(2) (Vernon 1972) and 13.110 (Vernon Supp. 1985).

California statutorily requires law enforcement agents to notify school authorities of the arrest of school personnel for specified sexual offenses. CAL. PENAL CODE § 291 (West Supp. 1985). See also UTAH CODE ANN. § 77-26-22 (Supp. 1983).

376. See the discussion of such an approach in Board of Education of Long Beach Unified School District of Los Angeles County v. M.I., 19 Cal.3d at 703–704, 139 Cal.Rptr. at 707, 566 P.2d at 609.

377. The Oregon Supreme Court rejected a similar suggestion in R.O. v. Springfield School District No. 19, 657 P.2d at 195.

   Such a suggestion with regard to the unconvicted may be in tension with legislation providing automatic sanctions for the convicted. See Board of Education of Long Beach Unified School District of Los Angeles County v. M.I., 19 Cal.3d at 700–702, 139 Cal.Rptr. at 705–706, 566 P.2d at 607–608.

   Cf. P.E. v. State Board of Education, 10 Cal.3d at 40, 109 Cal.Rptr. at 673, 513 P.2d at 897 (dissenting opinion): "The commission of a sex act, surreptitiously observed, not disclosed to fellow teachers or to pupils, not remotely adversely affecting plaintiff's teaching ability, must fail to support revocation of the certificate even though the act is labeled 'criminal' on the books."

378. See P.E. v. State Board of Education, 10 Cal.3d at 34–35, 109 Cal.Rptr. at 668–669, 513 P.2d at 892–893; M.E. v. State Board of Education, 22 Cal. App.3d at 990–991, 101 Cal.Rptr. at 87–88. (Some language in *M.E.* suggests that the criminal conviction was enough in itself to establish unfitness. See *id.* at 991, 101 Cal.Rptr. at 88).

379. *Cf.* M.O. v. Knowles, 482 F.2d at 1074: "[T]he board was entitled to conclude that with the indictments pending [the teacher] could not effectively perform in an eighth grade classroom. . . . "

   Of course, if fitness is adversely affected, that in itself will usually suffice for official action, without reliance on the criminal aspects of the conduct.

380. See Board of Education of Long Beach Unified School District of Los Angeles County v. M.I., 19 Cal.3d at 702, 139 Cal.Rptr. at 706, 566 P.2d at 608, n.6.

381. See W.I. v. McDonald, 500 F.2d at 1116.

382. See T.H. v. Southwest School District, 483 F.Supp. at 1182; M.S. v. State Board of Education, 1 Cal.3d at 229, 237, 82 Cal.Rptr. at 186, 192, 461 P.2d at 386, 392; W.E. v. Board of Education of Jefferson County School District No. R-1, 190 Colo. at 421, 547 P.2d at 1273.

383. *Cf.* A.N. v. Drew Municipal Separate School District, 507 F.2d at 615, where the court criticized a rule barring the employment of parents of illegitimate children, in part because it made irrelevant the amount of time elapsed since the birth, thus barring a person from employment forever; and P.E. v. State Board of Education, 10 Cal.3d at 39, 109 Cal.Rptr. at 672, 513 P.2d at 896.

384. Clay, *supra* note 18, at 933. For statutes limiting the time within which certain charges may be brought, see ME. REV. STAT. tit. 20-A, § 13020(2) (West Supp. 1984–85); NEW YORK EDUC. LAW § 3020-a(1) (1981).

   Conduct too remote to be considered directly in connection with fitness may be relevant for impeachment purposes. See P.R. v. Yakima School District No. 7, 632 P.2d at 66.

385. See M.S. v. State Board of Education, 1 Cal.3d at 218, 82 Cal.Rptr. at 177, 461 P.2d at 377 ("a single incident"); E.R. v. Iowa State Board of Public Instruction, 216 N.W.2d at 344 ("an isolated occurrence"); P.O. v. Kalama Public School District, No. 402, 644 P.2d at 1231 (teacher "persisted in his behavior").

386. Clay, *supra* note 18, at 933.

387. See T.H. v. Southwest School District, 483 F.Supp. at 1182; Board of Education of Long Beach Unified School District of Los Angeles County v. M.I., 139

Cal.Rptr. at 707–708, 566 P.2d at 609–610; M.S. v. State Board of Education, 1 Cal.3d at 229, 82 Cal.Rptr. at 186, 461 P.2d at 386; W.E. v. Board of Education of Jefferson County School District No. R-1, 547 P.2d at 1273; E.R. v. Iowa State Board of Public Instruction, 216 N.W.2d at 344. See the findings of the state board of education alluded to in P.E. v. State Board of Education, 10 Cal.3d at 36, 109 Cal.Rptr. at 670, 513 P.2d at 894, n. 7.

388. Clay, *supra* note 18, at 933 (citing W.I. v. McDonald, 500 F.2d at 1112; and M.S. v. State Board of Education, 82 Cal.Rptr. at 191, 461 P.2d at 391).

389. See P.E. v. State Board of Education, 10 Cal.3d at 36, 109 Cal.Rptr. at 670, 513 P.2d at 894, n. 7: "[T]he 'risk of harm' which justified revocation of [the teacher's] license . . . is not the likelihood that [she] will perform additional sexual offenses but instead that she will be unable to teach moral principles, to act as an exemplar for her pupils, or to offer them suitable moral guidance." See also T.O. v. Dade County School Board, 318 So.2d at 159–160.

390. See, *e.g.,* Board of Education of Long Beach Unified School District of Los Angeles County v. M.I., 19 Cal.3d at 698, 139 Cal.Rptr. at 703, 566 P.2d at 605; P.E. v. State Board of Education, 10 Cal.3d at 37, 513 P.2d at 894 (dissenting opinion); M.S. v. State Board of Education, 1 Cal.3d at 225–226, 82 Cal.Rptr. at 183, 461 P.2d at 383; *Cf.* A.N. v. Drew Municipal Separate School District, 507 F.2d at 615; K.R. v. Independent School District, 304 N.W.2d 338, 345–346 (S.Ct. Minn. 1981); G.A. v. Tacoma School District No. 10, 559 P.2d at 1347 (dissenting opinion); and E.R. v. Iowa State Board of Public Instruction, 216 N.W.2d at 344.

391. See Board of Education of Long Beach Unified School District v. M.I., 19 Cal.3d at 700, 139 Cal.Rptr. at 705, 566 P.2d at 607; E.R. v. Iowa State Board of Public Instruction, 216 N.W.2d at 344.

392. See T.H. v. Southwest School District, 483 F.Supp. at 1182; M.S. v. State Board of Education, 1 Cal.3d at 229, 236, 82 Cal.Rptr. at 186, 192, 461 P.2d at 386, 391; W.E. v. Board of Education of Jefferson County School District No. R-1, 190 Colo. at 421, 547 P.2d at 1273.

393. See E.R. v. Iowa State Board of Public Instruction, 216 N.W.2d at 344.

One danger is that the lack of remorse may merely reflect a disagreement with the school board over the morality of certain conduct: "The board's discretion to consider removal for misconduct does not include a right to revoke a teacher's certificate because he happens to disagree with the board as to the morality of any particular type of conduct." M.S. v. State Board of Education, 1 Cal.3d at 229, 82 Cal.Rptr. at 186, 461 P.2d at 386, n. 26. But see *id.* at 247, 82 Cal.Rptr. at 200, 461 P.2d at 400 (dissenting opinion).

394. See ILL. REV. STAT. ch. 122, ¶ 24-12, (Smith-Hurd Supp. 1984–85) and, *e.g.,* C.R. v. Board of Education, City of Chicago, 46 Ill. App.3d at 35, 360 N.E.2d at 539; R.E. v. Board of Education of Alton Community Unit School District No. 11, Madison and Jersey Counties, 19 Ill. App.3d at 483–484, 311 N.E.2d at 711–712; Y.A. v. Special Charter School District No. 150, Peoria County, 11 Ill. App.3d at 241, 296 N.E.2d at 75; L.O. v. Board of Education of School District No. 27, Cook County, 100 Ill. App. at 109, 241 N.E.2d at 495–496.

The finding of irremediability must be supported by reasons. R.E. v. Board of Education of Alton Community School District No. 11, Madison and Jersey Counties, 19 Ill. App. at 484, 311 N.E.2d at 712.

See also MINN. STAT. § 125.12, sub. 6 and 8 (1980); K.R. v. Independent School District No. 593, 304 N.W.2d at 345.

Cf. Board of Education of Alamo-Gordo Public School District No. 1 v. J.N., 98 N.M. 602, 651 P.2d 1037 (N.M. App. 1982).

But see P.O. v. Kalama School District No. 402, 644 P.2d at 1231, holding that WASH. REV. CODE § 28A.67.065, prohibiting, prior to the establishment of an evaluation and improvement plan, the discharge of a teacher for classroom-related deficiencies, does not apply to a male teacher's inappropriate physical contact with female students; and P.R. v. Yakima School District No. 7, 632 P.2d at 66.

395. The Minnesota Supreme Court has stated that the lack of actual (as opposed to threatened) harm is one consideration. K.R. v. Independent School District No. 593, 304 N.W.2d at 346.

396. *Id.* at 345.

397. See text accompanying notes 390–391, *supra.*

398. K.R. v. Independent School District No. 593, 304 N.W.2d at 345–346.

399. On hearing procedures generally, see Fleming, *supra* note 32, at 425.

For examples of hearing procedures, see ILL. ANN. STAT. ch. 122, ¶ 24-12 (Smith-Hurd Supp. 1984–85); N.Y. EDUC. LAW § 3020-a(3) (McKinney 1981); and WIS. STAT. ANN. § 118.23(3) (West 1973).

400. *Cf.* R.R. v. Robb, 662 S.W.2d at 260.

401. See M.O. v. Knowles, 482 F.2d at 1071.

402. Though it must be sufficiently specific to enable the teacher to prepare an adequate defense, the notice may be adequate even if the nexus between the alleged conduct and teaching responsibilities is not specifically set out, as long as that nexus may obviously be inferred from the facts alleged. S.H. v. Salem School District 24J, Marion County, 64 Or. App. 777, 669 P.2d 1172 (1983).

Apparently, most teachers, upon being charged by the school district, quickly resign. Winks, *supra* note 26, at 450, n. 66.

403. See M.C. v. Draper, 564 F.2d at 911.

404. Due process requires an opportunity to respond to charges *prior to* dismissal, not just a *review* of the dismissal. Cleveland Board of Education v. Loudermill, 105 S.Ct. 1487 (1985); B.R. v. Bathke, 566 F.2d at 592. *Cf.* M.O. v. Knowles, 482 F.2d at 1071.

405. A right to a hearing clearly applies to dismissals midcontract and to dismissals of teachers with tenure. However, even nonrenewal of a teacher without formal tenure may call for a hearing if *de facto* tenure exists or if a stigma is attached to the teacher by the nonrenewal. See, *e.g.,* Perry v. Sinderman, 408 U.S. 593 (1972); Board of Regents v. Roth, 408 U.S. 564 (1972); M.C. v. Draper, 639 F.2d at 643; G.R. v. Duganne, 581 F.2d at 224; A.U. v. Board of Education of Georgetown Community Unit School District No. 3 of Vermilion County, Illinois, 562 F.2d at 449, 450; M.O. v. Knowles, 512 F.2d at 72–73; *id.,* 482 F.2d at 1071–1072; B.U. v. Cascade School District Union High School No. 5, 512 F.2d at 854; S.E. v. Capital School District, 425 F.Supp. at 558, n. 30.

406. See S.E. v. Capital School District, 425 F.Supp. at 558–563; W.E. v. Board of Education of Jefferson County School District No. R-1, 190 Colo. at 425, 547 P.2d at 1276; Penn-Delco School District v. U.R., 382 A.2d at 168; ILL. ANN. STAT. ch. 123, ¶ 24-12 (Smith-Hurd 1984–85) (hearing officer must be from outside the district and accredited by a national arbitration organization).

If the board's attorney has served as "prosecutor," he should not be present at the deliberation. W.E. v. Board of Education of Jefferson County School District No. R-1, 190 Colo. at 425, 547 P.2d at 1276. *Cf.* Breitling v. Solenberger, 585 F.Supp. 289 (D. Va. 1984); R.R. v. Robb, 662 S.W.2d at 260; L.A. v. Lee, 639 S.W.2d 111, 115 (W.D. Mo. 1982).

The hearing should be public if the teacher so requests. See ILL. ANN. STAT. ch. 122, ¶ 24-12 (Smith-Hurd Supp. 1984–85) (public at request of teacher or of board); WIS. STAT. ANN. § 118.23(3) (West 1973) (public at teacher's request).

407. See M.C. v. Draper, 564 F.2d at 911.

408. For statutes authorizing the issuance of subpoenas, see, *e.g.*, ILL. ANN. STAT. ch. 122, ¶ 24-12 (Smith-Hurd Supp. 1984–85); MINN. STATS. ANN. § 125.17(6) (West 1979).

409. When a child is called to testify, special procedures to determine competence may be needed. See C.R. v. Board of Education, City of Chicago, 46 Ill. App.3d at 41, 360 N.E.2d at 542–543.

410. See S.U. v. Meade Independent School District No. 101, 530 F.2d at 806–807.

411. See M.C. v. Draper, 564 F.2d at 912; E.R. v. Iowa State Board of Public Instruction, 216 N.W.2d at 342; P.R. v. Yakima School District No. 7, 632 P.2d at 63. But see Penn-Delco School District v. U.R., 392 A.2d at 168, holding that, although findings of fact and a statement of reasons would facilitate review, the matter was one for the legislature.

The teacher should be provided a copy of the transcript without charge. See MINN. STAT. ANN. § 125.17(5) (West 1979).

412. *See* Mount Healthy City School District Board of Education v. Doyle, 429 U.S. 274 (1977); A.V. v. Homewood City Board of Education, 674 F.2d at 339–340; B.R. v. Bathke, 566 F.2d at 591; M.C. v. Draper, 564 F.2d at 916, n. 17.

413. *Cf.* M.O. v. Knowles, 482 F.2d at 1071.

414. See H.A. v. Governing Board of Roseland School District, Sonoma County, 46 Cal.App.3d 644, 653, 120 Cal.Rptr. 827, 832 (1975); R.S. v. Board of Education of School District No. 1, Denver Public Schools, 677 P.2d at 350; and L.A. v. Lee, 639 S.W.2d at 114. The teacher may be put in an awkward situation with regard to asserting his fifth amendment rights. See H.A. v. Governing Board of Roseland School District, Sonoma County, 46 Cal. App.3d at 652–653, 120 Cal.Rptr. at 832; and R.S. v. Board of Education of School District No. 1, Denver Public Schools, 677 P.2d at 350. But see L.A. v. Lee, 639 S.W.2d at 112–113. The hearing officer may have discretion to grant a continuance pending criminal proceedings. See, e.g., R.S. v. Board of Education of School District No. 1, Denver Public Schools, 677 P.2d at 350 (citing COLO. REV. STAT. § 22-63-117(6) (Supp. 1982)).

415. See Cal. App.3d at 653, 120 Cal.Rptr. at 832. *Cf.* M.O. v. Knowles, 482 F.2d at 1071–1074, where the Fifth Circuit approved delaying a hearing, following the teacher's indictment, and subsequent suspension with pay during the course of a one-year contract. "A hearing before the board on the issue of [the teacher's] guilt, or the issue of probable cause of guilt, would have placed the board in an unseemly position vis-a-vis the law enforcement structure.... Board findings in one direction would have injured the interests of the state, and in another direction would have damaged those of [the teacher]." *Id.* at 1073.

416. For statutes authorizing suspension, see *e.g.*, FLA. STAT. ANN. § 230.33(7)(e)

(West Supp. 1985) (suspension may be without pay with back pay granted if charges not sustained); ILL. ANN. STAT. ch. 122, ¶ 24-12 (Smith-Hurd Supp. 1984–85) (board may suspend without pay; teacher to be repaid if cleared); N.C. GEN. STAT. § 115c-325(f) (1983) (may suspend without pay); VA. CODE § 22.1-315 (1980).

417. See M.O. v. Knowles, 482 F.2d at 1071–1074. *Cf.* In the Matter of J.R., 35 N.Y.2d at 542–543, 364 N.Y.S.2d at 444–445.

Legislation may require one charged with certain crimes to take a leave of absence. See H.A. v. Governing Board of Roseland School District, Sonoma County, 46 Cal.App.3d at 650, 120 Cal.Rptr. at 830–831 (citing CAL. EDUC. CODE § 13409).

418. If a guilty plea is used, it should be clear that the plea procedure included an admission by the teacher concerning the problem conduct. *Cf.* S.A. v. State Board of Education, 249 Cal. App.2d at 61–62, 57 Cal.Rptr. at 71–72. A nolo contendere plea, of course, should be inadmissible at the civil proceeding since it implies no factual admission. Cf. *id.*

419. See J.E. v. Board of Education of District of Columbia, 294 F.2d at 261; H.A. v. Governing Board of Roseland School District, Sonoma County, 46 Cal. App.3d at 651–652, 120 Cal.Rptr. at 831; Board of Education of El Monte School District of Los Angeles v. C.A., 35 Cal. App.3d 490, 110 Cal.Rptr.916 (1974) (Neither res judicata nor collateral estoppel bars dismissal proceedings following acquittal on a criminal charge)

420. Board of Education of El Monte School District of Los Angeles County v. C.A., 35 Cal. App.3d at 495–496, 110 Cal.Rptr. at 920.

421. Y.A. v. Special Charter School District No. 150, Peoria County, 11 Ill. App.3d at 242, 296 N.E.2d at 76. Even if the hearing board erroneously kept the evidence of acquittal out, the error may be held harmless. See *id.*

422. See Governing Board of Mountain View School District of Los Angeles County v. M.T., 36 Cal. App.3d at 551, 111 Cal.Rptr. at 727–728; R.O. v. Springfield School District No. 19, 56 Or. at 207, 641 P.2d at 607. See also L.I. v. Board of Education of Twin Cedars Community School District, 350 N.W.2d 748 (Iowa App. 1984) (school board was entitled to consider polygraph results).

423. For an example of school board initiative in this regard, see S.U. v. Meade Independent School District No. 101, 530 F.2d at 807.

Chapter 5

THE STUDENT'S PERSONAL LIFE

INTRODUCTION

In 1928, Wanda Dodge Myers enrolled in the Moss Point, Mississippi high school. Before school began, however, the school superintendent discovered that Wanda was married and denied her admission, pursuant to an ordinance adopted by the Moss Point school trustees barring married persons from the schools. The ordinance was based on the idea that the presence of married students in the public schools would be detrimental to the good government and usefulness of the schools because "the marriage relation brings about views of life which should not be known to unmarried children."[1] Wanda sought judicial resolution of "whether the ordinance under which she was denied admittance was valid."[2] Disagreeing with the reasoning behind the ordinance, the Mississippi Supreme Court stated, "Marriage is a domestic relation highly favored by the law."[3] Thus, the Mississippi Supreme Court declared the ordinance barring married persons, otherwise eligible, from public schools unreasonable, an abuse of discretion and, therefore, void.

Wanda's case reflects the interest in the student's out-of-classroom activities which school officials have demonstrated. This chapter will explore the law's treatment of the married student, the pregnant student, the student mother, and the otherwise sexually active student.

THE MARRIED STUDENT

Although the courts do not generally interfere with the discretion of state school boards to run the public schools, the courts will, as Wanda's case illustrates, step in if a school board has abused its discretion or violated a student's constitutional rights. In *Tinker v. Des Moines Independent Community School District*,[4] the U.S. Supreme Court observed that "[s]tudents in school as well as out of school are 'persons' under our Constitution. They are possessed of fundamental rights which the State

169

must respect, just as they themselves must respect their obligations to the State."[5] Although no U.S. Supreme Court case has dealt specifically with the rights of married students to attend public high schools and to participate in extracurricular activities, other courts have begun according more protection to married students' rights.[6]

The Right to Attend School

Although courts have not looked favorably upon the complete exclusion of married students from high school,[7] the Tennessee Supreme Court in 1957 upheld a school board regulation requiring that any student who marries be temporarily excluded.[8] The court accepted the school board's argument that married students have a detrimental effect on other students for a few months immediately following the marriage and that, therefore, the rule was not arbitrary or unreasonable. The court distinguished *McLeod v. State,*[9] the decision in Wanda's case, on the grounds that the ordinance there involved permanently expelled the student.[10]

More recently, courts have disapproved even the temporary exclusion of married high school students. The Kentucky Court of Appeals, in *Board of Education of Harrodsburg v. Bentley,*[11] struck down as arbitrary and unreasonable a school board regulation requiring that any student who married withdraw from school subject to possible readmission after one year.[12] The *Bentley* court noted that although the school board purportedly enacted the rule to prevent the school disruption caused immediately before and after the marriage of a student, the school board in fact defeated this very purpose by allowing students who got married to remain in school for up to six weeks in order to complete the current term.[13] The resolution of a Texas school board which suspended for three weeks any student getting married met a similar fate, the court indicating that excluding a student for any length of time due to that student's marriage constituted an abuse of the school board's discretion.[14] As the court in *Anderson v. Canyon Independent School District*[15] said in voiding a school board rule requiring married students to withdraw from school for the rest of the school year: "If a student is entitled to admission, the question of length of exclusion is not material."[16]

The Right to Participate in Extracurricular Activities—The Old View

After courts began looking askance upon school board rules which kept married students out of school for any length of time, some school boards, in an effort to discourage marriage among high school students, sought to keep married students out of extracurricular activities. These boards felt such rules reduced the number of teenage marriages in part by preventing married students from becoming class idols through successful participation in extracurricular activities.[17] "If any married students are in a position of idolization," one court noted, "the more desirous is the group to mimic."[18] Courts were understandably reluctant to find an abuse of discretion on the part of school boards promulgating such rules: "Boards of education, rather than courts, are charged with the important and difficult duty of operating the public schools. . . . The Court's duty, regardless of its personal views, is to uphold the Board's regulation unless it is generally viewed as being arbitrary and unreasonable."[19] Until 1970,[20] consequently, courts upheld school board rules barring married students from extracurricular activities; in the courts' view, several legitimate purposes prompted such rules.

In *State v. Stevenson*,[21] the court noted that by enforcing laws forbidding underage couples from marrying without the consent of the "juvenile judge," the state of Ohio itself manifested its disapproval of teenage marriages.[22] The incidence of failure of such marriages justified the State's disapproval.[23] Accordingly, the court reasoned, any school board policy making teenage marriages unpopular, such as keeping married students from extracurricular activities, should be supported.[24]

School boards discouraged student marriages not merely because they occur "prior to the age set by law,"[25] or often fail, but also because many married students drop out of school.[26] Concern for the morals of unmarried high school students also caused school boards to restrict married students to the classroom. School officials worried that married students, whose "personal relationships . . . are different from those of non-married students",[27] could be a bad influence on unmarried students, especially during "informal extracurricular activities where supervision is more difficult."[28]

Finally, school boards adopted rules barring married students from extracurricular activities in order to protect the teenage marriage itself. Extracurricular activities take up time that married students need both for their marital obligations[29] and for their basic education,[30] an education "even more essential for married students."[31]

All of these reasons led courts to conclude that such rules were not arbitrary or unreasonable and did not, therefore, constitute an abuse of school board discretion.

Before 1970, courts concluded as well that such rules did not violate the equal protection clause of the Fourteenth Amendment, even though they created two separate classes of students for extracurricular purposes alone.[32] Not all classifications, after all, offend the equal protection clause: "Laws or regulations resulting in classifications having a sound and reasonable basis do not offend the equal protection clause of the United States Constitution."[33] Of course, it was important, even under the pre-1970 view, that the regulations were uniformly applied to all married students.[34]

Some courts, it should be added, viewed participation in extracurricular activities as a privilege subject to eligibility requirements:[35] "It is conceded, as plaintiff insists, that he has a constitutional right both to attend school and to get married. But he has no 'right' to compel the Board of Education to exercise its discretion to his advantage so he can participate in the named activities."[36]

The Right to Participate in Extracurricular Activities— The Modern View

Since 1970, courts have begun using equal protection analysis to strike down school board rules barring married students from extracurricular activities. Under this analysis, the action of a school board is considered state action because the school board is an arm of the State.[37] Although a classification usually offends the equal protection clause only if there is no rational basis for it, a "suspect" classification, or one infringing upon a fundamental right, calls for close judicial scrutiny and offends the equal protection clause unless justified by a compelling state interest.[38]

A school board classification based upon marital status is "suspect" because it impinges upon the right to marry, a right deemed "fundamental" by the United States Supreme Court.[39] Accordingly, in *Holt v. Shelton*,[40] the United States District Court struck down a school board regulation forbidding married students from participating in extracurricular activities. The right to marry, said the court, is a fundamental right under federal constitutional law,[41] one, therefore, whose infringement, in the absence of a compelling state interest, is constitutionally impermissible.[42] Other courts have followed the *Holt* lead.[43]

Interestingly, the *Holt* court could not find even a rational basis for the regulation restricting married students to the classroom,[44] and other courts as well have struck down such regulations solely on the strength of the rational basis test.[45] At least one court used an intermediate test, that is, whether the classification bears a fair and substantial relation to the object of the legislation,[46] to invalidate a similar rule.[47] Even that court, however, clearly suggested that the rule might not survive the rational basis test.[48]

Courts after 1970 thus concluded that justifications advanced by school officials for promulgating rules barring married students from extracurricular activities were insufficient to overcome the challenges to the classification.[49]

Responding to the argument that official policy should make student marriage unpopular in order to reflect state disapproval, some recent cases,[50] conceding that any state wishing to discourage teenage marriages may do so, have stressed that the school boards have no legislative authority to penalize couples who have legally married. In *Beeson v. Kiowa County School District RE-1*, for example, the court found "no specific legislative support for a policy which discriminates against married students."[51] Another court observed that state statutes had not explicitly or implicitly granted local school authorities the power to discourage teenage marriages.[52] Even if a school board had such authority, the implementing regulation may well be ineffectual. One court, sympathetic to the school board's purpose of discouraging teenage marriage,[53] nonetheless concluded that the school board's own statistics failed to show that the rule was significantly successful.[54]

Similarly, courts have found unpersuasive the argument that a regulation barring married students from extracurricular activities is needed to solve the serious high school drop-out problem.[55] There is, said the court in *Hollon v. Mathis Independent School District*, "no justifiable relationship between the marriage of high school athletes and the overall drop-out problem. . . . "[56]

School officials have continued to defend regulations barring married students from extracurricular activities on the ground that married students may in such informal settings be a bad influence on unmarried students.[57] More recent cases, however, have found no substantial evidence that the informal association of married students with unmarried students is likely to result in the "moral pollution" of the latter.[58] Further, if the purpose of the rule is to promote a "wholesome atmosphere," then the rule is both over- and under-inclusive. It is over-inclusive because it includes married students of good moral character who would not contribute to an unwholesome atmosphere, and it is under-inclusive because it does not include unmarried students of bad moral character who would contribute to an unwholesome atmosphere.[59] Therefore, under this analysis, the classification is unconstitutional due to the lack of a "fair and substantial relation between the classification and the objective sought."[60]

With regard to the contention that extracurricular activities consume time that married students should spend discharging their marital obligations, the court in *Moran v. School District #7, Yellowstone County,* said: "What married persons do with their time outside of school and how they discharge their matrimonial responsibilities is outside the statutory authority of the school board."[61] Indeed, one's marital responsibilities may best be served through postsecondary education, a prospect that may be significantly dimmed for a student prevented from participating in extracurricular activities.[62]

Courts have not been persuaded that such regulations are needed to enable married students to focus on their basic education. The opinions in both *Beeson*[63] and *Moran*[64] pointed out that an academic eligibility requirement on anyone's participation in extracurricular activities would ensure that all students involved in activities outside the classroom, married or not, keep up with their class work.

Finally, in response to the argument that participation in extracurricular activities is a privilege subject to eligibility requirements, the court in *Bell v. Lone Oak Independent School District*[65] pointed out that a state providing a privilege must do so without discrimination:

> [I]f the state and the local school provide free public education and an athletic program, it must do so in a manner not calculated to discriminate against a class of individuals who will be treated differently from the remainder of the students, unless the school district can show that such rule is a necessary restraint to promote a compelling state interest.[66]

Indeed, extracurricular activities may be considered not a privilege but rather an integral part of the student's education.[67]

In short, courts have lately been more willing to scrutinize the justifications advanced for such regulations and to find these justifications insufficient under the equal protection clause or, at least, beyond the legislatively authorized power of school officials.[68]

PREGNANCY, MOTHERHOOD AND STUDENT STATUS

Three different categories of student have confronted the courts with questions concerning the relevance of motherhood to student status: pregnant students, unmarried student mothers and married student mothers.

Pregnant Students

Some judicial authority supports the state's power to exclude pregnant students from the classroom. In *State v. Chamberlain*,[69] decided in 1961, a married high school junior who was pregnant challenged a school board regulation, partly based on the fear of disciplinary problems,[70] prohibiting any pregnant student, married or not, from attending regular classes. The court supported the school board, noting that its "primary purpose in adopting this regulation was to safeguard and protect the pregnant student whose physical well-being might be endangered as she went about, was subjected to and engaged in the day-to-day school work and activities."[71] The rule, concluded the court, did not constitute an abuse of the board's discretion.[72]

The speculativeness of the health argument in the typical pregnant student situation is indicated by a later case, *Ordway v. Hargraves*, involving a similar rule.[73] Both the pregnant student's attending physician and her obstetrician testified that nothing precluded her ability to attend classes until immediately before delivery.[74] The court agreed: "[N]o danger to petitioner's physical or mental health resultant from her attending classes during regular school hours has been shown. . . . "[75]

In *Ordway*, the principal's testimony implied that the rule reflected the board's reluctance to appear to condone premarital sex.[76] Relying on *Tinker's* teaching, however, the court found no reason to fear that the pregnant student's presence would cause any "disruption of or interference with school activities or pose a threat of harm to others."[77] Nothing, therefore, justified segregating her or otherwise giving her educational treatment inferior to that provided the rest of her class.[78]

Unwed Mothers

Some school boards have asserted the right to exclude unwed mothers on the grounds of moral character. In 1971, for example, in *Shull v Columbus Municipal Separate School District*,[79] the school board, pursuant to a district rule, denied high school admission to an unwed mother. The rule was based on fears that other students would be negatively influenced by associating with a person lacking in moral character.[80] Relying on its previous decision involving the same school district,[81] the federal district court held that unless the board accorded the student a hearing with "written specifications of charges upon which the school district relied to render plaintiff so lacking in moral character as to taint the education of other students with whom she might come in contact . . . ,"[82] she must be allowed to attend the high school; the fact alone of unwed motherhood is insufficient for exclusion.[83] The court emphasized that since the board had not charged any misconduct other than the status of unwed motherhood, the relief sought should be granted; the school board policy, the court concluded, violated the equal protection clause of the Fourteenth Amendment.[84]

In *Perry v Grenada Municipal Separate School District*,[85] the same court struck down, apparently on both due process and equal protection grounds, a similar rule. The court acknowledged the school board's right to exclude students lacking in moral character[86] and the possibility that the presence of unwed mothers in the school could imply society's approval of illegitimate births.[87] Nonetheless, despite past acts, one can reestablish a good reputation,[88] and unwed mothers, therefore, are entitled to admission unless a fair hearing establishes that "their presence in the schools will taint the education of other students."[89]

In *Houston v Prosser*,[90] a fifteen-year-old mother, apparently unwed,[91] challenged a high school policy barring parents[92] from regular daytime classes. Applying a "rational basis" test,[93] the court found no violation of equal protection. Since student-parents are "normally more precocious than other students. . . . it is *conceivable* that their presence in a regular daytime school could result in the disruption thereof."[94] Since an alternative night program was provided,[95] moreover, the policy did not penalize the student's exercise of her fundamental constitutional right of procreation.[96]

Married Mothers

Finally, in *Alvin Independent School District v. Cooper*,[97] the school district—again pursuant to a school board rule—denied admission to a married mother. The court concluded that as long as the student was of an age for which the state furnished school funds, the board lacked the "legal authority" to establish such a rule.[98] The only educational alternatives available to one in her position were adult education, which required one to be at least twenty-one years old, correspondence courses, which would not carry credit for college admission, or private schools at her own expense. The rule thus violated her right to a public education under state law.[99]

THE CURRENT OUTLOOK

Houston v. Prosser upheld a rule barring from regular classes all parents, male or female, wed or unwed.[100] Cases like *Ordway v. Hargraves*, on the other hand, illustrate the trend toward allowing educational opportunities to student mothers. Still other legal developments must be taken into account. The United States Supreme Court has found education not to be a fundamental right[101] but, rather, has placed it in an intermediate category requiring only a substantial, rather than a compelling, state interest for its denial.[102] Cases like *Prosser*, applying only a rational basis test, and like *Ordway*, relying on education as a "basic personal right or liberty," require, therefore, some reassessment. Moreover, restricting pregnant girls and student mothers to separate educational programs may not even constitute a *denial* of an education.[103]

Finally, plaintiffs challenging special school rules for pregnant students or for student mothers may have recourse not only to the federal Constitution, but also to state constitutions, state statutes, or federal or state regulations. Especially important today are Title IX regulations barring discrimination based on parental status.[104] Under these, a covered school district may operate special programs for pregnant students only if the programs are completely voluntary.[105] Otherwise, schools may not treat students differently because of their actual or potential parental status.[106]

SEXUAL MISCONDUCT OR ORIENTATION

Aside from cases dealing with pregnant students or student mothers, reported decisions involving the adverse official treatment of high school students for alleged sexual misconduct or orientation are rare. Nonetheless, a serious lack of morality justifies excluding students from a public school.[107] The *Perry* court, for example, although concluding that students could not be excluded solely for being unwed mothers, confirmed that a lack of moral character might justify exclusion.[108]

If the fact alone of unwed motherhood is not enough, what is? A very early case concluded that conduct amounting to prostitution would constitute a lack of morality sufficient to justify exclusion.[109] To the student's argument that she had not violated school rules and had not been guilty of misconduct in school,[110] the court responded that "open, gross immorality, in a female, manifested by licentious propensities, language, manners and habits, amounting even to actual prostitution" justified exclusion. The court felt that unsuspecting children should not be exposed to the "contaminating influence of those of depraved sentiments and vicious propensities and habits. . . . "[111]

In *Street v Cobb County School District*,[112] the student-plaintiff, who had left her mother's home to live with her eighteen-year-old boyfriend, was dismissed (1) because, since she did not live with a parent or guardian, she no longer was a "resident student," and (2) because her living arrangements could constitute a bad influence on other students.[113] Married minors, however, were allowed to attend school, although not living with a parent or guardian. Moreover, unwed pregnant students were allowed to attend school despite their possible bad influence on other students. Since neither of the justifications advanced by the district reflected a legitimate state interest, the dismissal failed equal protection analysis.[114]

In *Fricke v Lynch*,[115] finally, a federal district court held that a male homosexual high school student must be allowed to attend the senior prom with a male escort; excluding him, even on account of safety concerns, which could largely be alleviated, would violate the student's free speech rights under the first amendment.[116]

Several points seem clear in modern-day disciplining or other adverse treatment of alleged student sexual misconduct or sexual orientation by public school officials. First, the situation must be school-related in some manner. Presumably, what a student does in the privacy of his home, for example, may be of concern to his parents or even to the police, but, absent unusual circumstances, not to school authorities. Second, a school nexus is not enough; the state must have a legitimate reason for its rules, especially, in light of *Tinker,* if a speech right is involved. Third, appropriate procedural protections must be provided.

CONCLUSION

Public school authorities, as courts have recently recognized, are not justified in denying education or extracurricular activities to students merely because they marry or become parents. Every legitimate interest of the school can be protected through the enforcement of standards of performance applicable to all students. With regard to conduct generally, the school's interest is limited to the protection of the school community. To be sure, this interest includes warning students of the hazards and costs of marriage and of irresponsible sex, and prohibiting sexual activities during school hours, in connection with student functions, or on school property. States should follow the lead of Massachusetts, which has statutorily prohibited the expulsion, suspension or other discipline of a student on the grounds of marriage, pregnancy, parenthood or any conduct unconnected with school-sponsored activities.[117]

NOTES

1. McLeod v. State, 154 Miss. 468, 475, 122 So. 737, 738 (1929).
2. *Id.* at 472, 122 So. at 738.
3. *Id.* at 475, 122 So. at 738.
4. 393 U.S. 503 (1969).
5. *Id.* at 511.
6. Interestingly, some school boards have tried to compel married pupils to attend high school under state compulsory school attendance laws. The few cases considering whether married teenagers can be compelled to go to school have concluded, although for different reasons, that a married pupil is emancipated and no longer subject to state compulsory school attendance laws. See Knowles, *High Schools, Marriage, and the Fourteenth Amendment,* 11 J.FAMILY L. 711, 715–719 (1972).
7. See Nutt v. Board of Education, 128 Kan. 507, 278 P. 1065 (1929): McLeod v. State, 154 Miss. 468, 122 So. 737 (1929). But see Houston v. Prosser, 361 F.Supp. 295 (N.D. Ga. 1973) (dictum).
8. State ex rel. Thompson v. Marion County Board of Education, 202 Tenn. 29, 302 S.W.2d 57 (1957).
9. McLeod v. State, 154 Miss. 468, 122 So. 737 (1929).

10. State ex rel. Thompson v. Marion County Board of Education, 302 S.W.2d at 59.
11. Board of Education of Harrodsburg v. Bentley, 383 S.W.2d 677 (Ky. App. 1964).
12. *Id.* at 679.
13. *Id.* at 680–681.
14. Carrollton-Farmers Branch Indiana School District v. Knight, 418 S.W.2d 535, 542 (Tex. Civ. App. 1967).
15. Anderson v. Canyon Independent School District, 412 S.W.2d 387 (Tex. Civ. App. 1967).
16. *Id.* at 390.
17. See Cochrane v. Board of Education of Mesick Consolidated School District, 360 Mich. 390, 413, 103 N.W.2d 569, 581 (1960) (evenly divided court) (Kavanagh, J.); and State ex rel. Baker v. Stevenson, 27 Ohio Op.2d 223, 226, 189 N.E.2d 181, 185 (1962).
18. State ex rel. Baker v. Stevenson, 27 Ohio Op.2d at 227, 189 N.E.2d at 185.
19. *Id.* at 225, 189 N.E.2d at 184. See also Board of Directors of Independent School District of Waterloo v. Green, 259 Iowa 1260, 1267, 147 N.W.2d 854, 858 (1967); Estay v. LaFourche Parish School Board, 230 So.2d 443, 448 (La. App. 1969); Cochrane v. Board of Education of Mesick Consolidated School District, 360 Mich. at 400, 103 N.W.2d at 580 (Kavanagh, J.); McLeod v. State, 154 Miss. at 474, 122 So. at 738; State ex rel. Thompson v. Marion County Board of Education, 302 S.W.2d at 59; Kissick v. Garland Independent School District, 330 S.W.2d 708, 710 (Tex. Civ. App. 1959).
20. Indiana High School Athletic Association v. Raike, 164 Ind. App.169, 187, 329 N.E.2d 66, 78 (1975).
21. State ex rel. Baker v. Stevenson, 27 Ohio Op. at 223, 189 N.E.2d at 181.
22. *Id.* at 228, 189 N.E.2d at 187. See also Board of Directors of Independent School District of Waterloo v. Green, 259 Iowa at 1269, 147 N.W.2d at 859; Cochrane v. Board of Education of Mesick Consolidated School District, 360 Mich. at 411, 103 N.W.2d at 579 (Kavanagh, J.).
23. State ex rel. Baker v. Stevenson, 27 Ohio Op.2d at 228, 189 N.E.2d at 187.
24. See *id.:* "The school authorities, under whose supervision and control come the high school students, cannot be charged with abusing their discretion in promulgating rules which tend to make such marriages unpopular."
25. Board of Directors of Independent School District of Waterloo v. Green, 259 Iowa at 1268, 147 N.W.2d at 858.
26. State ex rel. Baker v. Stevenson, 27 Ohio Op.2d at 226, 189 N.E.2d at 184. See also Board of Directors of Independent School District of Waterloo v. Green, 259 Iowa at 1268, 147 N.W.2d at 859; Estay v. LaFourche Parish School Board, 230 So.2d at 449; Kissick v. Garland Independent School District, 330 S.W.2d at 710; Starkey v. Board of Education of Davis County School District, 381 P.2d 718, 720–721 (Utah 1963).
27. Board of Directors of Independent School District of Waterloo v. Green, 259 Iowa at 1268, 147 N.W.2d at 859. See also Estay v. LaFourche Parish School Board, 230 So.2d at 446.
28. Board of Directors of Independent School District of Waterloo v. Green, 259 Iowa at 1268, 147 N.W.2d at 859. See also Cochrane v. Board of Education of Mesick Consolidated School District, 360 Mich. at 393, 103 N.W.2d at 570–571 (Kelly, J.).

29. See Board of Directors of Independent School District of Waterloo v. Green, 259 Iowa at 1268, 147 N.W.2d at 859; Estay v. LaFourche Parish School Board, 230 So.2d at 447; Cochrane v. Board of Education of Mesick Consolidated School District, 360 Mich. at 394, 103 N.W.2d at 571 (Kelly, J.); State ex rel. Baker v. Stevenson, 27 Ohio Op.2d at 227, 189 N.E.2d at 186; Starkey v. Board of Education of Davis County School District, 381 P.2d at 720–721.

30. See Board of Directors of School District of Waterloo v. Green, 259 Iowa at 1268, 147 N.W.2d at 858; Estay v. LaFourche Parish School Board, 230 So.2d at 447; Cochrane v. Board of Education of Mesick Consolidated School District, 360 Mich. at 444, 103 N.W.2d at 581 (Kavanagh, J.); Kissick v. Garland Independent School District, 330 S.W.2d at 710.

31. Board of Directors of School District of Waterloo v. Green, 259 Iowa at 1268, 147 N.W.2d at 858.

32. Board of Directors of Independent School District of Waterloo v. Green, 259 Iowa at 1269–1270, 147 N.W.2d at 859; Estay v. LaFourche Parish School Board, 230 So.2d at 447, 450.

33. Estay v. LaFourche Parish School Board, 230 So.2d at 447 (citing State v. Winehill & Rosenthal, 147 La. 781, 86 So. 181 (1920)).

34. Estay v. LaFourche Parish School Board, 230 So.2d at 446. See also Starkey v. Board of Education of Davis County School District, 381 P.2d at 720.

35. See Board of Directors of Independent School District of Waterloo v. Green, 259 Iowa at 1270, 147 N.W.2d at 860; Estay v. LaFourche Parish School Board, 230 So.2d at 449; Starkey v. Board of Education of Davis County School District, 381 P.2d at 721.

36. Starkey v. Board of Education of Davis County School District, 381 P.2d at 721. See also Board of Directors of Independent School District of Waterloo v. Green, 259 Iowa at 1270, 147 N.W.2d at 860; and Estay v. LaFourche Parish School Board, 230 So.2d at 449.

37. West Virginia State Board of Education v. Barnette, 319 U.S. 624, 637 (1943): "The Fourteenth Amendment, as now applied to the States, protects the citizen against the State itself and all of its creatures—Boards of Education not excepted." See also Holt v. Shelton, 341 F.Supp. 821, 823 (M.D. Tenn. 1972).

38. Plyler v. Doe, 457 U.S. 202, 216–217, 217, n.15; San Antonio Independent School District v. Rodriguez, 411 U.S. 1, 17 (1972); Houston v. Prosser, 361 F.Supp. at 297–298; Holt v. Shelton, 341 F.Supp. at 823; Indiana High School Athletic Association v. Raike, 164 Ind. App. at 177–178, 329 N.E.2d at 72. See generally, K. ALEXANDER, SCHOOL LAW 428–429 (1980).

39. The U.S. Supreme Court, in Loving v. Virginia, 388 U.S. 1, 12 (1967), observed: "Marriage is one of the 'basic civil rights of man', fundamental to our very existence and survival." (Citing Skinner v. Oklahoma, 316 U.S. 535, 541 (1942)). See also Zablocki v. Redhail, 434 U.S. 374, 383–384 (1978): "The Court's opinion [in *Loving*] could have rested solely on the basis of race in violation of the equal protection clause.... But the Court went on to hold that the [miscegenation] laws arbitrarily deprived the couple of a fundamental liberty protected by the due process clause, the freedom to marry.... More recent decisions have established that the right to marry is part of the fundamental 'right of privacy' implicit in the Fourteenth Amendment's due process clause." See also Eisenstadt v. Baird, 405 U.S. 438, 454 (1972) ("We hold that by providing dissimilar treatment for married and unmarried persons who are

similarly situated, Massachusetts General Laws Ann., c. 272, §§ 21 and 21A [making it a felony for any one to sell contraceptives to an unmarried person] violate the equal protection clause.").

40. 341 F.Supp. 821 (M.D. Tenn. 1972).

41. *Id.* at 822–823 (citing Loving v. Virginia, 388 U.S.1 (1967)).

42. Holt v. Shelton, 341 F.Supp. at 823. The court found earlier cases upholding such regulations unpersuasive: "[They] are either inapposite or they fail to apply the appropriate constitutional standard." *Id.* at 822.

43. See Beeson v. Kiowa County School District RE-1, 567 P.2d 801, 805 (Colo. App. 1977); Bell v. Lone Oak Independent School District, 507 S.W.2d 636, 637–638 (Tex. Civ. App. 1974), *temporary injunction vacated on grounds of mootness,* 515 S.W.2d 252 (1974).

44. 341 F.Supp. at 823: "Indeed, they have failed to show that the regulation in question is even rationally related to — not to mention 'necessary' to promote — any legitimate state interest at all."

45. See Romans v. Crenshaw, 354 F.Supp. 868, 871 (S.D. Tex. 1972); Moran v. School District #7, Yellowstone County, 350 F.Supp. 1180, 1182 (D. Mont. 1972).

46. Indiana High School Athletic Association v. Raike, 164 Ind. App. at 179, 329 N.E.2d at 73 (citing Village of Belle Terre v. Boraas, 416 U.S. 1 (1974)). The court used an "intermediate scrutiny" test because the regulation "shackles two important rights," the right to marry and the right to participate in interscholastic athletics. 164 Ind. App. at 183, 329 N.E.2d at 75–76.

47. Indiana High School Athletic Association v. Raike, 164 Ind. App. at 188–189, 329 N.E.2d at 79,

48. *Id.* at 186, 329 N.E.2d at 77.

49. See Romans v. Crenshaw, 354 F.Supp. at 871; Moran v. School District #7, Yellowstone County, 350 F.Supp. at 1186–1187; Holt v. Shelton, 341 F.Supp. at 822–823; Beeson v. Kiowa County School District RE-1, 567 P.2d at 805–806; Indiana High School Athletic Association v. Raike, 164 Ind. App. at 186, 329 N.E.2d at 77; Bell v. Lone Oak Independent School District, 507 S.W.2d at 638.

50. Moran v. School District #7, Yellowstone County, 350 F.Supp. at 1186; Davis v. Meek, 344 F.Supp. 298, 301–302 (N.D. Ohio 1972); Holt v. Shelton, 341 F.Supp. at 823; Beeson v. Kiowa County School District RE-1, 567 P.2d at 805.

51. Beeson v. Kiowa County School District RE-1, 567 P.2d at 805.

52. Moran v. School District #7, Yellowstone County, 350 F.Supp. at 1186.

53. Davis v. Meek, 344 F.Supp. at 302.

54. *Id.* at 300.

55. See, *e.g.,* Bell v. Lone Oak Independent School District, 507 S.W.2d at 638: "In the present case, the evidence is legally insufficient to establish that the rule in question is a necessary restraint to promote a compelling state interest, that is, the prevention of dropouts from secondary schools."

56. Hollon v. Mathis Independent School District, 358 F.Supp. 1269, 1271 (S.D. Tex. 1973), *vacated on grounds of mootness,* 491 F.2d 92 (5th Cir. 1974).

57. See Moran v. School District #7, Yellowstone County, 350 F.Supp. at 1187; Indiana High School Athletic Association v. Raike, 164 Ind. App. at 184–185, 329 N.E.2d at 76; Bell v. Lone Oak Independent School District, 507 S.W.2d at 638.

58. Moran v. School District #7, Yellowstone County, 350 F.Supp. at 1187. See also Bell v. Lone Oak Independent School District, 507 S.W.2d at 638.
59. Indiana High School Athletic Association v. Raike, 164 Ind. App. at 185, 329 N.E.2d at 76–77.
60. *Id.* at 186, 329 N.E.2d at 77.
61. Moran v. School District #7, Yellowstone County, 350 F.Supp. at 1186.
62. See *id.;* and Beeson v. Kiowa County School District RE-1, 567 P.2d at 806.
63. Beeson v. Kiowa County School District RE-1, 567 P.2d at 806.
64. Moran v. School District #7, Yellowstone County, 350 F.Supp. at 1186.
65. 507 S.W.2d 636 (Tex.Civ.App. 1974).
66. *Id.* at 638.
67. Moran v. School District #7, Yellowstone County, 350 F.Supp. at 1184; Davis v. Meek, 344 F.Supp. at 301. See also Indiana High School Athletic Association v. Raike, 164 Ind. App. at 183, 329 N.E.2d at 75.

    But see Albach v. Ordle, 531 F.2d 983, 985 (10th Cir. 1976), stating that although a student has a property interest in the educational process, he does not necessarily have one in each component, such as varsity athletics. High school athletic programs, therefore, remain within the discretion of appropriate state boards unless the regulations deny an athlete a constitutionally protected right or classify on a suspect basis.
68. Federal regulations require that any school receiving federal funds not apply any rule concerning marital status that discriminates on the basis of sex. See 45 C.F.R. § 86.40(a) (1982). See *id.* at 86.21(c).
69. 175 N.E.2d 539 (Ohio Comm. Pleas 1961).
70. *Id.* at 542.
71. *Id.* at 541. See also Perry v. Grenada Municipal Separate School District, 300 F.Supp. 748, 753 (N.D. Miss. 1969) (dictum): "The court can appreciate that the Grenada School district might not have the funds to set up separate facilities for the education of pregnant girls. The purpose for excluding such girls is practical and apparent."
72. 175 N.E.2d at 542. See also Perry v. Grenada Municipal Separate School District, 300 F.Supp. at 753.
73. 323 F.Supp. 1155 (D. Mass. 1971).
74. *Id.* at 1156–57.
75. *Id.* at 1158.
76. *Id.*
77. *Id.*
78. *Id.*
79. 338 F.Supp. 1376 (N.D. Miss. 1972).
80. *Id.* at 1377.
81. See Smith v. Columbus Municipal Separate School District, No. E.C. 71-3-K (order dated Jan. 15, 1971).
82. 338 F.Supp. at 1378.
83. *Id.* See also Smith v. Columbus Municipal Separate School District, No. E.C. 71-3-K (order dated Jan. 15, 1971); and Perry v. Grenada Municipal Separate School District, 300 F. Supp. 748 (N.D. Miss. 1969).
84. Shull v. Columbus Municipal Separate School District, 338 F.Supp. at 1378.
85. 300 F. Supp. 748 (N.D. Miss. 1969).
86. *Id.* at 753.

87. *Id.* at 752.
88. Evidence at trial suggested that unwed mothers allowed to pursue their education are less likely to bear a second illegitimate child. *Id.* at 752.
89. *Id.* at 752–753. The court noted that state classification under the equal protection clause must have a rational purpose and must not arbitrarily discriminate. *Id.* at 750.
90. 361 F.Supp. 295 (N.D. Ga. 1973).
91. See *id.* at 297.
92. The policy covered expecting parents and married persons as well. *Id.*
93. *Id.* at 298.
94. *Id.* at 298–299 (emphasis added).
95. The court did hold that, since regular day school was free, barring indigents from the night program for inability to pay tuition or book fees violated equal protection. *Id.* at 299.
96. *Id.* at 298.
97. 404 S.W.2d 76 (Tex. Civ. App. 1966).
98. *Id.* at 77. See also State v. Chamberlain, where the court, although upholding the exclusion of a married pregnant woman from high school, noted that the school's regulation would permit the married student's return after giving birth. 175 N.E.2d at 543.
99. 404 S.W.2d at 77.
100. 361 F.Supp. at 296–297, 299.
101. San Antonio Independent School District v. Rodriguez, 411 U.S. 1, 29–39 (1972).
102. Plyler v. Doe, 457 U.S. 202, 221–24 (1982). *Cf.* San Antonio Independent School District v. Rodriguez, 411 U.S. at 23–24.
103. *Cf.* San Antonio Independent School District v. Rodriguez, 411 U.S. at 23–24; Houston v. Prosser, 361 F.Supp. at 298.
104. 45 C.F.R. § 86.40 (1982).
105. *Id.* § 86.40(b)(3).
106. *Id.* § 86.40(a).
107. See Sherman v. Inhabitants of Charlestown, 62 Mass. 160, 163 (1851); and Perry v. Grenada Municipal Separate School District, 300 F.Supp. at 753.
    In Dillon v. Pulaski County Special School District, 468 F.Supp. 54 (W.D. Ark. 1978), the court found that, if imposed pursuant to appropriate procedures, expulsion of a student for the lack of respect allegedly shown in his response to a teacher admonishing him to stop kissing a girl in the school hallway and for his alleged violation of the school regulation against public display of affection could be justified. (Under the circumstances, however, denying the student the right to call the accusing teacher as a witness violated procedural due process).
108. Perry v. Grenada Municipal Separate School District, 300 F. Supp. at 753.
109. Sherman v. Inhabitants of Charlestown, 62 Mass. 160 (1851).
110. *Id.* at 163.
111. *Id.* at 166, 167.
112. 520 F.Supp. 1170 (N.D. Ga. 1981).
113. *Id.* at 1171.

114. *Id.* at 1173.
115. 491 F.Supp. 381 (D.R.I. 1980).
116. *Id.* at 388.
117. MASS. ANN. LAWS ch. 71, §84 (Law. Co-op 1978).

Chapter 6

THE STUDENT PRESS

INTRODUCTION

In *Trachtman v. Anker*,[1] the editor-in-chief and a staff member of *The Stuyvesant Voice*, the student publication of New York City's Stuyvesant High School, submitted to school officials a plan to survey student sexual attitudes at Stuyvesant and to publish the results and some interpretation of them in the *Voice*. As ultimately rejected by school officials, the plan called for a written questionnaire of twenty-five queries eliciting personal information concerning the student respondent's sexual attitudes, preferences, knowledge and experience. Its topics included premarital sex, contraception, homosexuality and masturbation. The proposed cover letter outlined the nature and purpose of the project, encouraged candid responses, and advised that the student need not respond to any of the questions.[2] The plan also called for random distribution on school grounds, anonymous returns, and confidentiality.[3] On First Amendment grounds the editor-in-chief and his father challenged in federal court the rejection of the plan by school officials.

Such situations mandate a consideration of the limits of school board power with regard to the treatment of sexual matters in the student press. This chapter will explore to what extent, and under what conditions, freedom of speech cloaks sexually-oriented pronouncements in the student press.

The United States Supreme Court, in *Tinker v. Des Moines Independent Community School District*,[4] recognized the first amendment rights of high school students: "It can hardly be argued that either students or teachers shed their constitutional rights to freedom of speech or expression at the schoolhouse gate."[5] However, the Court was alert to the special discipline problems encountered by educators: "[T]he Court has repeatedly emphasized the need for affirming the comprehensive authority of the States and of school officials, consistent with fundamental constitutional safeguards, to prescribe and control conduct in the schools."[6] In line with this tension, the contours of the free speech right in the context of school newspapers remain elusive. The news fit to print in the *New York Times* may not be fit to print in the high school paper.

FREEDOM OF SPEECH GENERALLY

Courts have traditionally granted much leeway to speech, remaining "profoundly skeptical of government claims that state action affecting expression can survive constitutional objections."[7] As one court has noted, "Indeed, we have granted First Amendment protection to much speech of questionable worth, rather than force potential speakers to determine at their peril if words are embraced within the protected zone."[8] Nonetheless, the right to free speech is not absolute[9]—if the state's concerns are paramount, even speech content may be regulated.[10] Accordingly, obscenity,[11] libel[12] and incitement[13] fall beyond the protection of the First Amendment.[14] Moreover, although the state may enforce reasonable regulations of the time, place or manner of speech occurring in a public forum, the enforcement must be without regard to the content of the speech.[15] Otherwise, the state might restrain unpopular, offensive or dissident speech under time, place or manner pretexts.[16]

Although the state can punish unprotected speech such as obscenity after it has been uttered, it remains extremely difficult for the state to restrain such speech prior to any utterance.[17] Such prior restraint provides fewer procedural inhibitions to the state than after-the-fact criminal proceedings, tempts courts to overpredict the potential danger from the speech, and prevents the message from ever being heard; it thus more effectively chills speech than does punishment after the fact.[18] The United States Supreme Court itself has warned that any system of prior restraint comes to court with a heavy presumption against its constitutionality.[19] Nonetheless, prior restraint applied to alleged obscenity, while still suspect, is generally more tolerated than other forms of prior restraint.[20]

In *Freedman v. Maryland,*[21] the United States Supreme Court considered the validity of a film censorship system. The Court concluded that a noncriminal process mandating the prior submission of films to a censor must provide procedural safeguards "designed to obviate the dangers of a censorship system,"[22] including: (1) placement upon the censor of the burden of proving that the expression is unprotected;[23] (2) a specified, brief period during which the censor issues the license or seeks a court order against exhibiting the film;[24] and (3) assurance of a prompt and judicial final decision.[25] Indeed, the Court later noted,[26] exhibition must be allowed pending the judicial determination of obscenity, and would-be exhibitors lacking a copy due to an official seizure must be permitted to copy the seized film.[27]

FREEDOM OF SPEECH AND STUDENT PUBLICATIONS

School boards, as arms of the state, may establish rules punishing students for publishing and distributing on school grounds unprotected speech such as obscenity and libel.[28] Under *Tinker,* any student conduct, in class or out, which "materially disrupts classwork or involves substantial disorder or invasion of the rights of others" presumably falls beyond the protection of the First Amendment.[29] Looking to these grounds for official disapproval of speech, one court voided the expulsion of two high school students for distributing at school a publication critical of the school administration.[30] The authorities had not alleged that the writing was libelous,[31] the language was not objectionable for students[32] and the school board could not reasonably foresee from the publication and distribution of the paper any substantial or material interference with school activities.[33]

A system of prior restraint is more easily justified in the secondary school environment than in the adult world because children's First Amendment rights are not coextensive with those of adults,[34] and school officials may be entitled to ensure that the student press is not only free, but responsible.[35] Although even in secondary school contexts prior restraint systems come to court with a presumption against their constitutionality,[36] school authorities may exercise reasonable prior restraint not only with regard to student obscenity and student libel, but also with regard to certain other student expression.[37] Following the lead of *Eisner u Stamford Board of Education,*[38] most courts[39] have interpreted *Tinker* to allow censorship by authorities who reasonably anticipate that the student expression at issue will result in material disruption, substantial disorder or invasion of the rights of others.[40] For example, in *Trachtman u Anker,*[41] the sex survey case whose facts introduced this chapter, the Court of Appeals for the Second Circuit emphasized that school officials need not wait until the harm occurs before acting. The Court concluded that the threatened psychological harm warranted prohibiting distribution of the survey.[42]

The Court of Appeals for the Seventh Circuit, however, has not been persuaded: "We believe the Court erred in *Eisner* in interpreting *Tinker* to allow prior restraint of publication—long a constitutionally prohibited power—as a tool of school officials. . . . "[43] The court felt that the forecast called for by *Tinker* related to the result of allowing existing conduct to continue.[44]

Even courts authorizing prior restraint in certain student cases, however, stress the need for procedural safeguards. The *Eisner* court adapted to the school environment the procedural safeguards specified by the United States Supreme Court in *Freedman*.[45] Referring to *Tinker* and other[46] federal decisions, the court made clear that when challenged in court, the school board bears the burden of proving that interference with student expression was reasonable.[47] The *Eisner* court concluded that although a final judicial determination is not required prior to censorship, an "expeditious review procedure" is.[48]

Moreover, when prior restraint, as opposed to a postpublication sanction, is involved, regulations must define more precisely what type of material is prohibited.[49] The challenge is a formidable one. In *Leibner v Sharbaugh*,[50] the court found that the failure of proscriptions against the distribution of "obscene" or "libelous" material to define these terms contributed to the unconstitutionality of the regulations.[51] In *Nitzberg v Parks*,[52] a federal Court of Appeals, criticizing a prior restraint regulation for vagueness, faulted it for giving "no guidance whatsoever" with regard to what would constitute substantial disruption or material interference and for failing to specify the criteria by which officials might predict such disruption.[53] One concern is that prior restraint might be used to censor criticism of school officials or school policies because school authorities find the criticism disrespectful, tasteless or offensive.[54]

Obscenity in the Student Context

Since specificity concerning what is prohibited will be required, at least in prior restraint schemes, the school board must define obscenity in the student context. In *Miller v California*,[55] the United States Supreme Court described as obscene and therefore outside first amendment protection works which, taken as a whole, the average person, "applying contemporary community standards," would find appealing to the prurient interest; which depict or describe in a patently offensive way sexual conduct specifically defined by state law; and which, again taken as a whole, lack serious literary, artistic, political or scientific value.[56]

In *Ginsberg v New York,*[57] however, the same Court, noting that the power of the state over children exceeds its authority over adults,[58] approved a variable and constitutionally broader obscenity standard for minors. The New York penal statute upheld in *Ginsberg,* adjusting the *Miller* standard, defined obscenity with regard to minors as a description or representation that "(i) predominantly appeals to the prurient, shameful or morbid interest of minors, and (ii) is patently offensive to prevailing standards in the adult community as a whole with respect to what is suitable material for minors, and (iii) is utterly without redeeming social importance for minors."[59]

In *Jacobs v Board of School Commissioners,*[60] Indianapolis school authorities told the student plaintiffs that their unofficial newspaper could no longer be distributed because, according to the authorities, it contained obscene material. The publication contained "a few earthy words relating to bodily functions and sexual intercourse" and one cartoon depicting "a sequence of incidents in a bathroom."[61] In the absence of a specific school board definition of obscenity, the Court of Appeals for the Seventh Circuit alluded to both the *Miller* and *Ginsberg* standards in determining whether the student publication could be considered obscene. Even with Ginsberg's "variable obscenity concept" softening the *Miller* constraints on the state, concluded the court, the student publication, although perhaps containing profanity,[62] was not obscene even as to minors.[63] The newspaper appealed to the prurient interest of neither adult nor minor:[64] "Making the widest conceivable allowance for differences between adults and high school students with respect to perception, maturity or sensitivity, the material pointed to by [school authorities] could not be said to fulfill the *Miller* definition of obscenity."[65]

Because it based its decision on "the facial constitutionality of the school board's regulation," the court in *Nitzberg*[66] did not have to decide whether the contents of the student publication in question were obscene.[67] Nonetheless, the court noted its disagreement with school officials who considered obscene a description of cheerleaders as "sex objects."[68]

In *Koppell v Levine,*[69] a federal district court, calling the penal provision upheld in *Ginsberg* an acceptable definition of obscenity for minors,[70] stated that school officials could not censor as obscene a high school literary magazine story containing four-letter words and describing a movie scene in which a couple "fell into bed":[71] "The magazine contained no extended narrative tending to excite sexual desire or constituting a predominant appeal to prurient interest."[72]

The "Tinker" Standard

Presumably, however, speech not obscene even under *Ginsberg* may still run afoul of the *Tinker* standard if the speech threatens substantial disruption.[73] The *Trachtman* case presents the most intriguing example. The plaintiff submitted statements from five experts alleging variously that the survey might benefit many students, that barring the survey could have harmful effects, that the topics alluded to in the questionnaire were commonly discussed by, and of normal interest to, students, that students in Manhattan were constantly exposed to sexually explicit matters, and that any harm to a student from answering the questions was highly unlikely. Two of the plaintiffs' experts did concede some possibility that answering the questionnaire could cause emotional damage to some students.[74]

The defendant school officials countered with the affidavits of four experts who stated, variously, that some of the questions were highly inappropriate; that high school students presented wide variations in physical and psychological development; that answering the questions would very likely cause anxiety, tension and self-doubt for certain students, and indeed, for some students with a "brittle" sexual adjustment, could occasion a panic state or even psychosis; that serious injury was likely to result to at least some students; and that the methodology proposed would make it impossible to provide support or protection to those students experiencing anxiety.[75]

The Court of Appeals for the Second Circuit relied heavily on *Tinker's* observation that student expression is not immunized when it collides with or invades the rights of others.[76] The Court stated that *Tinker* and its progeny only required school officials to show reasonable cause to believe that distribution would result in significant psychological[77] harm to some students.[78] Nor did officials need to wait until the harm occurred before acting; the fact that psychological diagnosis may be imprecise does not preclude officials from shielding students against foreseen injuries. The question, furthermore, was not the wisdom of the officials' action, but the existence of a substantial basis for their conclusion. The court found that the record did establish a substantial basis for the school officials' concern and held constitutional their prohibition of the survey.[79]

The *Trachtman* decision may raise as many questions as it answers. First, it gives little guidance concerning the number of students who need be at risk of psychological harm. Are two or three such students enough? The court refers only to "a number" of students believed by authorities to be jeopardized.[80] Does all speech have to be harmless to virtually all students in order to be protected? The standard urged by the dissent would look not to the "effect of the questionnaire upon one or even a few exceptionally immature and impressionable students but its effect on the average."[81]

Second, to what other subjects might the Court's holding extend? Again, the dissent is instructive, voicing its fear that psychological harm, as compared with physical disruption or violence, constitutes too "vague and nebulous" a concept; if the questionnaire at issue in *Trachtman* could be banned under such a concept, so too could a wide variety of other writings.[82] It may be that articles which merely convey information are not within the court's pronouncement, that the crux of the case is the probing of private feelings and attitudes. Indeed, the Court specified that the "desire to use Stuyvesant students as research subjects" distinguished the case from other student press cases.[83] Even so, the problem does not disappear. Could a similar questionnaire probing students' feelings about fighting in Vietnam meet the same fate if expert opinion suggests that some students might be psychologically affected?

Third, the school officials maintained that their interest was in protecting the students, yet conceded that if the plan had called for off-campus distribution of the questionnaire no effort would have been made to stop it.[84] But would not the jeopardy to the students have been the same? Would distribution fifty feet from the school grounds by staffers of a school newspaper substantively change the situation? If the school officials felt a lack of authority to prohibit off-grounds conduct, could they not have indirectly stopped the distribution by prohibiting the publication of any resulting material? A distinction based upon where the distribution takes place seems overly formal.[85]

Fourth, does the opinion give undue weight to the possible psychological harm? Should we not balance against any anticipated harm any anticipated good from the activity in question? One expert noted that the questionnaire might serve as an important outlet for certain youngsters,[86] another that enormous benefit would inure to students discovering that their worries were both common and normal, and a third that the questionnaire presented "positive mental health implications".[87] Further, "squelching" the project might give the students "a cause to do battle with authority figures."[88]

The *Trachtman* result has perhaps been indirectly buttressed by the United States Supreme Court's decision in *New York v. Ferber*,[89] holding constitutional a criminal statute which prohibits "knowingly promoting sexual performance by children under the age of 16 by distributing material which depicts such performances."[90] Despite the recognized threat presented to protected expression,[91] the Court noted the state's compelling interest in protecting the physical and psychological well-being of minors.[92] The spirit of *Ferber* is surely not inconsistent with that of *Trachtman* and may well broaden the power of school boards over material distributed to students. *Ferber* and *Trachtman*, conversely, are easily limited since both involve not the mere exposure of the young to sexual material but their very participation in its production. With regard to mere expression, of course, *Ginsberg*'s variable obscenity standard remains the most likely constraint.

In other cases, claims that student speech fell within the *Tinker* standard have failed. In *Jacobs*, the Court, after dismissing the argument that the student newspaper contained obscenity, went on the find that "the occasional presence of earthy words . . . can not be found to be likely to cause substantial disruption of school activity or materially to impair the accomplishment of educational objectives."[93] Similarly, in *Vail v. Board of Education of Portsmouth School District*,[94] profanity[95] in a publication distributed at school by students not only did not constitute obscenity but also was not likely to "substantially disrupt normal educational activities."[96]

Vulgarity and Profanity

As indicated earlier,[97] school boards apparently retain broad power to prevent the appearance of at least pervasive vulgarity in the curriculum and in the library. In light of this, these limits on their power over vulgarity or profanity in student publications may seem surprising.[98] Several reasons may be advanced to explain the court results to date, however. First, the cases discussed here were decided prior to the United States Supreme Court's handling of *Pico*, which is the most striking suggestion concerning school board power vis-a-vis pervasive vulgarity. Second, the lower courts in these pre-*Pico* cases would perhaps not find the vulgarity to be "pervasive." Finally, and perhaps most critically, the curriculum and library situations involve speech by the state itself directly through its employees or indirectly through its libraries. Whatever the ultimate contours of one's right to receive information,[99] those situations do not directly impinge upon the speaking rights of students. Moreover, the more independent the student publication involved, the less is the state's inculcative prerogative at issue and the less the state can be seen as impliedly approving the publication's content.[100]

Indeed, at least one court has focused on the concept of vulgarity itself, rather than obscenity, in overseeing the school's authority to control speech content. In *Baker v. Downey City Board of Education*,[101] the United States District court upheld the suspension of students for vulgarity appearing in the off-campus newspaper they wrote and distributed. Relying on *Ginsberg* for the notion that state power over children is greater than over adults, the court concluded that neither legally defined pornography nor obscenity was a prerequisite to the establishment of a violation of rules against profanity or vulgarity or to concerns by experienced officials that the educational process was impaired by the speech involved.[102] Declaring that "freedom of speech is not the right to say anything one may please in any manner or place," the court found that the students were disciplined not for their criticism of school administrators and faculty but for the "vulgar manner" of their expression.[103]

Put this way, such regulation seems only to reflect a time, place or manner restriction, and such restrictions, when otherwise reasonable, are upheld by the courts.[104] Accordingly, most courts[105] have acknowledged the school board's power reasonably to regulate the time, place and manner of student expression. "Manner," however, should involve the method of distribution of the expression, for example its volume level in the case of sound,[106] not, like in *Baker*, its content.[107] The *Vail* court, for example, noted that its ruling did not prevent the board from enforcing reasonable, specific rules concerning the time, place and manner of distribution of written materials when the only purpose is the orderly conduct of school activities through the prevention of disruption and not the stifling of the freedom of expression.[108] The particular words used, however, seem more like content than like manner, especially when one considers that even vulgarity, like other rhetoric, may be inseparable from the message.[109] Clearly, the restriction in *Baker* ran afoul of the usual requirement that the regulation be a "narrow means of protecting important interests *unrelated to content*".[110]

SPEECH OR INSUBORDINATION?

In some cases involving student speech, the courts have seized upon a discrete part of the transaction, separable from the speech, to deny relief to the student.[111] In *Schwartz v. Schuker*,[112] for example, the student defied a school official's request that he not bring copies of the newspaper onto school grounds and, following his suspension, came to school admitting his defiance of the superintendent's order. The court held that the student's First Amendment rights were not violated by the suspension, which was due more to flagrant disobedience than to distributing an off-campus newspaper on school premises:

> While there is a certain aura of sacredness attached to the first amendment, nevertheless these first amendment rights must be balanced against the duty and obligation of the state to educate students in an orderly and decent manner to protect the rights not of a few but of all of the students in the school system. The line of reason must be drawn somewhere in this area of ever expanding permissibility. Gross disrespect and contempt for the officials of an educational institution may be justification not only for suspension but also for expulsion of a student.[113]

SEXUAL INFORMATION

Several courts have considered whether the distribution of sexual information in high schools by students may be barred as disruptive or obscene.[114] In such cases, protesting school officials have met with little success. In *Gambino v. Fairfax County School Board*,[115] secondary school censorship regulations were used to stop the publication in the school newspaper of an article entitled, "Sexually Active Students Fail to Use Contraception." The federal court, expressing surprise at the "innocuousness" of the article,[116] held the interference unconstitutional. In *Shanley v. Northeast Independent School District, Bexar County, Texas*,[117] the Court of Appeals for the Fifth Circuit held that the application of the school board's prior restraint law to the student plaintiffs who were suspended for distributing off-campus[118] an "underground"[119] newspaper that was neither obscene[120] nor disruptive[121] was unconstitutional. Although the paper provided information on birth control (and advocated a review of marijuana laws),[122] the court described it as "probably one of the most vanilla-flavored ever to reach a federal court."[123] In *Boyer v. Kinzler*,[124] the court found unconstitutional the high school principal's seizure of a sex education supplement to the high school newspaper.

Although the supplement consisted primarily of articles dealing with contraception and abortion, the court noted that they were serious in tone, were intended to carry information rather than appeal to prurient interests and, therefore, were not obscene.[125] The seizure, not reasonably necessary to avoid material and substantial interference with the operation of the school, violated the plaintiff's First and Fourteenth Amendment rights.[126]

The "Intrusion into the Curriculum" Argument

The school board in *Gambino* argued that since it was written and published on campus as part of a student activity, the paper constituted part of the curriculum. Consequently, the argument continued, students allowed to publish articles on birth control would effectively override the decision of the school board not to include birth control in the sex education curriculum.[127] Without questioning the board's authority to "prescribe course content,"[128] the court concluded that the paper was established as a "vehicle for first amendment expression" and not as an "official publication"; the paper did not, therefore, constitute an integral part of the curriculum.[129] Another court similarly found the "intrusion into the curriculum" argument no justification for interference with student speech, noting that since social studies are part of the curriculum the suggested theory would support seizure of newspapers dealing with political topics.[130] The intrusion into the curriculum argument presumably carries more weight when the publication, for example a student newspaper or yearbook, is itself produced as an integral part of a credited course.[131] Even in such a case, however, constitutional values could be implicated.[132]

The "Captive Audience" Argument

In *Gambino*, the school board also argued that regulation of the paper was justified by the fact that the students exposed to it constituted a "captive audience," a theory resorted to by the United States Supreme Court in *Lehman v. City of Shaker Heights*.[133] In *Lehman*, the Court had focused on "the lack of free choice which effectively compelled the users of the city transit system to receive the messages displayed on the system's vehicles. . . ."[134] The *Gambino* court noted, however, that Justice Brandeis, in *Packer Corp. v. Utah*,[135] had distinguished such a situation from that of newspapers and magazines, which require some seeking out by the reader.[136] Despite the paper's official status, its homeroom distribution, and peer pressure, the court concluded that the school newspaper did not create a captive audience situation.[137]

CONCLUSION

Students in public schools should be afforded as much freedom of speech as is consistent with the criminal law, the rights of others, the orderly running of the school, the age of the students involved and fundamental decency. Accordingly, only obscenity, libel, speech threatening substantial disorder or harm to others and perhaps pervasive vulgarity or profanity are candidates for exclusion. Freedom of expression should be more expansive in upper grade levels and, at least for such levels, should be affirmatively proclaimed by regulation or even statute.[138]

In administering policies covering expression in the schools, school officials should adhere to several basic principles. First, adverse action with regard to speech should occur only pursuant to clear procedures and subject to narrowly-drawn standards. Second, prior restraint should be viewed with skepticism and employed only as a last resort. Third, the demonstration of tolerance for a variety of outlooks itself teaches students to be tolerant. Fourth, censorship which is constitutional may still be undesirable; a school district need not exert all its power. Finally, a wide variety of speech—even speech that is shrill, unpleasant, critical or misguided—contributes to a lively learning environment.

NOTES

1. 563 F.2d 512 (2d Cir. 1977).
2. *Id.* at 514–515 ("You are not required to answer any of the questions and if you feel particularly uncomfortable—don't push yourself.")
3. *Id.* at 515.
4. 393 U.S. 503 (1969).
5. *Id.* at 506.
6. *Id.* at 507. See also Vail v. Board of Education of Portsmouth School District, 354 F.Supp. 592, 597 (D.N.H.), *aff'd in part,* 502 F.2d 1159 (1st Cir. 1973).
7. Thomas v. Board of Education, Granville Central School District, 607 F.2d 1043, 1047 (2d Cir. 1979). See also Federal Election Commission v. Central Long Island Tax Reform Immediately Committee, 616 F.2d 45, 54 (2d Cir. 1980).

8. Thomas v. Board of Education, Granville Central School District, 607 F.2d at 1048.

9. Thomas v. Board of Education, Granville Central School District, 607 F.2d at 1047; Vail v. Board of Education of Portsmouth School District, 354 F.Supp. at 598; Schwartz v. Schuker, 298 F.Supp. 238, 242 (E.D.N.Y. 1969).

10. Thomas v. Board of Education, Granville Central School District, 607 F.2d at 1048 (citing New York Times Co. v. Sullivan, 376 U.S. 254 (1964); Miller v. California, 413 U.S. 15 (1973); and Brandenburg v. Ohio, 395 U.S. 444 (1969)).

11. Miller v. California, 413 U.S. 15 (1973).

12. New York Times Co. v. Sullivan, 376 U.S. 254 (1964).

13. Brandenburg v. Ohio, 395 U.S. 444 (1969).

14. Thomas v. Board of Education, Granville Central School District, 607 F.2d at 1047–1048.

15. See, *e.g.*, Linmark Associates, Inc. v. Township of Willingboro, 431 U.S. 85, 93 (1977); and Madison School District v. Wisconsin Employment Relations Commission, 429 U.S. 167, 176 (1976). See generally NOWAK, ROTUNDA & YOUNG, CONSTITUTIONAL LAW 977 (2d ed. 1983).

16. NOWAK, ROTUNDA & YOUNG, *supra* note 15, at 977.

17. See Vance v. Universal Amusement Co., Inc., 445 U.S. 308, 316 (1980).

18. See generally NOWAK, ROTUNDA & YOUNG, *supra* note 15, at 886–90.

19. Bantam Books, Inc. v. Sullivan, 372 U.S. 58, 70 (1963).

20. NOWAK, ROTUNDA & YOUNG, *supra* note 15, at 887, 890.

21. 380 U.S. 51 (1965).

22. *Id.* at 58.

23. *Id.*

24. *Id.* at 59.

25. *Id.* at 58–59.

26. Heller v. New York, 413 U.S. 483 (1973).

27. *Id.* at 492–493.

28. See Baughman v. Freienmuth, 478 F.2d 1345, 1351 (4th Cir. 1973); Fujishima v. Board of Education, 460 F.2d 1355, 1359 (7th Cir. 1972); Eisner v. Stamford Board of Education, 440 F.2d 803, 809 (2d Cir. 1971); Sullivan v. Houston Independent School District, 307 F.Supp. 1328, 1341 (S.D.Tex. 1969).

    The use of obscenity may trigger enforcement of the criminal law. See, *e.g.*, LA. REV. STAT. ANN. § 14:106A(3) (West Supp. 1985). Moreover, many states statutorily authorize the suspension or expulsion of students who use obscene or profane language or the like. See, *e.g.*, CAL. EDUC. CODE § 48900 (West Supp. 1985) (obscene acts, habitual profanity or vulgarity); LA. REV. STAT. ANN. § 17:416A(1) (a)(iv) (West Supp. 1985) (unchaste or profane language); and OR. REV. STAT. § 339.250(4) (Supp. 1981) (profane or obscene language).

29. Tinker v. Des Moines Independent Community School District, 393 U.S. at 513.

30. Scoville v. Board of Education of Joliet Township High School District 204, 425 F.2d 10 (7th Cir. 1970), *cert. denied*, 400 U.S. 826.

31. 425 F.2d at 12.

32. *Id.* at 14.

33. *Id.* at 15.

34. See Ginsberg v. New York, 390 U.S. 629 (1968). See also New York v. Ferber, 102 S.Ct. 3348 (1982); FCC v. Pacifica Foundation, 438 U.S. 726 (1978); Tinker v.

Des Moines Independent Community School District, 393 U.S. at 515 (concurring opinion); Nicholson v. Board of Education [of] Torrance Unified School District, 682 F.2d 858, 863 (9th Cir. 1982); Nitzberg v. Parks, 525 F.2d 378, 382 (4th Cir. 1975); Baughman v. Freienmuth, 478 F.2d at 1348; Quarterman v. Byrd, 453 F.2d 54, 58 (4th Cir. 1971); Gambino v. Fairfax County School Board, 429 F.Supp. 731, 734 (E.D. Va. 1977); and Vail v. Board of Education of Portsmouth School District, 354 F.Supp. at 598.

35. *Cf.* Nicholson v. Board of Education [of] Torrance Unified School District, 682 F.2d at 863.

36. Baughman v. Freienmuth, 478 F.2d at 1348.

37. See Baughman v. Freienmuth, 478 F.2d at 1349; Shanley v. Northeast Independent School District, Bexar County, Texas, 462 F.2d 960, 971 (5th Cir. 1972); Quarterman v. Byrd, 453 F.2d at 58; Eisner v. Stamford Board of Education, 440 F.2d at 809; and Vail v. Board of Education of Portsmouth School District, 354 F.Supp. at 599.

Prepublication review of student articles may be "for accuracy rather than for possible censorship or official imprimatur." See Nicholson v. Board of Education [of] Torrance Unified School District, 682 F.2d at 863.

38. 440 F.2d at 810.

39. See Nitzberg v. Parks, 525 F.2d at 382–383; Baughman v. Freienmuth, 478 F.2d at 1349; Shanley v. Northeast Independent School District, Bexar County, Texas, 462 F.2d at 969; Quarterman v. Byrd, 453 F.2d at 58; Reineke v. Cobb County School District, 484 F.Supp. 1252, 1257 (N.D. Ga. 1980); Boyer v. Kinzler, 383 F.Supp. 1164, 1165 (E.D. N.Y. 1974); and Vail v. Board of Education of Portsmouth School District, 354 F.Supp. at 598.

40. See Tinker v. Des Moines Independent Community School District, 393 U.S. at 513. *But see* Shanley v. Northeast Independent School District, Bexar County, Texas, 462 F.2d at 973, suggesting that not even reasonably forecast disruption is *per se* justification for prior restraint or subsequent punishment of student expression.

41. 563 F.2d 512 (2d Cir. 1977).

42. *Id.* at 517, 520.

43. Fujishima v. Board of Education, 460 F.2d at 1358.

44. *Id.* "The *Tinker* forecast rule is properly a formula for determining when the requirements of school discipline justify *punishment* of students for exercise of their First Amendment rights. It is not a basis for establishing a system of censorship and licensing designed to prevent the exercise of first amendment rights." *Id.*

45. Eisner v. Stamford Board of Education, 440 F.2d at 810–811.

46. Blackwell v. Issaquena County Board of Education, 363 F.2d 749 (5th Cir. 1966); and Burnside v. Byars, 363 F.2d 744 (5th Cir. 1966).

47. Eisner v. Stamford Board of Education, 440 F.2d at 810. See also Shanley v. Northeast Independent School District, Bexar County, Texas, 462 F.2d at 969; and Vail v. Board of Education of Portsmouth School District, 354 F.Supp. at 597.

48. Eisner v. Stamford Board of Education, 440 F.2d at 810.

49. Baughman v. Freienmuth, 478 F.2d at 1349. See also Stanton v. Brunswick School Department, 577 F.Supp. 1560 (D.Me. 1984); and Leibner v. Sharbaugh, 429 F.Supp. 744, 748–749 (E.D. Va. 1977).

50. 429 F.Supp. 744 (E.D. Va. 1977).

51. *Id.* at 748. See also Baughman v. Freienmuth, 478 F.2d at 1350.

52. 525 F.2d 378 (4th Cir. 1975).

53. *Id.* at 383. See also Leibner v. Sharbaugh, 429 F.Supp. at 748 (citing Baughman v. Freienmuth, 478 F.2d at 1348): "Proscriptions against distributing obscene or libelous material do not define those terms. This, too, renders the regulation unconstitutionally vague."

54. Baughman v. Freienmuth, 478 F.2d at 1351. In Baker v. Downey City Board of Education, 307 F.Supp. 517, 527 (C.D. Cal. 1969), the court, apparently alert to this problem, emphasized that the students had been disciplined not for criticizing the school administrators and the faculty but for the vulgar manner of expression.

55. 413 U.S. 15 (1973).

56. *Id.* at 24.

57. 390 U.S. 629 (1968).

58. *Id.* at 638.

59. *Id.* at 646, quoting N.Y.PENAL LAW § 484-h, enacted by L.1965, ch. 327. For the current provision, see N.Y.PENAL LAW §§ 235.20–235.22 (McKinney 1980).

60. 490 F.2d 601 (7th Cir. 1973), *vacated as moot,* 420 U.S. 128 (1975).

61. 490 F.2d at 610.

62. Referring to the United States Supreme Court's decision in Cohen v. California, 403 U.S. 15 (1971), the *Jacobs* court emphasized the difference between "obscene materials and non-obscene materials containing profanity." 490 F.2d at 610. See also Fujishima v. Board of Education, 460 F.2d at 1359; Vail v. Board of Education of Portsmouth School District, 354 F.Supp. at 599; and Sullivan v. Houston Independent School District, 333 F.Supp. 1149, 1165 (S.D. Tex. 1971), *vacated on other grounds,* 475 F.2d 1071 (5th Cir. 1973), where the court observed that in *Cohen* the United States Supreme Court "finally laid to rest the argument that the indiscriminate use of 'fuck' is necessarily tantamount to obscenity." In *Sullivan,* the court, reviewing vulgar material under the *Ginsberg* standard, noted that the United States Supreme Court "never suggested that material which has no relationship to a minor's 'prurient interest' can qualify as 'obscene material' ". *Id.* at 1163.

63. Jacobs v. Board of School Commissioners, 490 F.2d at 610.

64. *Id.*

65. *Id.*

66. Nitzberg v. Parks, 525 F.2d 378 (4th Cir. 1975). See text accompanying notes 52–53, *supra.*

67. 525 F.2d at 380, n.1. Significantly, however, the *Nitzberg* court did not fault the regulation's *Miller*-based obscenity definition for vagueness. Its only reference to the obscenity definition occurs in a footnote observation that it found no clear reason for including in the definition a reference to the Maryland criminal obscenity law. See *id.* at 383, n.4.

68. 525 F.2d at 380.

69. 347 F.Supp. 456 (E.D. N.Y. 1972).

70. *Id.* at 459.

71. *Id.* at 458.

72. *Id.* at 459.

73. See text accompanying note 29, *supra.*
74. 563 F.2d at 514–515, 518–519.
75. *Id.* at 517–518.
76. *Id.* at 516 (citing *Tinker,* 393 U.S. at 512–513).
77. See *id.* at 520 (concurring opinion): "[A] blow to the psyche may do more permanent damage than a blow to the chin."
78. *Id.* at 519.
79. *Id.* at 517, 519, 520.
80. *Id.* at 520.
81. *Id.* at 522 (dissenting opinion)(citing Roth v. United States, 354 U.S. 476, 489 (1957); and Butler v. Michigan, 352 U.S. 380, 383–384 (1957)).
82. *Id.* at 521 (dissenting opinion).
83. *Id.* at 516, n. 2. See also *id.* at 519–520: "The First Amendment right to express one's views does not include the right to importune others to respond to questions when there is reason to believe that such importuning may result in harmful consequences." See also *id.* at 520 (concurring opinion).
84. *Id.* at 517, n. 3.
85. Two curious aspects of the court's opinion bear mention. First, the court suggests in a footnote that, since other kinds of communication concerning sex matters were allowed at the school, the banning of the sex survey project amounted to a "time, place or manner" regulation. *Id.* at 517, n. 3. Curious as well is the suggestion that the school board might have justified its action on the ground that "the proposed article will attempt to make 'scientific' conclusions about the sexual habits of Stuyvesant students that might be misleading." *Id.* at 516, n. 2. Absent the possibility of these conclusions causing a disruption or interference meeting the *Tinker* test, it is difficult to see the constitutional relevance of the court's suggestion.
86. *Id.* at 524 (dissenting opinion).
87. *Id.* at 525 (dissenting opinion).
88. See *id.* (dissenting opinion).
89. 102 S.Ct. 3348, 3354–3364 (1982).
90. *Id.* at 3350.
91. *Id.* at 3354.
92. *Id.* at 3354–3355.
93. Jacobs v. Board of School Commissioners, 490 F.2d at 610.
94. 354 F.Supp. 592 (D.N.H.), *aff'd in part,* 502 F.2d 1159 (1st Cir. 1973).
95. See note 62, *supra.*
96. 354 F.Supp. at 599–600. See also Sullivan v. Houston Independent School District, 307 F.Supp. at 1341.
97. See Chapters 1 and 3, *supra.*
98. See Jacobs v. Board of School Commissioners, 490 F.2d 601 (7th Cir. 1973), *vacated as moot,* 420 U.S. 128 (1975); Vail v. Board of Education of Portsmouth School District, 354 F.Supp. 592 (D.N.H.), *aff'd in part,* 502 F.2d 1159.
    Statutes in some states, whatever their constitutionality in particular applications, authorize the disciplining of students using vulgarity. See, *e.g.,* CAL. EDUC. CODE § 48900 (West Supp. 1985).
99. See Chapters 1 and 3, *supra.*
100. See text accompanying notes 127–128, *infra.*
    A Massachusetts statute provides that no student speech is deemed to express

school policy and protects all school officials from civil or criminal liability for any student speech or publication. The provision applies only to secondary schools. MASS. ANN. LAWS ch. 71, § 82 (Lawyer Co-op 1978).

101. 307 F.Supp. 517 (C.D.Cal. 1969).
102. *Id.* at 526–527.
103. *Id.* at 527.
104. See text accompanying note 15, *supra.*
105. See Jacobs v. Board of School Commissioners, 490 F.2d at 608–609; Baughman v. Freienmuth, 478 F.2d at 1348; Shanley v. Northeast Independent School District, Bexar County, Texas, 462 F.2d at 969; Fujishima v. Board of Education, 460 F.2d at 1359; Eisner v. Stamford Board of Education, 440 F.2d at 805; Vail v. Board of Education of Portsmouth School District, 354 F.Supp. at 598; and Sullivan v. Houston Independent School District, 307 F.Supp. at 1340.
106. See, *e.g.,* Saia v. New York, 334 U.S. 558 (1948) and Kovacs v. Cooper, 336 U.S. 77 (1949).
107. See NOWAK, ROTUNDA & YOUNG, *supra* note 15, at 977 and text accompanying note 15, *supra.*
108. 354 F.Supp. at 598.
109. See text accompanying notes 163, Chapter 1, *supra,* and text accompanying notes 154–156, Chapter 3, *supra.*
110. NOWAK, ROTUNDA & YOUNG, *supra* note 15, at 977 (emphasis added).
111. See Sullivan v. Houston Independent School District, 475 F.2d 1071 (5th Cir. 1973); Graham v. Houston Independent School District, 335 F.Supp. 1164 (S.D. Tex. 1970); and Schwartz v. Schuker, 298 F.Supp. 238 (E.D. N.Y. 1969).
112. 298 F.Supp. 238 (E.D. N.Y. 1969)
113. *Id.* at 242.
114. Shanley v. Northeast Independent School District, Bexar County, Texas, 462 F.2d 960 (5th Cir. 1972); Gambino v. Fairfax County School Board, 429 F.Supp. 731 (E.D.Va. 1977), *aff'd,* 564 F.2d 157 (4th Cir. 1977); and Boyer v. Kinzler, 383 F.Supp. 1164 (E.D.N.Y. 1974).
115. 429 F.Supp. 731 (E.D.Va. 1977), *aff'd,* 564 F.2d 157 (4th Cir. 1977).
116. 429 F.Supp. at 734.
117. 462 F.2d 960 (5th Cir. 1972).
118. Both Thomas v. Board of Education, Granville Central School District, 607 F.2d at 1045, and Sullivan v. Houston Independent School District, 307 F.Supp. at 1341, make a point of the distribution being off-campus. See text accompanying notes 84–85, *supra.*
119. 462 F.2d at 964.
120. *Id.* at 971.
121. *Id.* at 974–975.
122. *Id.* at 972.
123. *Id.* at 964.
124. 383 F.Supp. 1164 (E.D.N.Y. 1974), *aff'd without opinion,* 515 F.2d 504 (2d Cir. 1975).
125. 383 F.Supp. at 1165.
126. *Id.* at 1165–1166.
127. 429 F.Supp. at 733–736.
128. *Id.* at 736.
129. *Id.*

130. Boyer v. Kinzler, 383 F.Supp. at 1166.
131. Kuhlmeier v. Hazelwood School District, 578 F.Supp. 1287, 1294–1295 (E.D. Mo. 1984). *Cf* Nicholson v. Board of Education [of] Torrance Unified School District, 682 F.2d at 863, calling pre-publication review by school officials appropriate due to the "special environment, particularly one involving students in a journalism class that produces a school newspaper...."
132. See Kuhlmeier v. Hazelwood School District, 578 F.Supp. at 1291, 1294–1295.
133. 418 U.S. 298 (1974).
134. 429 F.Supp. at 735.
135. 285 U.S. 105 (1932).
136. 429 F.Supp. at 735–736 (citing 285 U.S. at 110).
137. *Id.* at 736.
138. See MASS. ANN. LAWS ch. 71, § 82 (Law. Co-op 1978), granting secondary students the right to publish their views as long as disruption or disorder does not result.

TABLE OF CASES

INDEX

ABORTION
(*see also* under SEX EDUCATION)
unwed parents and, 124
ACADEMIC FREEDOM
(*see also* under STUDENTS and under
    TEACHERS)
generally, 18
CENSORSHIP
frequency, 73
symbolic effect, 35(n.35), 75–76, 85
wisdom of, 90
CHILDREN
(*see also* STUDENTS)
generally, 94(n.77)
rights of, as opposed to parents, 14, 39(n.103),
    66(n.90), 67(n.103), 76, 92(n.40), 188, 190, 193
CLASSROOM
(*see* CURRICULUM and LIBRARY)
COMPLAINTS
generally, 19, 22, 25, 30, 126, 128, 129, 133, 134
parents', 5–6, 19–20, 126, 129, 133, 134
CRIMINAL IMPLICATIONS
generally, 134–135, 141(n.39), 145(n.92), 156(n.268),
    160(n.337), 163(n.375), 168(n.417), 198(n.28)
CURRICULUM
comparing other material or authors, 24–26
generally, 3–35, 47–60, 74, 86
right to receive information (*see* under FIRST
    AMENDMENT)
school plays, 35(n.5)
sex education (*see* SEX EDUCATION)
DUE PROCESS
(*see* under FOURTEENTH AMENDMENT)
EQUAL PROTECTION
(*see* under FOURTEENTH AMENDMENT)
ESTABLISHMENT CLAUSE
(*see* under FIRST AMENDMENT)
EVOLUTION
generally, 30, 45(n.228), 50, 59
EXCUSAL
as precedent, 57
generally, 6, 22, 27–28, 51, 52–53, 55–56, 56–58
number invoking, 57

EXPERTS
generally, 28–29, 31–32, 86, 90, 112, 113–116, 135,
    191–193
EXTRACURRICULAR ACTIVITY
married students and, 171–175
worship as, 66(n.90)
FIRST AMENDMENT
(*see also* STUDENT PUBLICATIONS)
comparing other material, 24–26
"employee model", 11–12
establishment clause 42(n.164), 47, 49–51
flag salute, 16
free exercise, 42(n.164), 47, 51–52, 54
generally, 8, 11–18, 28, 30, 32, 54, 58, 59, 72, 73, 74,
    77, 78, 79, 81, 82, 84, 87, 107, 120–122, 186–197
juveniles, 15
marketplace of ideas, 6–8, 9, 73
notice, 32–33, 189
obscenity, 20–21, 33, 78, 80, 84–86, 187, 188
    —as cause of harm, 92(n.51)
    —exemptions from prohibitions against,
        42(n.158), 98(n.151)
prior restraint (*see* under STUDENT
    PUBLICATIONS)
profanity, 21, 190, 193, 197
right to association, 108
right to receive information, 17, 77–78, 194
sexual explicitness, 84–86
sliding scale, 7, 8, 23
speech, 4–5, 87, 108
    —advocacy of illegal conduct, 152(n.208)
    —inducement to antisocial conduct, 21
    —symbolic, 121
style versus content, 21, 85, 86, 194
text of, 62(n.22)
time, place or manner restrictions, 187, 194
"Tinker" test, 15, 18, 29–31, 75, 80, 121, 179, 188–189,
    191, 196, 197
universities versus schools, 7–8
vagueness, 32, 189, 192
vulgarity, 21, 33, 84–86, 197
FITNESS TO TEACH
(*see* under TEACHERS)

215

ABOUT THE AUTHOR

Fernand N. Dutile, Professor of Law at the Notre Dame Law School, was born in Lewiston, Maine, in 1940. Following graduation from Assumption College and the Notre Dame Law School, he joined the United States Department of Justice in Washington. He has served on the law faculty at the Catholic University of America and, since 1971, at the University of Notre Dame. Professor Dutile has published five books and numerous articles. A member of the Maine Bar, he is married, has two children and makes his home in South Bend, Indiana.